*Research practices in the
study of kinship*

ASSOCIATION OF SOCIAL ANTHROPOLOGISTS

ASA Research Methods in Social Anthropology

Panel of Honorary Editors

A. L. Epstein   James J. Fox   Clifford Geertz
Adam Kuper   Marilyn Strathern

Series Editor

R. F. Ellen, University of Kent at Canterbury

Research practices in the study of kinship

Alan Barnard

and

Anthony Good

Department of Social Anthropology
University of Edinburgh
Edinburgh, Scotland

With a Foreword by
Professor Sir Raymond Firth

1984

Academic Press
(Harcourt Brace Jovanovich, Publishers)
London · Orlando · San Diego · San Francisco · New York ·
Toronto · Montreal · Sydney · Tokyo · São Paulo

ACADEMIC PRESS INC. (LONDON) LTD
24/28 Oval Road, London NW1 7DX

United States Edition published by
ACADEMIC PRESS INC.
(Harcourt Brace Jovanovich, Inc.)
Orlando, Florida 32887

British Library Cataloguing in Publication Data

Barnard, Alan
Research practices in the study of kinship. –
(ASA Research methods in social anthropology; no. 2)
1. Kinship – Handbooks, manuals, etc.
I. Title   II. Good, Anthony   III. Series
305.9′04   GN480
ISBN 0-12-078980-9
LCCCN 83-72314

Typset by Oxford Verbatim Limited
and printed in Great Britain
by St Edmundsbury Press,
Bury St Edmunds, Suffolk

Foreword to the series

Writing about research methods in social anthropology may have several functions. An anthropologist presents a mass of information about some issue, with reflections upon its significance; it may be of prime importance for his colleagues to know just how the information was collected, its representativeness, the manner of communication between all the parties, the type of systematic record, in order that the author's interpretation may be fairly judged. An account of research methods can also stimulate comparative interest, and aid in the evaluation of similar or contrasting views on a problem. It can perhaps serve a most useful function in suggesting to a prospective or actual fieldworker more fruitful ways of tackling an enquiry. This *Research Methods* series is designed to cover a wide range of interest, including that of colleagues outside the discipline of anthropology who legitimately want to know what is the justification for what we so broadly and confidently say about the human condition. But understandably, it is directed strongly towards fellow anthropologists who are grappling with problems of this fascinating, exasperating, rewarding, always unique experience known vaguely as "the field".

Writing about research methods in anthropology is a bold undertaking. While it may be gratifying to the ego either to explain one's own procedures or to tell other people how to improve theirs, an account of methods does mean often an exposure of the self from which many anthropologists have shrunk. Social anthropology in its field work phase demands a commitment of the self to personal relationships of a wide variety, with qualities hard to define, often ranging from casual encounter to prolonged and serious communication, perhaps of an emotional character which can be properly characterized as friendship. Data are collected by observation and discussion, not in neutral situations of mechanical action, but in situations of vivid human interaction in which the anthropologist is often directly involved in a complex interplay of judgement, sympathy and personal statement. To generalize from this in terms of more abstract procedures or even practical rules for conduct is not easy. Nevertheless the attempt at generalization has to be made if anthropologists are to retain credibility in the face of charges that their work is primarily a series of aesthetic constructs, a set of ego-trips into the exotic.

In social anthropology we are faced by a fundamental dilemma: we work at three levels or in three dimensions. The declared object of our study is some aspect of the ideas and institutions of a society – often exotic but not necessarily so – and there is a professional obligation upon us to describe, represent or interpret such ideas and institutions as accurately as possible. Whatever be the talk about models or the social conditioning of perception, whatever the obscurity in relation between portrayal and portrayed, we are trying to perceive and make statements about the order of an actual, not an invented society. But our perceptions and statements must inevitably pass through a personal lens, with all the individual assumptions and mode of thought which our specific upbringing and our general literature training have helped to establish. The individual component in the study of the actual society is involved in an historical time-flow, a series of particular incidents which in themselves may be trivial and unilluminating. Yet anthropologists deem themselves to be concerned with more than a record of past events; their work should relate to more general human issues. So while a contribution to social anthropology can be a rendering of personal experience in an identifiable social milieu, it should not be purely idiosyncratic; it must carry an implication of generality. As I see it, this dilemma is ultimately not resolvable. But it is not unique – there is something akin to it for example in the efforts of Asian or African novelists to write about their own natal societies. It is inherent indeed to some degree in any relationship of the Self to the Other. In all human relationships we operate with sets of assumptions if not about the reality at least about the viability of our observations and inferences, and with convictions that however approximate our models of other people's character and behaviour may be, at least some fair degree of consistency in relations with the Other is predictable.

This *Research Methods* series has been and is being composed in clear realization of the difficulties faced by anthropologists in these and allied sensitive areas. With sophistication and without dogmatism the volumes aim to face the problems and indicate where some solutions may be found. In this way they attempt to reduce the burden of uncertainty that often lies on anthropologists facing the fieldwork situation. Each book sets out in varying detail the framework upon which our work has been built so far, and indicates the kinds of lines on which improvement is needed if our conclusions are to hold their validity. One can always argue about the value of such guides, which have a long history in our discipline. Some anthropologists of great experience have argued that it is useless to try and teach the craft, that each neophyte must find his or her own solution. I myself have never held this opinion. Not only have I tried to publish at least some brief account of my field condition and methods in Tikopia and again in Kelantan (and Rosemary Firth has given more extended and more penetrating examination of some aspects of our joint work in the latter field), but I have also collaborated with Jane Hubert and Anthony Forge in a systematic exposé of the methods adopted in a team research project in North London. Again, in cooperation with colleagues at the London School of Economics and University College, London, I was involved for upwards of 20 years in seminars on fieldwork methods. Anthropologists in other institutions have done likewise. But I think we have all shared the view of the uniqueness and intensely personal character of a field experience, and that any training for the field is therefore not injunction but example, not prescription but suggestion. This seems also to be the spirit of these volumes.

What I can say here is that looking back over my own field experience, I am very aware of how much my own enquiries would have benefited from use of monographs such have been prepared or are planned in this series. They combine theoretical stimulus and practical suggestion in fertile ways, and though I may not agree with all their formulations I find them definitely thought-provoking. Of some vocal economic historians R. H. Tawney once said "I wish these fellows who talk so much about method would go and *do* some of it". The contributors to volumes in this series have already completed a great deal of field research, and the methods they advocate are a distillation from a very wide experience.

I look at these research method volumes much as a cook looks at a recipe book. They are no substitute for individual ingenuity and skill, but they can offer a range of alternative suggestions about procedure, and warnings about pitfalls, that are most unlikely to have occurred in such fullness to the practitioners. To change the analogy, if I can conclude on a light-hearted note, their role is parallel to that ascribed by a Kelantan religious man to his ritual and formula for securing fish. In terms almost reminiscent of Malinowski he said he could not turn an unskilled fisherman into a skilled one, but through the bounty of Allah he could "help" a competent fisherman to get a better catch. Fisherman or cook – and figuratively an anthropologist is sometimes both–anyone in our profession should keep these volumes to hand.

Raymond Firth

Preface

No fieldworker, and indeed no social anthropologist, can afford to ignore the study of kinship. It is central both to the lives of the people we study and to the theoretical development of the discipline we practise.

There was a time when it was enough for fieldworkers to collect genealogies, fill out relationship term charts, and label social institutions under such headings as "patrilineal descent", "cross-cousin marriage" or "Omaha terminology". This approach is certainly no longer considered adequate. Yet basic kinship text books still tend to gloss over some really important and interesting areas of the subject. In this book we try to redress the balance by bringing alive some of the theoretical problems which too often lie submerged below the worn-out labels of introductory texts. This is a crucial first step in carrying out satisfactory fieldwork, for ethnographers have to be aware of the limitations of the check-list approach just mentioned. For example, to label a social institution, let alone an entire society, as "partrilineal" often creates more difficulties than it solves. It encourages spurious "comparisons" with other, equally arbitrarily labelled "patrilineal" institutions in other societies, when what is really needed is consideration of the particularities of the institution in question, and its links to other aspects of local society.

We make similar points in the main text, so here we need give only a general outline of our position. Briefly, we see no real division between the theory and practice of anthropology. It is quite wrong to imagine that "data" can be obtained in advance of, or isolation from "theory". The questions you ask, and even your choice of issues about which to ask, depend upon the theoretical stance you adopt, because this tells you in the first instance where the interesting or significant problems lie. The only alternative to an explicit theory is an implicit, unexamined, and probably inadequate one, so it is essential to have a good grounding in kinship theory *before* undertaking research. If not, you may fail to ask certain questions, or ignore certain aspects of kinship behaviour, which later prove highly significant. But if your "theory" helps determine what kinds of "data" you collect, it is equally the case that your "data" lead you to refine, modify or abandon certain aspects of your "theory". That, of course, is the nature of progress in a cumulative social science like anthropology. We think that social anthropology *is* a science in Popper's (1972) sense. That is, it develops theoretical hypotheses which are empirically testable. These can be falsified, but never conclusively or universally "proven". The development of the subject stems, therefore, from the constant interplay of theory and practice.

Kinship theory is not just something to be memorized in a second-year anthropology course. It is a challenging branch of the discipline, and indeed the one in which most of its senior practitioners first made their mark. We hope to impart to our readers some of the excitement to be found in the study of kinship. At the same time, where appropriate, we try to prepare them for the kind of fieldwork which will lead to genuine understanding of their chosen field areas. As just explained, this is not exclusively, or even primarily, a matter of applying standardized procedures, but rather of sophisticated theoretical awareness.

For many students, the greatest barrier to the study of kinship is its jargon. Not only are there many technical or specialized phrases in use, but different authors have different definitions for these (often reflecting their own particular fieldwork situations). Definitions change subtly over time even in the works of individual authors, and terms come and go with fashion. For this reason we have chosen to discuss such issues directly in the text, rather than try to list *all* traditional, current and idiosyncratic usages in a glossary. The index should help you find our discussions of relevant concepts. Very often, we define such concepts polythetically, in which case it is virtually impossible to distinguish the "definition" from the theoretical issues surrounding the concept. This, perhaps more than anything else, distinguishes our book from any previous work of this length on kinship. We hope that this approach will make the study of kinship both clearer and more interesting, by clarifying and revitalizing issues which in the past may have been muddled and dead for many readers.

Our own fieldwork in South Asia and Southern Africa has, naturally enough, influenced our theoretical stances and our views on which theoretical issues are significant enough to merit treatment here. Yet at the same time we have tried to make our discussions as widely applicable as possible. This task has been made easier by the fact that our respective field experiences were so different, and by the fact that we ourselves are not fully in agreement on all the theoretical issues we discuss. We have also tried to draw examples from as wide a geographical range as possible.

We are happy to express our gratitude to our editor Dr Roy Ellen and foreword writer Professor Sir Raymond Firth, both of whom read the manuscript and made valuable comments and suggestions on a number of issues. Their advice helped clarify our arguments in many places, and ensured that our topical coverage was as wide as possible. Naturally, the responsibility for any remaining errors or omissions is entirely ours.

We thank Professors John Barnes and Sir Edmund Leach for allowing us to use Figs 2.2 and 5.2, which closely resemble diagrams in J. A. Barnes (1967a) and Leach (1961a[1967]) respectively. We also thank Dr Dennis McGilvray for permission to cite an unpublished paper. Dr Eric Hanley gave invaluable advice on the preparation of the manuscript by word processor. Finally, we thank all our colleagues – and in A. G.'s case, his family – for their patience and support.

Edinburgh   Alan Barnard
October, 1983   Anthony Good

Contents

1 _Introduction_

1.1 Why study kinship?

Kinship is perhaps the most esoteric and specialized branch of social anthropology. Yet every ethnographer, whether kinship specialist or not, is expected to come home from the field with a description of "the kinship system" of the people he or she has been studying, and a clear knowledge of how this system relates to other aspects of their culture and social organization. The main purpose of this book is to acquaint non-specialist fieldworkers and anthropology students with the problems of collecting kinship data, with details of the kinds of data required, and with suggestions on how to analyse such data. We hope that it will be useful to the kinship specialist, as a checklist of things to look out for; to the undergraduate, as a review of the connections between theory, methods, and data; and to specialists in other disciplines, such as demography.

So what _is_ "kinship"? The leading introductory kinship textbook is _Kinship and Marriage_ by Robin Fox (1967). In using this book for teaching purposes over recent years, we have found that one section attracts special interest – that in which Fox deals with what he calls the four basic principles of kinship (ibid: 31). These are:

Principle 1   The women have the children.
Principle 2   The men impregnate the women.
Principle 3   The men usually exercise control.
Principle 4   Primary kin do not mate with each other.

What is immediately striking is that these principles are not all of the same order. Principles 1 and 2 seem obvious physiological facts, which may well be at the root of _all_ kinship systems, however one defines "kinship". But for that very reason they cannot explain the observed differences between kinship systems. Moreover, the status of these two principles – especially the second – is not as unproblematic as might at first appear (§8.4, §8.7).

By contrast, principles 3 and 4 are either wholly or partly sociological in character. Even if you agree with Fox that principle 3 is "rooted in primate nature" (ibid: 32) and that principle 4 originated among early hominids and has been preserved because of "inhibitory responses" which may be bio-logically based (ibid: 75–76), the fact remains that *patriarchy* and *incest* are explained and institutionalized very differently in different societies. In the latter case especially, there is serious doubt over whether incest constitutes a cross-culturally definable phenomenon at all, so varied are the ways in which societies may define these tabooed "primary kin" (§6.2.1).

No doubt Fox's general principles hold particular appeal for those whose interest in kinship stems from an explicit or implicit quest for universality. That is, their primary object of study is "the Human species" rather than "human beings", or "Society" rather than "societies". We would not quarrel with this as an ultimate objective, but in our view the more immediate concerns of social anthropology lie with the *differences* between societies, not with the biological or other similarities between them.

Another fascination of kinship for some is that it appears to be the one area of anthropological discourse where the ground rules are clearly laid down (though ecological anthropologists and Marxists may disagree). In what other branch of social anthropology could anyone even begin to present a set of universal principles, much as a geometry teacher might set out Euclidean axioms? What other branch of the subject is so "scientific" that the puzzles it presents, to both fieldworkers and undergraduates, are "problems that only their own lack of ingenuity [keeps] them from solving" (Kuhn 1970: 37)? That kinship is widely regarded as the most "difficult" area of anthropology is undeniable. Yet this reflects the unwillingness of many anthropologists to achieve the necessary conceptual and logical rigour, rather than the im-penetrable nature of the topic itself. In the truly difficult areas of social anthropology – the study of religion, for instance – vagueness is often mistaken for profundity. In kinship, the emperor's clothes are much more readily seen to be transparent.

There is, finally, a more substantive issue. In most cases, kinship is an extremely important aspect of social organization. Almost invariably, in fact, it is more important in the society which the anthropologist studies, than in that from which he or she originates. Moreover, as "kinship" is something which every society has, it lends itself to (and indeed *demands*) comparative study. For both these reasons, every anthropologist is, as we mentioned, required to investigate it. We hope that readers setting out for the field will find this book useful for that most basic and essential of fieldwork tasks. And for those not envisaging fieldwork of their own, we hope to convey some idea of the intellectual stimulation, and practical understanding of the human condition, to be obtained from studying this quintessential anthropological phenomenon.

1.2 Problems of representation and meaning

A kinship specialist and senior colleague once told one of us, who was about to set off to do fieldwork for the first time: "Forget about kinship for the first few months; think about why you became an anthropologist." This was, and is, very sound advice. We take it to mean, in part, that a fieldworker should forget about "kinship" as an academic discipline with its internal theoretical premises and controversies, and focus instead upon understanding the lives of the people with whom he or she is living. Nevertheless, there comes a point when the fieldworker must abandon this purely personal perspective, and come to grips with "kinship" in the more formal sense. The rest of the book is directed towards the making of that most difficult transition.

1.2.1 *Abbreviations for kin types*

Among Anglophone anthropologists, there are at least four simple systems using letters as abbreviations for kin types. These are given in Table 1.1. In every system, most abbreviations speak for themselves, though they have different ways of overcoming the minor problem of distinguishing "son" from "sister". We strongly recommend system *A*, use of which is virtually universal among contemporary British anthropologists, and common even among French writers (but see §2.5). System *B* is more common in the United States, though even there system *A* is gaining strength. Systems *C* and *D* are now virtually obsolete: *C* uses capital letters for males and lower-case letters for females, whereas *D* uses capitals for steps up or across in genealogical level, and lower-case letters for steps down in level. Systems using mathematical symbols instead of letters are also found in the literature (e.g. Radcliffe-Brown 1930), but we do not feel that they have any particular advantages (see also Needham 1971a:xxi–xxxi).

The most likely sources of difficulty arise when you wish to record relative

Table 1.1   *Systems of kin type notation*

	System			
Kin type	*A*	*B*	*C*	*D*
father	F	Fa	F	F
mother	M	Mo	m	M
brother	B	Br	B	B
sister	Z	Si	s	S
son	S	So	S	s
daughter	D	Da	d	d
husband	H	Hu	H	H
wife	W	Wi	w	W
parent	P	Pa		
child	C	Ch		
sibling	G	Sb		
spouse	E	Sp		

age, the sex of ego, or the relative sex of ego and alter. System *A* is particularly convenient in such cases, because it uses upper-case symbols throughout. Lower-case letters can then be employed for these further refinements. Thus, relative ages are indicated by using the symbols "e" and "y" for "elder" and "younger", respectively. These are placed so that they denote the age of the person whose symbol immediately follows them, relative to the person denoted by *all* the symbols preceding them. This sounds more complex than it is, as some examples will illustrate.

Thus, FyBWB denotes the "father's younger brother's wife's brother", i.e. the wife's brother of ego's father's younger brother, whereas FBWyB denotes the "father's brother's wife's younger brother". When age relative to ego is to be indicated, the lower-case symbol is best placed at the end. For example, FBWBy denotes the "father's brother's wife's brother who is younger than ego". Notice that for the sake of consistency, it is better to denote ego's elder brother by Be rather than the more usual eB. We shall do so throughout.

Sometimes the sex of ego may be relevant to the definition of a particular relationship. That is, different relationship terms may be used by male and female speakers. In such cases, the suffixes "ms" and "ws" (or "m.s." and "w.s.") can be added, to denote either a "man" or a "woman speaker". For some reason, the use of "fs" ("female speaker") is rare, though it might be thought more logical. These symbols may be either placed in brackets or given as subscripts, at the end of the string of genealogical symbols. We shall adopt the first of these procedures: thus, the FZS(ws) denotes the "father's sister's son" as referred to or thought of by a woman speaker (in this case, his

MBD). These addenda are required only in cases where "sex of speaker" *is*, in fact, a significant variable. Their omission implies that it is not, at least for the genealogical position concerned.

Relative sex only enters into the notation when one is using the more abstract symbols for "parent", "child", "sibling" and "spouse". These are useful for depicting a large number of relationships economically. Here, the symbols "os" and "ss" (or "o.s." and "s.s.") are used to indicate "opposite sex" and "same sex", respectively. Again, these may be placed in brackets or as subscripts. Thus, one can write G(os) to denote both B(ws) and Z(ms). These relative sex indicators can also be inserted at other points in the notation. For instance, PosGC denotes all the "cross-cousins", that is, the FZS, FZD, MBS and MBD, while PosGC(ss) denotes cross-cousins of the same sex as ego, i.e. the FZS(ms), MBS(ms), FZD(ws) and MBD(ws).

So as to avoid ambiguity, we make frequent use of this notation, not only in figures and tables but also in the text itself. In fact, we use three different forms of notation throughout, to convey three distinct kinds of meaning. For example:

(i) MB refers to the specified, etically-defined genealogical position;

(ii) *mother's brother* is the composite English-language relationship term, which a native speaker of the language might use to specify one particular kind of *uncle*: we shall italicize such usages throughout, just as we italicize such terms from other languages;

(iii) "mother's brother" is used as a simple-minded translation of some foreign-language relationship term: it indicates the nearest English equivalent *in that context*, but the foreign term in question may have a broader or narrower overall semantic range than (English) *mother's brother*.

1.2.2 *Triangles and circles*

Most readers of this book will already be familiar with kinship diagrams. Nevertheless, in this section we shall take a brief look at common practices in drawing such diagrams, since a few symbols or conventions may be unfamiliar. Lest you be tempted to skip this section and forge ahead, remember that even in geometry definitions are formulated heuristically, with knowledge of the problems to come (Lakatos 1976: 144). A book can be written with hindsight, but can only be read with foresight.

A man is usually represented by a triangle, and a woman by a circle. Deceased persons have oblique lines drawn through their symbols: sometimes they are indicated by shading-in the corresponding circles or triangles, but we shall not follow that practice here. Instead, shading in our diagrams serves merely to draw attention to certain individuals. If the sex of a person is unknown or irrelevant, a diamond or square shape may be used. In the next section, we shall discuss the implications of diagrams using these symbols, and the various levels of abstraction which can be represented by them, but for the moment we confine ourselves to the case in which our triangles and circles represent individual men or women in a genealogy.

Siblingship is represented by a continuous horizontal line, below which are attached the full siblings of either sex. Relative age is often indicated by arranging siblings in birth order from left to right, but this is not universal practice, and if you adopt it you should say so explicitly. In Fig. 1.1a, *A* is the eldest sibling, and *D* the youngest: the sex of *B*, who has died, is unknown.

Marriage is sometimes represented by an equals sign. We prefer the alternative notation, whereby spouses are attached *above* a continuous horizontal

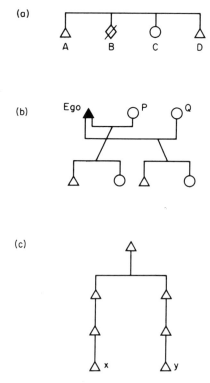

Fig. 1.1 *Notation in kinship diagrams.*

line. This is also connected vertically downwards to the line linking the sibling group of their offspring. Polygamy may be indicated by linking the man or woman concerned to *all* their spouses in a similar way. You should indicate the relative seniority of these spouses, in cases where such distinctions are relevant, and should show which children are the offspring of which two parents. Thus in Fig. 1.1b, ego has two wives P and Q. P is the senior, and each has two children.

If you want to draw attention to a particular genealogical feature, then the persons or relationships irrelevant to your purpose can be omitted. For instance, if you wish to trace a man's pedigree (§2.3.1) in a strongly patri- lineal society (§5.2), then you might be able to make the point more clearly if you include his male ancestors and their other descendants, but omit the wives and sisters of all such men, as in Fig. 1.1c. Finally, it may be necessary to devise other symbols or forms of notation, to cope with the peculiarities of your own fieldwork situation. There is no reason at all why you should not do this, so long as you make quite clear what you are doing. After all, such matters are purely conventional.

1.2.3 *Degrees of abstraction*

Despite what has been said in the previous section, kinship diagrams are not always intended to be understood in such a way that each triangle or circle represents one *real* man or woman (cf. Leach 1961a [1951]: 61–64). They may, for instance, be used to represent *fictive* genealogies of imaginary persons, and be so constructed as to bring out certain structural features to which you wish to draw attention. Our Fig. 1.1 is of this kind: the letters A, B, P, Q, etc., are not pseudonyms for actual people whose anonymity we wish to preserve, but purely notational devices for depicting and illustrating certain kinds of possible relationship.

Both the "real" and "fictive" uses of "genealogical-type" diagrams seem perfectly legitimate, provided of course that you make it absolutely clear which is which. But diagrams in this format have frequently been used for still other purposes, with much less happy results. For instance, many anthro- pologists have used them to depict the *structures of relationship termino- logies*. This is so prevalent a practice that any example can only be invidious, but Korn (1973), for instance, displays a number of terminological structures in this way. The procedure seems to us quite illegitimate, for a number of reasons. In the first place, the form of the diagram fosters belief in the primacy of genealogically close denotata, or at least encourages one to visualize terminologies in such terms. Many apparent features of kinship systems, and many of the apparent "problems" which arise in the study of relationship terminologies, are in fact merely concomitants of the genealogical format rather than real characteristics of the kinship systems themselves (see §6.3.1 in particular). Another problem with these types of diagram is that they accord relationship terminologies a degree of consistency which they do not always possess in reality. Usages which do not fit neatly onto a systematically structured "genealogical" diagram, are simply ignored, as comparison between Korn's tables and figures soon makes clear. In this book, we shall *not* use "genealogical" diagrams for such purposes, but you are certain to encounter them elsewhere, and should be on your guard.

Finally, and even more misleadingly, such figures have often been used to depict the forms of *marriage alliance relationships* between groups. Each triangle then represents not just one man, but all the male members of a given group in that particular generation. This leads to errors of two kinds. In the first place, the mistaken impression is again created that such alliances inevitably concern persons who are already close (genealogical) relatives. Even more serious in its effect on the development of kinship theory, has been the assumption, which such diagrams apparently bear out, that the groups engaging in these alliances comprise persons related to each other by common descent. As Leach (1961a [1951]: 56) argues, systematic alliance relationships almost always involve *local residence groups* rather than descent groups (although members of many such societies *conceptualize* these residential groupings in kinship terms). We shall use diagrams in this way (Chapter 6), but only when reviewing the work of others, and in order to demonstrate more fully the erroneous conclusions to which they may lead.

So in our view, diagrams in genealogical format should only be used when you intend to portray the inter-relationships of real or imaginary *individuals*. Even then, the significance of these diagrams is still not fully established, because we have still to clarify the *nature of the relationships* between these individuals. At the most concrete level, we have "biological reality". As we saw (§1.1), this is the level at which the first two of Fox's "principles" are intended to apply. What could be more consistent with everyday, Western common sense than the assumption that genealogies are historical records of biological relationships, brought into being by physiological acts of mating, engendering, giving birth, etc.?

One of us, at least, has been so recently emancipated from this particular relic of a natural science background, that the conceptual struggle involved is still vividly remembered. We find that the distinction between "biology" and "kinship" is one of the hardest for beginners in anthropology to grasp, and yet we believe that such a grasp is essential to their understanding of the nature of the subject. For that reason, we raise the issue very briefly here, even though it is more fully explored in the final chapter. The matter is immensely complex, so the rest of this paragraph is a general statement of our position, rather than a properly argued case. Let us be clear from the very beginning, though, that genealogies are not historical records of biological relations, but contemporary models for *social* relations. The "true" biological links, if any, between the persons depicted are not only irrelevant to social anthropology, but are mostly unknowable even to geneticists. As anthropologists we are concerned primarily with the social links between people. In so far as physiological "facts" are important, it is the indigenous version of those "facts" which matters, not our own, allegedly objective view. In sum, genealogical diagrams do *not* depict etically-defined biological relationships; they do *not* (unless this is specifically stated) even depict putative or emically-defined biological relationships; what they *do* depict are networks of real or possible social relationships between particular individuals, or particular types of individual.

All of the levels of study we have mentioned, and no doubt others too, provide us with valid perspectives on the complexities of human kinship. But not all these perspectives are anthropological ones. Even those which are must be kept distinct from each other at all times if misunderstandings are to be avoided. That is why we have gone to such lengths in this section, to argue against the indiscriminate use of diagrams which serve admirably at certain levels and for some analytical purposes. When reading this book, therefore, and even more so the works of other authors, you should always take note of the levels at which discussions are phrased, and to which diagrams are intended to apply. Such information ought always to be stated explicitly in anything you yourself may write or draw: in the next section we make our own position clear.

1.3 Levels of data

One analytical device which permeates the entire book, surfacing in virtually every chapter, is our division of kinship *data* into three distinct types, these being located at what we shall call the *categorical*, the *jural* and the *behavioural* levels, respectively. It seems necessary, therefore, to explain at this early stage the reasons behind our adoption of this approach. First, we shall review the history of its development in anthropology, in a very brief and no doubt over-simplified way.

1.3.1 *Relationship terms and social structure*

Early writers on kinship took it for granted that all levels of kinship data were mutually congruent, if not now then in some hypothetical past state of the society concerned. To give a prime example, Morgan assumed that relationship terminologies, or "systems of consanguinity" as he called them, were conservative aspects of culture which reflected earlier socio-structural forms. He wished

> to draw attention to the singular permanence and persistence of systems of consanguinity, and to the value of the evidence they embody with respect to the condition of ancient society. (1877: 389)

His main interest, therefore, in his pioneering study of contemporary relationship terminologies from around the world, was to develop a model of the evolutionary stages through which the kinship institutions of mankind as a whole had passed.

Although he rejected Morgan's evolutionist assumptions, especially the idea that "primitive promiscuity" was the earliest human state (ibid: 500), Rivers (1968 [1914]: 90) *did* agree that the study of relationship terminologies gave information about the histories of the groups using them. He placed particular emphasis on the importance of archaic forms of marriage in structuring contemporary terminologies.

> I hope to have shown that . . . it is possible to infer with certainty the ancient existence of forms of marriage from the survival of their results in the terminology of relationship. (ibid: 73–74)

Ever since Morgan, and particularly since Rivers, anthropologists have debated the connection between relationship terminology and social structure. In a famous paper, to which the passage just cited was a direct response, Kroeber had contradicted Rivers, arguing that there was in fact very little correlation between relationship terminologies and either past or present social structure. In his view:

> Terms of relationship reflect psychology, not sociology. They are determined primarily by language and can be utilized for sociological inferences only with extreme caution. (1909: 84)

Had that final point been widely accepted at the time, several decades of theoretical confusion might have been prevented. But it was not, partly because other aspects of Kroeber's approach were less satisfactory. For instance, his emphasis upon the linguistic determination of relationship terms, coupled with his playing-down of the congruence between terminology and social structure, led generations of American anthropologists to analyse such terminologies "in terms of formal components as distinct from social forms" (Schneider 1968c: 16). Such views held (and still hold) little appeal for the far more sociologically inspired British and French anthropologists. Perhaps understandably, they responded at the time by throwing out the incongruent baby along with the linguistic bath-water.

Whereas early writers had been interested mainly in the historical origins of relationship terminologies, which they imagined to have been the result of archaic, and now vanished, forms of marriage, their more empirically oriented successors focused attention upon the *present* connections between marriage practices and systems of classification. From this perspective, the causal link seemed to operate in the opposite direction. For instance, Hocart's comment on the famous case of "dual" or moiety organization was:

> The system then is not based on marriage, but marriage is regulated by the system. (1933: 258)

Such views came much closer than did Kroeber's to answering the needs of contemporary anthropological fieldworkers, who were seeking above all to explore synchronic inter-relationships rather than diachronic ones. A similar approach had allowed even such a staunch anti-evolutionist as Radcliffe-Brown to cling to the notion of congruence. He argued that relationship terms reflected *existing* social facts, especially in the sphere of kinship ideology (which he termed "behaviour", thereby confusing norms with practices). He stated:

> The general rule is that the inclusion of two relatives in the same terminological category implies that there is some significant similarity in the customary behaviour due to both of them, or in the social relation in which one stands to each of them, while inversely the placing of two relatives in different categories implies some significant difference in customary behaviour or social relations. (1950: 9)

So when ego addresses persons of two (etically-defined) distinct types by the same relationship term, that indicates that these two types of person are in some sense structurally equivalent, using "structure" in Radcliffe-Brown's substantive sense, to refer to empirically-observable phenomena "of which the component units are human beings" (1952 [1940]: 190). This view has tended to be tacitly adopted by most fieldworkers, not so much because they accept the full implications of Radcliffe-Brown's theoretical position, but rather because his approach lends itself so readily to the fieldworker's search for correlations between relationship terms and other aspects of social life.

Finally in our short survey, Lévi-Strauss tended to take for granted the interchangeability of terminological structures on the one hand, and the marital alliances of social groups on the other. So obvious did this seem to him, that even after many of the theoretical developments to be described in the following section, the question of whether the "elementary structures of kinship" were terminological or jural in character was laconically dismissed. The sole criterion of an "elementary structure"

> rests in the fact that, preferred or prescribed, the spouse is the spouse solely because she *belongs to an alliance category or stands in a certain kinship relationship* to Ego. (Lévi-Strauss 1969: xxxiv; emphasis added)

Yet in fact his tendency to mix up terminological data with information on rules of marriage, accounted for many of the confusions in his argument. It was also largely responsible for the furore to which his kinship writings led, because it allowed readers to draw very different conclusions, according to their own theoretical interests. Homans and Schneider (1955), for example, took his arguments to apply to relationships between genealogically close individuals, an error fostered by his use of pseudo-genealogical diagrams in the ways criticized above (§1.2.3). Needham (1962), on the other hand, took him to be dealing with structured terminological classifications, applicable also to very distant relatives, and even to persons not related at all in genealogical terms. We discuss this issue in more detail later (§6.3).

1.3.2 *Categories, rules and behaviour*

Dumont followed in the footsteps of Lévi-Strauss at first, but the implications of his work proved quite different. When he stated that "kinship terminologies have not as their function to register groups" (1964: 78), he drew attention to a crucial fact that had long been apparent in the available ethnography without having been fully digested theoretically. There is in fact *no* necessary correspondence between the structure of a society's relationship terminology, and the structure of the alliance relationships among its social groupings. This is true of "elementary" kinship systems as well as "complex" ones.

At that time, Dumont posed the problem in terms of a distinction between "ideology" and "behaviour", the latter being to some degree, but never entirely, directed by the former (1980: 343, fn 1a). This is still not sufficiently discriminatory, however, and the level of "ideology" needs to be further sub-divided into its "categorical" and "jural" components. This point was first clarified by Needham (1967: 43), who showed that terminological structures (categorical) need not necessarily be congruent with inter-group alliance structures (jural). For example, there are societies whose members use symmetrically structured terminologies, but who none the less practise asymmetric marriage alliance, or vice versa. Even in the absence of systematic forms of inter-group alliance, one may have symmetrical terminological prescriptions co-existing with asymmetric behavioural preferences (§6.3).

In short, there appear to be *three* levels of data which, since they can vary independently, need to be examined and analysed independently (Needham 1973a). The first (in descending order of abstraction, not decreasing importance) is the *system of categories* whereby people conceptualize and classify the world around them. In the field of kinship, this consists pre-eminently, though not exclusively, of their relationship terminology (Chapters 3 and 4). Then there is the set of *jural* or normative precepts and *preferences*. These legally or morally binding rules and values are phrased in terms of the system of terminological categories. Whereas the individual terms which go to make up each system of classification are largely taken for granted and un-examined, the jural rules convey the explicitly recognized ideology of the people concerned. Examples in the field of kinship are the rules governing the choice of an ideal spouse. The difficulty is that jural rules may take an indefinitely large number of cultural guises, so that their study, particularly their comparative study, is very difficult. Partly for this reason, such data are especially problematic, as we shall see in Chapter 8. Finally, there is the level of *behaviour*, which is conceptualized by the actors in terms of their systems of categories, and wholly or partly justified by them with reference to the prevailing jural norms. It is necessary to distinguish *collective behaviour*, that is, overall trends expressible in statistical terms ("20% of local men had married their FBD"), from *individual behaviour*, which needs to be explained in the light of the unique social context within which it occurs. Except in Chapter 8, we shall concentrate mainly upon behaviour in the first, collective sense.

Although, as we said, these three levels have a degree of independence, they are not *wholly* independent of each other. Any satisfactory analysis of a given kinship system must ultimately take account of them all. It seems to us that many of the controversies to which the study of kinship has been so prone, arose between writers apparently dealing with "the same" ethnographic evidence, but in fact approaching that evidence at different levels of under-standing and analysis. For example, it could be argued that the "descent theory"/"alliance theory" debates of the 1950s and 1960s – some of which are rehearsed below – reflected the emphases of those two approaches upon jural and categorical data, respectively. Though no doubt too simplistic to be a full explanation, this does make sense of most of the arguments which occurred.

Notice that the three levels have been defined *formally* rather than *substantively*. That is, we have distinguished them in terms of their mutual inter-relationships as a structured set, rather than according to their content, which has been mentioned only for purposes of illustration. Another strand running throughout the book is this concern with relationships rather than essences, and with structures rather than contents. This also entails a lack of interest in precise "real" definitions of concepts such as "marriage" (§6.1), or even "kinship" itself. We are perfectly content with a situation in which many of these key anthropological notions are polythetically – and therefore, from some viewpoints, imprecisely – defined, a position which we justify more fully at the end (§8.8).

1.4. The aims of this book

Finally, some explanation of our aims in writing this book. It is *not* a kinship textbook. No adequate, comprehensive work of that kind has been produced so far, though there have been numerous attempts. Those instructional books which *are* authoritative, such as Fox's *Kinship and Marriage* (1967) and Dumont's brilliant *Introduction à deux théories d'anthropologie sociale* (1971), aim only at partial coverage. Other, broader, textbooks have generally reflected only a limited range of theoretical views, or have been surprisingly prone to basic errors. While not claiming freedom from inadvertent error, we do feel that this book is different in what it sets out to do.

If you are soon to embark upon fieldwork, you are likely to be particularly interested in the practical and methodological suggestions which form the main subject matter of Chapters 2 and 3, and which are also scattered throughout the rest of the book. But although there are a few standard techniques for investigating kinship, and although you should always be systematic in whatever you do, the topic does not lend itself, by and large, to mechanical procedures. So this is not, and could not be, purely an instruction manual either. Our endeavour has been to explain the field of kinship studies in terms of its problems, issues and debates, not to avoid these. While making our own views clear on such matters, we have tried to present both sides of the story. For one thing, we cannot expect our readers to agree with all our personal conclusions. For another, polemic seems out of place in a book of this kind. We have no axe to grind, then, except that of good fieldwork, and full, clear, comprehensible ethnography.

Kinship cannot easily be distinguished from other aspects of society. Nor should it be. In our last two chapters, for example, we examine the economic and political sides of kinship, as well as the cosmological and biological theories of the people whom anthropologists study. Earlier chapters deal directly, though not narrowly, with "kinship" in its more conventional senses. Writers on kinship tend to divide up their subject matter under broad sub-headings such as "relationship" terminologies", "descent systems", "marriage", and so on, a fact reflected in our chapter and section titles. But this is primarily a matter of convenience, for ease of presentation. No ethnographer can afford to neglect any of these areas, and almost every aspect of any kinship system will involve more than one such theme. Marriage, for example, crops up at several different places in the book, and in a variety of contexts. Chapter 6 deals with "marriage" in itself, but it also appears (under the guise of "complementary filiation") in Chapter 5, and its political concomitants take up a large part of Chapter 7.

So the sub-divisions of the book, and the section headings used, indicate pragmatic changes in emphasis rather than truly different topics. To underline this, we often use the same data from the same society several times over, drawing out different aspects on each occasion, according to context. You will notice that anthropologically classic peoples like the Trobrianders, Tallensi, Nuer and Kachin, are particularly in evidence here, though we draw upon our own fieldwork experiences too. Furthermore, although we say little explicitly about studies of kinship in industrial societies, we see no great divide between these and more traditional kinds of ethnography. The theoretical issues raised are similar in both situations, though the fact that kinship institutions are often less central or well-defined in the former case requires certain modifications in the methods used, and may demand greater skill and sensitivity (§2.6).

Our aim is to explain how, in our view, kinship may be most effectively studied and analysed. The principle requirement, whether you are an undergraduate, a desk-bound or fieldworking postgraduate, or indeed a Professor of Social Anthropology, is a capacity for clear, logical and *open-minded* thought. Theoretical debate is the lifeblood of anthropology, but petty disagreements based on blinkered reasoning, ambiguity or conceptual confusion, threaten it with pernicious anaemia. Before forming an opinion on any of the controversies which fill the kinship literature, ask yourself one simple, diagnostic question: does the argument truly concern rival interpretations of views or practices in any given society, or is it merely a squabble over differing definitions? As we said, many writers do not comprehend what their "opponents" have written, because the premises from which they start are so different. Moreover, once you have "defined" a particular term, the only argument possible is the sterile one of whether the society in question does or does not contain the "real" phenomenon, "out there", to which the term is naively assumed to apply. Our true concern should be to *understand* the fascinating variety of human kinship institutions, not merely to label them.

2 *Collecting census data and genealogies*

2.1 Introduction

Wherever you do fieldwork and whatever your interests, you will almost certainly find it necessary to carry out a census of some kind, and to collect genealogical information about the people you study. This chapter discusses the status of such data, evaluates the methods for obtaining them, and deals with some of the theoretical and practical difficulties which may be encountered. Regrettably, the possible problems are as varied as kinship systems themselves, and it will certainly not be possible to anticipate every eventuality.

If time is limited, census and genealogical data may be gathered together, but there are advantages in collecting them separately if at all possible. A census by itself takes up relatively little time, whereas genealogy collection is not only much slower in each case, but also involves interviewing a larger proportion of the population. For instance, census information can generally be obtained from a single informant in each household, but a genealogical study will almost certainly call for information from both spouses, at the very least. Another advantage of separating the two processes, is that momentary lapses of memory or random mistakes by particular informants become obvious and can be enquired into. All information should ideally be checked by comparing statements from the same person on different occasions, or by questioning others. More significant cases of "structural amnesia" will of course remain (§2.4).

2.2 Doing a Census

In our experience, there is much to be said for carrying out a census as your first task upon arrival in a new fieldwork location. Until you have some idea of the size, occupations, social composition, and so on, of the local population, you can neither make sense of your first, fragmentary impressions nor frame possible lines of enquiry with any precision.

Census-collection is indirectly useful in another way. A fieldworker newly arrived in some remote or exotic spot inevitably attracts great interest and attention from the local people. In fact, the early flow of information may be in quite the opposite direction from the one you naively anticipated. Even if you do not find this sudden and drastic loss of privacy disturbing, sensible conversation with local people is impossible under such conditions. There is no way in which this period of mutual *rapprochement* can be avoided, but how is it best minimized and most quickly overcome? The most obvious answer is that you should be visible as often as possible to as many people as possible during the early stages of fieldwork. A census, by its very nature, fulfils these criteria.

The first step in any census, assuming that you are dealing with a sedentary population in fixed dwelling-sites, is likely to be the preparation of a map of the locality. Clearly, the accuracy and sophistication with which this is done will depend upon the aims of the research (see Monkhouse and Wilkinson (1963) for advice). These will also dictate whether it is merely areas of settlement which are depicted or whether, for instance, agricultural land must also be mapped. The latter almost certainly requires training in surveying (R. Spier 1970) if quantitatively meaningful results are to be obtained: on the other hand, it may prove the only reliable source of information on land-holding. Official data (even if available) may be outdated, inaccurate or, at the very least, not a true reflection of the *de facto* control of land resources. Informants may for their part be unwilling to divulge such crucial information to an outsider.

Preparing a sketch-map of inhabited dwellings, to an approximate scale obtained by, say, pacing out distances, presents few problems when a nucleated or otherwise bounded settlement is to be studied (though it goes without saying that this geographical segregation is bound to be to some extent illusory from the sociological perspective). On the other hand, geographical boundaries may be of little significance in certain kinds of study, for instance those of dispersed minorities spread throughout a metropolis, or of nomadic populations with few material possessions and fluctuating band composition.

Whatever the peculiarities of the local situation, it will not be possible to "bound" your fieldwork area with any confidence until much later, so it is better to cast the cartographic and census net widely in the early stages.

Where there are permanently-located dwellings and other buildings, these may be mapped first. The nature or purpose of the building, and the name of its owner, tenant or householder, should be recorded. Significant or immediately apparent variations in size or type of dwelling can be noted straight away. It is useful to assign each building a provisional code number when it is added to the map. This may need modification later, if there turns out to be multiple occupancy, or so that the dwellings of socially significant groups or categories may easily be distinguished. At this stage it is not especially important to speak to every householder in person. Passers-by and neighbouring children may be consulted, and even if their information ultimately proves inaccurate, there will be ample opportunity to correct it later. The most important things at this stage are speed and completeness of coverage.

A second visit must then be made to carry out the actual census. Naturally, the details you require are best obtained from a senior adult, preferably the household head. As a minimum, the names of all household members should be recorded, together with their relationship to the household head, and their ages or dates of birth, if either are known. If you wish, you can also obtain details of their occupations, membership of socially significant groups and categories, and so on, but there are advantages in postponing the collection of most of this additional information. The sooner you visit every house, and the more often you return thereafter, the better – within reason and given the constraints of time. Data on place of birth, clan, lineage, or similar affiliations, and so on, are best obtained in conjunction with the genealogy, and as already mentioned, details on income and property are unlikely to be volunteered accurately at this early stage. We deal with the collection of such economic data in a later section (§7.2).

At the beginning, then, only a fairly rudimentary set of data need be collected. The questions – about names, ages, and close family relationships – are not only innocuous but simple and repetitive. Asking them not only provides essential basic information, but also gives you a chance to explain, or at least illustrate, the purpose of your stay. With luck, this will help quash any wild rumours concerning ulterior motives. Moreover, the visit provides a first opportunity for developing personal relationships, whereby the two parties eventually come to see each other not as exotic creatures to be studied, but as people to be befriended and understood. These first visits have yet another advantage when you are not fluent in the local dialect. Constantly repeating the same questions, and comprehending a fairly standard set of replies, provides an ideal opportunity for building up proficiency and – equally important – confidence in your use of the language. For all these reasons, even fieldworkers who employ local interpreters or assistants would be well-advised to undertake much of this work personally, however tedious and time-consuming the prospect might appear.

There is always the risk that your arrival in the field will have been received with suspicion – as evidence that you are a government agent or foreign spy, for instance. In that event you will probably have to suspend the census proper until your *bona fides* are properly established. The need to meet and quickly get to know as many people as possible will become still more acute, but you will have to accomplish this without appearing too inquisitive.

Census data perhaps constitute the nearest approach made by anthropology to the chimerical world of "hard facts". They are not, however, unproblematic. It is by no means as simple as one might think to decide who are members of particular communities or households and who are not. Some individuals may work and normally reside elsewhere, but return for festivals, family occasions or harvests. They may or may not hold land or other property locally. Others in similar positions may not return for years on end, but intend to do so once they have reached retirement age, saved enough money to get married, or become widowed. Relatives of various kinds may come to stay, often for extended periods. They may contribute significantly to the economy of the household during their visit, yet not be regarded as permanent members of it. Government officials or other workers may live locally, but have family homes and community loyalties elsewhere. People may live locally but work elsewhere, or vice versa. Clearly, there is no general, foolproof way of defining community membership. The decision depends in every case upon the time for which it is relevant and the context in which the question is posed. Individuals who are excluded for one purpose may well have to be included for another, and you must judge every case on its merits.

The indigenous definition of "residence" may not always accord with the situation on the ground. In that event, it is important to notice what status people have in the community or section of the community in which they are staying. In the language of modern nation states, there may be "visitors", "temporary residents", "permanent residents", and "citizens", for instance. Where individuals hold long-term rights of residence in a place which is not their "home", this may reflect patterns in the developmental cycle of local residential groups (§5.7). It is also important to watch out for seasonal or random events bringing about significant changes in the size or composition of the population, at different times during your fieldwork.

2.3 Genealogical Knowledge

2.3.1 *Form*

Societies differ greatly with regard to the extent of the genealogical knowledge held by a typical member, and in the form that knowledge takes. Here it is helpful to follow J. A. Barnes' distinction between "genealogy" and "pedigree" (1967a: 103). The *genealogy* is the "scientific" (though as we shall see, not necessarily biologically-based) record made in standard format by the anthropologist, with random errors removed, evidence duly verified, and the testimonies of different informants combined and consolidated. The *pedigree* is the information provided by informants, in culturally-specific fashion. This distinction is ultimately only relative, since genealogies are merely our form of pedigree, but it is nevertheless useful to distinguish etic and emic perspectives, as long as the context is specified.

Even genealogical pedigrees may be expressed or depicted in many different ways, and Barnes (ibid: 113–118) discusses some of the methods employed in other societies and in our own past, including the familiar notion of the "family tree". Another interesting example is the written "family history" found among white South Africans (Preston-Whyte 1981: 192–195). On the other hand, pedigrees need not be genealogically-based at all. In a celebrated article, Hocart (1937) pointed out that Fijian hill-people classify on the basis of age-set (there are two which alternate) and "line" (cross or parallel). Offices are inherited by the next most senior member of the previous incumbent's age-set, irrespective of genealogical propinquity. The cultural possibilities are endless, but whatever the details you are always performing a more or less drastic act of translation when converting local pedigrees into standard genealogical form.

2.3.2 *Extent*

Generally speaking, the extent of genealogical knowledge is likely to be determined largely by the degree to which it is useful in various aspects of life. People do not usually remember such information purely for its own sake. One might expect, then, that members of societies having structurally-important descent groups or pronounced lineal ideologies, should display a considerable depth of genealogical knowledge. Conversely, members of societies in which marriage alliance is structurally and conceptually as important as descent, should have broad, rather than deep genealogies. Evidence from India supports these suggestions to some extent, while providing some important caveats.

In North India, exogamous patrilineal clans are widespread, while marriage rules include the requirement that *sapiṇḍa* (persons related through males within, typically, six generations on the paternal and four on the maternal side) should not marry. Clearly, at least this depth of genealogical knowledge might be anticipated, and is sometimes found in practice. However, and this is a very common feature, genealogically-distant local residents are more likely to be included in a person's remembered genealogy than are closer relatives who have moved away (Parry 1979: 136). There are, moreover, several reasons why genealogical knowledge should be still more restricted. Like knowledge of all kinds, it will be unevenly distributed among the population (§8.2.1). This uneven distribution is likely to correlate with other socio-structural features. It is important to note any systematic variations of this kind. For instance, do the old know significantly more than those actually of marriageable age, on average? Who are better informed, men or women? Are there other, culturally-defined categories of person, who are unusually well or badly informed on these matters? Some North Indian castes, for example, employ professional genealogists to record and keep the necessary information for them (Mayer 1960: 194–201). This can be recovered only upon payment of a fee, and may prove wholly inaccessible – or at best, extremely expensive! – to the fieldworker, because genealogists will naturally hesitate to reveal the information which provides their livelihood.

There may often be alternative, non-genealogical ways of working out such matters as marriageability. Thus, the particular North Indian marriage rules just mentioned can be applied in practice simply by prohibiting marriage with anyone having the same clan title as one's F or M. This includes all the *sapiṇḍa* and, just to be on the safe side as it were, adds numbers of other people to the *de facto* exogamous unit. It is also, of course, much easier to remember two clan names, rather than all the ramifications of a six-generation genealogy (Madan 1965: 145; Berreman 1972: 157–158).

In South India a very different situation exists. Marriage is frequently confined within localized sub-castes, displaying little stress on unilineality. The preferred spouses are often cross-cousins, and marriage is in almost every case prescribed with a member of the terminological category to which such cousins belong. The relationship terminology is logically ordered and highly symmetric (see Fig. 3.5), so that the marriageability of a given couple is easily ascertained if the terminological relationships between their respective parents are known. Thus, the children of any two male parallel relatives, are themselves parallel relatives and so cannot marry. But if two men are cross relatives, their children will also be cross relatives, and can marry so long as the groom is senior to and one "terminological level" above his bride ("generation" is here too ambiguous a word, cf. Good 1980: 490–491).

So the practicalities of South Indian marital and other kinship behaviour do not require genealogical knowledge to extend any further back than the level of one's parents. People do normally know the identities of their grandparents, but even this is not universal. On the other hand, as would be expected, people have a very broad spread of genealogical knowledge, embracing not merely their own parents' immediate affines (parents' opposite sex siblings and their spouses), but their parents' affines' affines and so on.

As with the North Indian case, there are limits to this spread, which again arise because the relevant knowledge may be held in non-genealogical form. Here it is the logical symmetry of the terminology which is turned to advantage. In a prescriptive system, the *terminological* relationship between the parents expresses the marriageability of the children (§6.3.2), so it is not necessary for the exact genealogical links to be known. Indeed, none need exist. As a consequence, South Indians can easily specify their terminological relationships to many members of their local caste group, without being able to say precisely how they are related to these people genealogically.

These Indian examples illustrate that genealogical knowledge does indeed tend to correlate with other, structural aspects of the kinship system, but that there are always contingent limitations on the extent to which this is so. Most limitations are culture specific, and so cannot be catalogued in advance, but there are some general points to watch out for. There is first the question of the sociology of genealogical knowledge: who knows what? Secondly, much of this knowledge may take ostensibly non-genealogical forms. And thirdly, remember the fundamental point that genealogies are always *sociological* statements.

2.4 Types of genealogical kowledge

Genealogies are not accounts of biological relationships but sociological artefacts whose relevance for demographic, genetic, and other kinds of would-be objective or quantitative study is often problematic. That said, one can go on to distinguish:

(1) *Objective genealogies*, which aim to state as accurately as possible the "true" sociological relationships actually existing "out there". These are

obtained by checking, comparing and combining the statements of informants, so as to eliminate errors and distortions, and overcome gaps in individual knowledge. These may be supplemented, in societies with written
records, by recourse to the local equivalent of Somerset House. The intention
here is to produce an historically-accurate account.

(2) *Subjective genealogies*, which reflect the situation as perceived by
particular persons or groups at particular times. These should correlate to
some extent with the ages, sexes, social statuses, and aspirations of the people
concerned.

Notice that this distinction is not the same as that between genealogy and
pedigree. The concern there was with the format in which knowledge was
expressed, whereas here it is a matter of its etic historical status. A third type
of distinction may be made between *jural genealogies*, which express idealized or normative relationships between persons or groups, and *behavioural
genealogies* expressing the way things actually work out in practice.

It is crucial to be clear just where each piece of information fits into this
cross-cutting matrix, because this determines its intrinsic significance and
hence the analytic uses to which it may be put. For instance, officially
recorded "objective" information may well be relevant to studies of, say,
long-term emigration patterns, divorce rates, or infant mortality, but there is
probably little point in seeking out information unknown to those concerned,
if the sole intention is to explain their current, observed behaviour. In fact,
subjective genealogies of either jural or behavioural kind are the stock-in-
trade of most social anthropologists most of the time.

It is therefore always possible that, knowingly or not, people may adjust
their genealogical statements to emphasize important or sought-after links,
disguise others which may be discreditable, eliminate remote or structurally
unimportant ancestors, and so on. You should always be on the look-out for
these kinds of selective recall or structural amnesia. They can be distinguished
from mere random forgetfulness, to some extent, by rechecking the information later on.

One systematic feature to look out for, especially in societies for which
lineages or lineal pedigress are important, is the use of genealogies to describe
or order *contemporary* relationships among putatively kin-based social
groupings or local communities. Among many others, Evans-Pritchard,
Peters and Andrew Strathern have described such situations for the Nuer,
Bedouin and Melpa respectively. The political implications of kinship are
considered later (§7.4, §7.5, §8.3.1). Here we need mention only the possibility that more than one type of genealogical information may be dis-

tinguishable in the pedigrees provided by informants. Thus, particularly in their lower (more recent) levels, pedigrees will be behavioural statements about interpersonal relationships: "X is the son of Y", where X and Y are identifiable living or historical persons. By contrast, higher levels of the same pedigrees may be mythologically-based jural statements about primeval ancestors of the people as a whole, and their major contemporary sub-divisions (tribes, clans, etc.). Though very different in purpose and status, both types of genealogy tend to be fairly stable in structure, at least in the short term. After all, there is little possibility of denying very close genea-logical ties, and little cause to revive basic cosmology. But in between these extremes the situation is necessarily subject to change and reinterpretation. As contemporary groupings wax and wane in size, status, or power; as they form alliances or split into hostile factions; so their members may consciously or unwittingly adjust their genealogical connections, perhaps emphasizing links with new allies or downplaying those with newly-formed hostile factions. Members of the other group may of course repudiate such activities, and there are likely to be instances where two parties assert quite different views of their mutual relationship. Such situations clearly demand careful investigation. When an individual omits to mention a relationship to a particular person or grouping, this may indicate an avoidance relationship, a ban on speaking certain names, or a personal dispute, but is also quite likely to be mere forgetfulness. But where all members of an entire lineage or similar grouping assert a relationship which the other parties do not acknowledge or admit only reluctantly, this is almost certain to indicate sociologically-significant manipulation of the etic evidence by one or both parties.

Even when this does not happen, the intermediate reaches of the genealogy are often places where "etic facts are sorted and reassembled to form shifting emic statements" (A. Strathern 1972: 93). The borderline between historical and mythological ancestors is bound to be fluid, as members of successive generations have to fit their ever-changing genealogical and demographic situations onto a constant emic grid. People in such societies have to have ways of papering over the cracks, which you will need to elucidate. Bedouin, for instance, tend to fuse together deceased persons bearing the same name, so that lines of descent are telescoped, and members of extinct lines are provided with heirs by their namesakes (Peters 1960: 33–35). Melpa have their men's house group idiom (Strathern 1972: 48), whereby prolonged co-residence comes to be accorded the same *de facto* status as common descent. Nuer not only permit Dinka to be adopted into their captors' lineages (Evans-Pritchard 1940: 221), but also have ways of allowing the emic framework to pre-empt the etic "facts" very directly, by means of "ghost" and "woman" marriage (Evans-Pritchard 1951: 108–109). Here the emic groupings (the descent lines) are maintained even when their members do not produce the necessary offspring, by the device of ascribing to them in advance the offspring of certain others. The cultural possibilities are again limitless. In general, such different types of genealogical connection must be looked out for, and any systematic discrepancies investigated with the above ideas in mind. It should at least be clear by now that genealogical information is by no means as mundane, factual and unproblematic as might at first appear.

2.5 Collecting pedigrees and genealogies

The standard technique for obtaining genealogical information has long been the "*genealogical method*" developed by Rivers during the Torres Straits expedition of 1898–1899 (Rivers 1910, 1968 [1910]). This method was succinctly described by him in the 4th edition of *Notes and Queries on Anthropology* (1912), and its latest (6th, 1951) edition contains instructions which, though unsigned, are still largely as Rivers wrote them. Subsequently J. A. Barnes (1967a) has suggested going about things in a slightly different order. Both systems are described below. Rivers' has been more widely used and contains more precise instructions, but there is one initial procedure which only Barnes recommends and which seems highly desirable. Before either etic method is applied, you should first discover, through observation and less formal questioning, how people conceive of, talk about, and portray their genealogies. If it turns out that they have their own ways of diagramming or talking about kinship, record them. At the very least they will have a distinctive relationship terminology (see Chapter 3). Do not prompt them, or constrain them to express ideas in etic, genealogically-based terms, at least until you have mastered their own idiom. Often you will be able to collect information couched in this idiom, which is inaccessible in genealogical form. Thus the indigenous system is important in two ways: (i) as an aid to fieldwork, since it uses terms and concepts which both the informants and the fieldworker understand; (ii) as data – more specifically, as a native representation of kinship ideology.

It is crucial, for both theoretical and practical reasons, that you pay attention to how people phrase their discussion of genealogical points of reference. For example, Nharo Bushmen do not string possessives together, as we do in phrases such as "*mother's brother's daughter*". Instead, they start at the top genealogically, with a sibling pair, and trace downwards (Barnard

1978b). In unilineal societies people frequently start a generation above that, with a common ancestor or ancestral married couple. Even the French, because of the normal rule of possessive formation in their language, have a different system from the English. They trace not from ego to alter, but from alter to ego: *le frère de ma mère*, "the brother of my mother". Some French anthropologists reflect this in their abbreviations for genealogical positions, e.g. "FM" for *frère de la mère*, meaning "mother's brother", not "father's mother". Dumont and others, however, employ the ego-to-alter method and the English abbreviations even when writing in French.

The *Notes and Queries* account begins by pointing out that even those local words used as the equivalents of *mother, father, brother* and *sister* may have quite different semantic ranges from their English counterparts. It recommends (1951: 54) that you first ascertain the identities of "the woman from whose womb [the male ego] was born", and the man "who begot him". This biblical phraseology is designed to specify biological parents and so overcome the obvious difficulty that local terms for *mother* and *father* may have wider meanings. The exact idiom will have to conform with local usage. In South India, for instance, one might distinguish genealogical from classificatory siblings by referring to the former as "having been born in the (same) house".

Ego should be asked how he addresses each of these persons and how they address him (1951: 55). He is then asked: "Did *A* and *B* (these being his parents' *names*) have any children besides yourself?" The names and sexes of full siblings are thus obtained, and ego is asked how he addresses them, and they him. The account continues:

> Thus a genealogical record of an *elementary family* . . . is obtained, with the terms for father, mother, child and *sibling*. (ibid; original emphasis)

In fact, of course, it is strictly the term for S which has been obtained, not that for C, and probably those for B and Z rather than for G. The procedure may need to be more complicated if siblings are distinguished according to relative age, relative gender, birth order, etc., but *Notes and Queries* does not consider these problems.

Ego is then asked whether he is married, and his wife's name is recorded, together with the relationship terms for H and W. The names of ego's children "borne him by his wife" (ibid) should then be obtained, and although the account itself does not specifically say so, it is at this point that the possibility of obtaining the relationship term for D first presents itself.

By this time, the investigator has collected ego's most immediate genealogy, and with it the relationship terms for F, M, H, W, S and D. *Notes and Queries* suggests that more extended enquiry be conducted entirely by means of these basic terms, avoiding the local equivalents of *brother, sister, aunt, grand-father, cousin*, etc. It is rightly pointed out that such terms may be used in a variety of genealogical senses, as when *uncle* applies to FB, MZH, etc. However, comparative evidence reveals that exactly the same may be true of local terms for *father, son*, etc. Why then does *Notes and Queries* treat some genealogical positions as less problematic than others? The answer may be that there is an implicit lineal bias pervading the entire method. Lineal relationships are consequently seen as less potentially ambiguous than col-lateral and (especially) affinal ones.

The next stage is to collect information about any other spouses whom ego's parents may have had, and thereafter about ego's half or step-siblings. From here on, individuals are consistently to be referred to by name, and their relationships to ego denoted only by combining the elementary terms already collected. Thus, if ego's M is named X, her B must always be described as "X's brother" rather than "your mother's brother" or, worse still, "your uncle". One would imagine that the spouses and children of ego's half- and step-siblings would be recorded at this point, but *Notes and Queries* does not specifically say so. Instead, it moves straight on to consider ego's parents' parents, and their children, then the spouses and children of the latter, and so on. The order in which this is to be done is not entirely clear, but Fig. 2.1 lists the various relatives in the numerical sequence apparently envisaged. The basic movement is, first, up one generation to a new apical ancestor, and thence downwards to cover all of this person's descendants not already recorded. The process is repeated for as far as a person's knowledge extends. The instructions end: "The genealogy of the informant's wife may be recorded next" (ibid).

As already mentioned, all this takes for granted that every genealogy is based on certain kinds of lineal relationship. Somewhat surprisingly, that assumption is even more clearly evident in J. A. Barnes' account. Figure 2.2 displays his suggested order of procedure for a patrilineal society, with the matrilineal sequence in parentheses: he recommends that the "dominant line of ascent" be recorded first in each case (1967a: 110). The relatives shown are taken as apical ancestors in numerical order, so that in the patrilineal case ego's own descendants are recorded first, then those of his F, FF etc. To allow for the possibility that, say, ego might know of his FFB but not his FFF, the siblings of the highest known apical ancestor should also be investigated (ibid: 110–111).

Barnes' extended diagram (ibid) makes clear something already evident in Figs 2.1 and 2.2, namely that the genealogy is conceived of as a set of unilineal

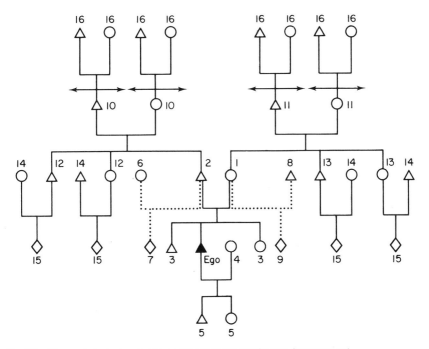

Fig. 2.1   *The genealogical method according to* Notes and Queries *(1951: 54–55).*

segments, to be mapped out one by one. Clearly there are many societies for which such assumptions and procedures are entirely justified. Moreover, both methods discussed so far will work after a fashion whenever and wherever they are applied. Yet our two figures reveal a number of gaps, particularly regarding affines. Only the spouses and daughters of males in these lineal segments are recorded: neither method, rigidly applied, investigates such pre-eminent affines as ego's child's spouse's parents. Of course, such information may ultimately be obtained by indirect means, at least for those of ego's children and their spouses who happen to live locally, but the fact remains that the apparent form and extent of ego's genealogical knowledge are moulded and constrained by these etically-inspired techniques of questioning. For instance, the large reservoir of knowledge about affines (and affines' affines, etc.) held by the average South Indian, would be left almost completely untapped. In short, although many of the procedures and warnings contained in both accounts are valuable and justified, the methods as a whole cannot be applied to many societies without the risk of considerable distortion.

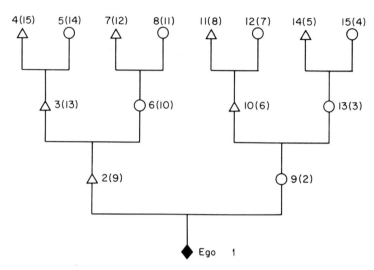

Fig. 2.2 *Sequence of apical ancestors in the method of J. A. Barnes (1967: 110). The numerical sequence assumes patrilineal descent. For matrilineal societies the order should be that given in parentheses.*

We suggest that you begin with a more open mind concerning the likely "shape" of an informant's genealogical knowledge, and that questions be phrased with a view to exploring as many avenues of genealogical knowledge as possible. This is particularly necessary in the early stages of investigation. It is especially important that a more even balance be struck between agnatic and/or uterine relatives on the one hand, and affines on the other.

So as to make the technique more general in this way, you might begin by asking ego about the relatives listed in Table 2.1. It may prove convenient to

Table 2.1   *Suggested order of procedure in genealogy collection*

---

(1) F, (2) FP, (3) FG, (4) FGE, (5) FGC, (6) FGCE, (7) FGCC

(8) M, (9) MP, (10) MG, (11) MGE, (12) MGC, (13) MGCE, (14) MGCC

(15) E, (16) EP, (17) C, (18) CE, (19) CEP, (20) CC, (21) CCE, (22) CCEP

(23) EG, (24) EGE, (25) EGEP, (26) EGC, (27) ECGE

(28) G, (29) GE, (30) GEP, (31) GC, (32) GCE, (33) GCEP, (34) GCC, (35) GCCE

(36) GEG, (37) GEGE, (38) GEGC, (39) GECGE.

---

investigate them in this particular numerical order, but what really matters is that all these possible relationships are explored in a reasonably systematic way. Possible variations on the order given in the table, which might prove easier to apply in the light of local circumstances, include: (i) the collection of matrilateral relatives before patrilateral ones, a procedure which may have advantages in matrilineal societies; and (ii) investigation of ego's siblings before ego's spouse's relatives, particularly perhaps in strongly unilineal contexts.

Although these 39 types of relationship, shown pictorially in Fig. 2.3, represent an *a priori* bare minimum which every investigation should aim to include within its scope, this is not to say that any ego will be able to provide all this information in practice. For one thing, of course, not everyone has relatives of all these possible types. If, more significantly, it becomes clear that there are certain types of relative that *no-one* knows anything about, and that there are obvious socio-structural reasons for this – as might well be the case for, say, spouses' siblings' spouses' parents (EGEP) in societies like the North Indian ones considered earlier – then you may eventually decide to drop these particular questions in order to save time. Conversely, enquiries may be pushed further in whichever directions prove fruitful. For instance, the greater lineal depth provided by the methods of Rivers and Barnes will clearly be appropriate in many situations. Table 2.1 should not, therefore, be seen as regulating or restricting the scope of genealogical enquiry, but rather as a signpost to avenues of investigation which these other methods neglect. The essential improvement which it contains is that, for every new person added to the genealogy, one asks about not merely their spouse(s) and children, but also their spouse's parents, etc. To put it another way, while the earlier methods limit themselves to working downwards from a set of apical ancestors, this technique also works upwards from a set of ultimate descendants. This greatly facilitates the collection of information about affines, and makes it easier to piece together the genealogical fragments collected from different people. These are considerable advantages where there is much intermarriage, or where affinal links are otherwise important.

Whatever the precise method adopted, there is in principle no limit to the amount of information that can be collected at the same time. For every person added to the genealogy, you may wish to record their names, ages, places of birth and current residence, wealth, occupation, clan or lineage membership, etc., etc., depending upon which social indices seem important for the society concerned. Clearly though, there are limits to the patience and goodwill of every informant. These vary from person to person, but may be to some extent characteristic of the society as a whole. In general, the more

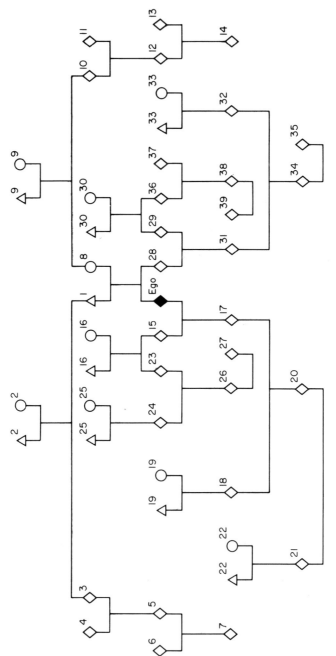

Fig. 2.3 *Modified genealogical method, involving affinal as well as lineal relationships.*

extensive a person's genealogical knowledge, the less supplementary information can be collected along with it, otherwise the procedure very quickly
assumes daunting proportions. On the other hand, especially in cases where
identical or similar names recur frequently, it may be more certain precisely to
whom a piece of information refers, if that information is obtained during
genealogy-collection. This tension between your desire for systematic
information, and your need to retain the goodwill of bored informants, arises
in all aspects of fieldwork. You will have to use your judgement, based on
sensitivity to the situation and accumulated experience, to decide how far to
press your questioning.

Whereas that particular problem is to some degree universal, there may be
other, culturally-specific difficulties which cannot be anticipated in advance.
Nharo Bushmen, for instance, do not like to speak of the dead by name, and
may resent being pressed. In other societies, there are namesake avoidances or
prohibitions on using the personal names of certain categories of relative.
Thus, South Indian women will not speak their H's name. In Good's case,
these women solved this problem for him, by telling one of their children to
say the name. Not every difficulty can be so easily overcome though, and
special strategies may need to be adopted in cases where informants tell
systematic and deliberate lies (Chagnon 1974: 88–101), or simply refuse to
answer. You can only meet such problems as and when they arise.

2.6. Kinship studies in urban settings

Raymond Firth (1956: 11) long ago remarked on the paucity of studies of
kinship in urban, industrial societies. Sociologists in Western countries have
concerned themselves almost exclusively with *family studies* rather than
kinship *per se*. That is, they have focused upon the elementary or nuclear
family, seen as a self-contained unit. Kinship links outside that unit have been
ignored, or treated as comparatively unimportant: alternatively, the wider
context has been seen in terms of "a series of interlocking nuclear families"
(Turner 1969: 35). Though ostensibly concerned with "scientifically
oriented" methods (Anderson 1971: 12), many such studies prove ultimately
trivial because, despite their frequent mathematical sophistication, they
merely "reproduce data in the same (cultural) terms as informants perceive
them" (M. Strathern 1982: 73; orig. gloss). This happens, of course, because
observers and observed share broadly the same kinship culture, *or think that
they do*. As Anderson admits, the family sociologist working in his own
society "knows too much" (1971: 8). None the less, much of this work is

clearly relevant for anyone engaging in urban research. Its volume (particularly concerning "the American family") has been so great, however, that we cannot possibly deal adequately with it here.

We shall therefore concentrate upon matters more central to "kinship" as generally understood by anthropologists. Firth's comments are still broadly applicable today, but in this section we refer briefly to some work which *has* been done in this area. As we have already said (§1.4), the basic theoretical considerations remain the same wherever one does fieldwork. On the other hand, the methodological emphasis has to shift somewhat in urban studies, and the more elusive and *elective* character of kinship in many such societies calls for greater skill, subtlety and persistence on the part of the fieldworker.

Generally speaking, the kinship system is less central to society as a whole than in isolated or small-scale communities, because other kinds of institution regulate – for example – economic and political affairs. Kinship tends, therefore, to be much less evident in the public domain: kinship relationships become above all *domestic* relationships. It often follows that questions concerning a person's relatives are regarded as intrusive, and that those who ask them – if not already well-known to the respondent – are liable to be viewed with suspicion. Moreover, participant observation becomes much more difficult when so many family activities take place in the home, behind closed doors (Firth *et al.* 1969: 36). You will still find public gatherings of kin, of course, most notably in connection with life crisis rituals. These must naturally be studied, as in societies of all kinds (§6.5). Relationship terms can be obtained in the usual way (§3.3), though their importance is likely to lie more at the cognitive level (§8.5) than in what they tell you about social structure or social organization. Genealogies, too, should be collected (§2.5). Their range is often restricted, though this cannot be assumed: as usual (§2.3.2), genealogical knowledge may be considerable if advantages are to be gained thereby, or interests safe-guarded. For example, one of us – like many Americans – knows much more about his British ancestors, including their place of origin and approximate date of migration, than does the average Briton, who is unlikely to be able to name even his FFF (Firth *et al.* 1976: 166–167). Likewise, South African families of European origin often maintain family histories going back 300 years. In them

> the myth of white purity is celebrated and validated by the strict genealogical tally of white marriages and births down the generations (Preston-Whyte 1981: 195).

But routine domestic life is very likely to remain almost inaccessible to you except in a very few cases, and your dependence upon formal interviewing and questionnaire techniques is likely to be greater than in most fieldwork.

Moreover, relatives are less likely to be locally resident than in isolated, rural communities, though this need not always be the case, as studies in the East End of London have shown (Young and Willmott 1957: 117). It is therefore unlikely that you will be dealing with a community displaying neat geographical or social boundaries. Whereas anthropologists have stressed (perhaps too much (§5.4)) the "corporate" character of kinship units in many societies, kinship in Western, urban society is characterized by its amorphous nature.

> The kin groups outside the elementary family are not structural groups but organisational groups. They are assemblages *ad hoc* from among the total kin (Firth 1956: 14).

In short, once you move beyond the individual family or household, you are likely to be dealing not with neatly bounded or structurally constituted corporations, but with *quasi-groups* (Boissevian 1968: 550) or kinship networks.

All these characteristics suggest that the object of study will not usually be an entire community in the traditional anthropological fashion, but rather a *sample* community, selected from among the total population of the locality at random (either literally, or in the statistical sense), or according to some other statistical criteria. The method of sampling chosen will of course depend upon the purpose of your study (see Mitchell 1967: 30–35), although practical considerations of much more mundane kinds are almost certain to intrude. For example, Firth *et al.* (1969: 42), wishing to study a heterogeneous North London housing estate, used the local electoral roll to select by lot a sample of 60 *households*. A number of reserves were chosen, to replace households which dropped out or had to be eliminated: there were as many as 32 of these. Young and Willmott (1957: 204) used the Bethnal Green roll similarly, picking out every thirty-sixth *person*: over 150 of these had died, moved away, or refused to take part, leaving them with a total sample of 933. Later, however, they carried out more detailed studies using a sub-sample which comprised all 45 people from the families in which they were particularly interested, those including two or more children under the age of 15. This technique of "multi-stage sampling" (J. C. Mitchell 1967: 34) avoids some of the difficulties anthropologists commonly face in drawing statistically valid samples from inadequately defined populations. Whatever the method adopted, problems are bound to arise concerning the typicality of your sample, and hence the degree to which you can generalize from your findings about it.

Because the kinship links of your sample population are very likely to extend far beyond the area you are actually studying, you require research techniques which will enable you to deal with such situations. One possibility here is the use of *social network analysis* (J. C. Mitchell 1969). The aim of this is not so much to discover the total range of an individual's genealogical knowledge, but rather the ways in which selected relationships (with both kin and non-kin) serve as resources, which may be mobilized for particular purposes into *action sets* (Mayer 1966). A. L. Epstein (1969: 97, 1981: 226–227) produces just such a genealogical network, obtained not by any of the methods discussed in §2.5, but by asking his informant about the people whom he met over a given period of time, and about the content of the interactions which took place. This kind of study therefore gives some indication of a person's *effective kin network* (Firth *et al.* 1969: 195), and makes it possible to compare this with the total *kin universe* (ibid: 154), namely, that person's entire range of genealogical knowledge obtained in the usual way.

Clearly, such studies require detailed consideration of the formal properties of networks, and techniques for assessing not merely the *number* of active kin relationships which an individual may have, but also their *strength*, with respect both to each other and to relationships with non-relatives (J. C. Mitchell 1969: 12). The strength of a kinship link may be assessed in several possible ways according to context: for example, the content, durability, intensity, or frequency of the relationship may all be important to some degree (ibid: 20–29).

A. L. Epstein (1969, 1981: 224–238) has used network analysis to show how urban migrants utilize a wide variety of kinship ties to gain some measure of security and stability in the fluid, unpredictable environment of a burgeoning Zambian township. Boswell (1969) demonstrates that this happens even in Lusaka, particularly at times of crisis, such as bereavement. Bott, working in central London, used network studies as the basis for her hypothesis that the degree to which a British urban couple segregate their conjugal roles, is proportional to the density of their social network (1971: 60, 321). "Density" here refers to the extent to which other members of that network actually know and interact with each other, independently of the focal couple. Note that the networks involved are therefore demarcated initially on an ego-centric (or more accurately, couple-centric) basis. It is important to distinguish clearly between ego-centric and socio-centric networks, though this is not always easy (J. A. Barnes 1969: 57; Bott 1971: 319–323).

3 *Relationship terminologies 1*

3.1 Introduction

In this chapter we discuss the collection and analysis of "relationship terminologies". This designation is nowadays widely regarded as preferable to the more traditional phrase "kinship terminology", because it defines the field of relevance more broadly and does not assume that persons denoted by such terms are "kin" as we understand them, nor indeed that they are "related" in any genealogical sense whatever. A contrary view has been expressed by Scheffler and Lounsbury (1971: 71), who argue that "kinship" *is* a matter of genealogical connection, and that if "relationship terms" do not refer to genealogical categories, then there is no reason to regard them as aspects of kinship in the first place. They draw a distinction between genealogically based "kinship terminologies" and society-wide "relationship terminologies" of the kinds just mentioned, but we shall not do so here, for reasons partly explained in §3.6.1.

The investigation of such terminologies has been, and remains, central not only to the study of kinship, but to the theoretical development of anthropology in general. All the more surprising then, that so little has been written on the crucial matter of how to collect them. If only a fraction of the effort which has gone into developing formal, analytical procedures, had been devoted to the question of how to *obtain* the data, much theoretical and conceptual confusion could have been avoided. For as we shall see, the methods used to collect relationship terms partly determine the status of the terms collected. This is hardly surprising. What *is* remarkable is that so few fieldworkers make their methods explicit. We would urge all those who collect, analyse, and discuss relationship terminologies to make it absolutely clear how their information was obtained.

After a brief discussion of definitional and bounding problems, we shall describe and evaluate the methods available for collecting terminological data. Once again it will be impossible to anticipate all possible problems; indeed, this limitation is particularly acute here, precisely because authors have so rarely discussed the particular difficulties they encountered. We go on to suggest some basic tests to which your data may be subjected, with a view to determining the overall structure of the terminology in question.

3.2 What is a relationship terminology?

The techniques of data-collection and analysis discussed in this chapter assume, at least provisionally, that the notion of "relationship terminology" is meaningful cross-culturally, and that such terminologies constitute bounded systems, at least for the purposes of abstract, structural analysis. Both assumptions require examination.

First, *do* all societies have relationship terminologies? Every society must have ways of classifying its members, but this by no means always (and doubtless never exclusively) involves genealogically-based labels. The question is, under what circumstances do such classifications constitute relationship terminologies? To debate this fully would mean taking into account the tremendous differences in structure, range of applicability, and context of use, found even among those relationship terminologies universally recognized as such. We would also need to consider such phenomena as personal naming, teknonymy, necronymy and Australian section systems. But although this is clearly a matter of great interest and importance, we do not pursue it here for the following reasons.

The fact that the broad subject-matter of this chapter is apparent from its title, shows that the notion "relationship terminology" conveys something to anthropologists in general. It is only when one attempts an essentialist, monothetic definition of the concept that difficulties arise (§8.8.2). We do not believe it necessary, useful, or even possible to define the notion in any precise way, and prefer to operate with a working definition which we suspect is generally, if implicitly held. It is that relationship terminologies are ego-centred, consistent, and reciprocal systems of classification covering, though by no means exclusively, ego's socially-defined "family relationships".

The second problem concerns the bounding of terminological systems. In many if not all societies, relationship terms are also used in ways which are clearly not intended to express "normal" kinship, whatever that may mean for the society concerned. Such usages may be explicitly metaphoric, as when a shop-steward addresses his union "brothers" on the shop-floor, or a penitent his "father" in the confessional, but it may be less clear to the fieldworker, as a cultural outsider, just when this is so. Moreover, there may be more difficult cases for which such distinctions are not readily drawn. For example, the Bengali term *svāmī* means "husband", but also "lord", "master", and even "god" (Inden and Nicholas 1977: 68). There is no reason to think that the kinship meaning is the primary one here. If anything, *it* constitutes the metaphor, because the other usages are much more widely disseminated throughout India. On the other hand, *svāmī* is clearly a relationship term in Bengal, since there is no other word for "husband". We shall have more to say on "fictive kinship" in §7.6. As far as the collection of terminological data is concerned, all you can possibly do is judge every case on its merits.

Deciding what constitutes a separate relationship term is by no means always straightforward, either. For instance, suppose one term contains another within it, as with the English *grandfather* and *father-in-law*. Do we have only one term here (*father*), modified in several structurally insignificant ways, or are there three distinct terms? Most would take the latter view, since the terms all denote different kinds of relationship, but things may not always be so clear. For instance, Dumont (1953) argues that the distinction between "consanguines" and "affines" in Tamil terminologies of the type shown in Fig. 3.5, is less basic in the − 1 than in the + 1 level. In the latter case, the terms are completely distinct lexically, but in the former, "affines" are distinguished from "consanguines" by the mere addition of a prefix. Thus, S = *makan* and ZS(ms) = *marumakan*. Is this argument a valid one, or is the resemblance simply an accident of linguistic history? After all, the respective reciprocals of *makan* and *marumakan* are quite distinct, as we said.

To take a slightly different case, most English-speaking people know and interact socially with their EGE, yet they are able to refer to such people only by composite terms such as *wife's sister's husband* which, unlike *grandfather,* are entirely composed of more basic terms. Should we regard these composites as distinct terms, on the grounds that people recognize the relationships involved?

What happens if there is no relationship term whatever for categories of person who are none the less recognized, or whose existence is apparent to the fieldworker? In all these cases, it is important to distinguish between a *category*, or "structural region in a system of classification" (R. H. Barnes 1978: 475), and the *term* which labels that category. It is quite conceivable that there are categories which lack labels of any kind. This may become particularly apparent in comparative studies within "culture areas", when one society has an explicit term for a category which another leaves un-named (§3.6). There is no easy way of deciding how far to go in considering composite terms or postulating un-named categories. All the more necessary, then, that you should explicitly keep the issue in mind from the beginning.

A more generalizable problem of similar type is raised by the distinction between *terms of reference* used when alter is a third party, and *terms of address* used when ego speaks to alter directly. These may differ both in the genealogical range over which they are applied, and in their assignation of terms to particular relatives. To illustrate the first point, *cousin* is used as a term of reference far more broadly than as a term of address, in which context it is virtually obsolete. To illustrate the second, many British people address their *mother-in-law* as *mother* (Firth *et al.* 1969: 419).

The methods described below collect information primarily on terms of reference. This is as it should be for the purposes of formal analysis, because such terms are likely to be the more systematic. On the other hand, terms of address are the important ones in most day-to-day behaviour, and you will certainly need to investigate them. This is best done by detailed, prolonged observation, rather than positive questioning. It is a matter of listening carefully, throughout your fieldwork, to the ways in which people address each other in conversation. In other words, this is an aspect of kinship behaviour rather than a feature of the system of classification itself.

Perhaps an easier situation to resolve is that in which relationship terms take several grammatical forms, through the addition of case endings, posses-sives and so on. Some anthropologists from Morgan onwards have reported such forms separately from their roots. This seems unnecessary for the purpose of formal analysis, unless these variants have different sets of denotata, but it is of course necessary to know and understand the use of all such forms in order to interpret people's conversations and behaviour.

To summarize, it is always necessary to distinguish named from un-named categories, basic from composite relationship terms, terms of reference from terms of address, and literal usages from metaphoric ones. The systematic methods we shall describe are designed principally to collect data on the first of each of these dichotomous pairs. Other types of data are equally important, but by their nature are susceptible only to painstaking and time-consuming participant observation.

3.3 The collection of relationship terminologies

3.3.1 *The "genealogical method"*

Once again *Notes and Queries* is the main methodological source, and, also once again, its suggestions are traceable directly to Rivers (compare the table in Rivers 1968 [1910]: 101 with *Notes and Queries* 1951: 81–82). The technique is a development of the "genealogical method" already discussed (§2.5), and we have already partly anticipated it for the simple reason that collecting genealogies is impossible without using at least the relationship terms for ego's closest relatives. However, once the terminology becomes the *end* of the investigation rather than simply its means, matters have to be carried much further.

Genealogies are first collected as already described, using only the minimal set of relationship terms and referring to people by name as far as possible. Afterwards, "the terms of relationship should be obtained by asking the informant what he calls the various other members recorded in his genealogy" (ibid: 79). In every case, ego should also be asked what term each of these persons uses in return, so that it is never one isolated relationship term which is obtained, but a *reciprocal pair* (ibid: 80). This is of course essential, because such terms apply in the context of relationships which cannot be entirely defined with reference to one party alone. If we are told that a British ego uses *sister* to refer to a particular alter, this by itself does not allow us to specify the relationship involved. We also need to know whether alter responds with *sister* or *brother*. English presents few problems where reciprocals are concerned but the complexities may be much greater in other societies, and it is vital that you never merely assume that a given reciprocal would apply. Always ask about it specifically, and if you can check both usages with the alter involved, so much the better.

Obviously it is most unlikely that a single ego will have relatives in all the genealogical positions about which information is required, and so several persons will have to be interviewed. At the very least, both men and women must be included in the sample, but other social statuses, too, may give rise to distinct terminological usages. For instance, if more than one language or dialect is spoken locally, each must be investigated: the same applies if there are distinct classes, castes, or ethnic groups. Taking all these possibilities into account, the minimum of three genealogies suggested in *Notes and Queries* (1951: 80) seems far too small even for the most socially homogeneous populations.

The method can be applied in two ways. Relationship terms may be recorded either at the same interview as the genealogy itself, or on a later occasion. The latter procedure is desirable in some ways, since it allows the genealogy itself to be double-checked and helps overcome momentary lapses of memory. On the other hand it is much more time-consuming, and there is greater likelihood of confusion on ego's part, especially when relationships are complex or certain personal names recur frequently. Again, the peculiarities of your local situation must play the determining role.

3.3.2 *The "hypothetical question" method*

Notes and Queries naturally envisages the possibility that not all the required genealogical positions can be covered in the above way, and suggests that in such cases you ask questions such as: "If So-and-so (named) had a child [etc.], what would you call that person, and reciprocally what would he or she call you?" (1951: 80). The method we shall discuss here is even less tied to ego's own genealogy, and although it has obvious deficiencies its use is none the less necessary in many cases.

The method is quite simple. Ego is asked a series of purely hypothetical questions, without reference to his or her genealogy or to particular, named persons. Each question takes the form: "What term would you use for your 'mother's brother' (say), and what term would he use for you?" In this way, every desired genealogical position can be denoted by combinations of the primary terms mentioned in §3.3.1, in whatever way makes sense for the language and society concerned.

This technique involves a number of difficulties. First, as just implied, not everyone finds it easy to think in terms of genealogical steps, and some informants will inevitably become confused. It is less easy to spot mistakes here than in the genealogical method, though this is possible to some extent if every question is put again in reverse. Thus, the above question would be followed a little later on by: "What term would you use for your 'sister's son', etc.?" The same two terms should be elicited as in the first case, but in reverse order. Secondly, not all languages permit easy construction of the kinds of composite terms needed. Finally, anthropologists rightly tend to suspect such "idealized" data collected outwith specific social contexts. Despite all these valid criticisms, we feel that this technique is necessary to supplement (though not replace) the genealogical method, for the simple reason that it provides information of a different kind (§3.4).

3.3.3 *Other methods*

Both techniques discussed so far assume that genealogical position determines the choice of relationship term. This is not necessarily the case. Needham (1966) pointed out that relative age could be the criterion, as for the Siwang of Malaysia. Similar findings have since been reported from South and Central America (Rivière 1969; Boremanse 1981: 28), and from South India (Good 1980). In these instances, relative age does not entirely replace genealogical position as the determinant of usage, but does so within certain limits (cf. §7.5.5). Even when terminologies *are* genealogically grounded, they may be used as alternatives to genealogical knowledge rather than as expressions of it (§2.3). This is particularly likely for "universal" systems, in which ego classifies every person in his social universe on the basis of the relationship terminology, without necessarily knowing their exact genealogical relationship (Barnard 1978a).

No doubt there are other, localized peculiarities which might cause the first two methods to yield distorted results. Fortunately, a third technique is available to help circumvent such difficulties. Again, it complements rather than replaces the genealogical method, of which it constitutes a systematic development.

The technique here depends upon the ethnographer having collected other relevant information, usually including a full genealogy, from as many people as possible, and having thereafter constructed a consolidated "master genealogy" for the entire tribe, local community, or other relevant social universe. This often makes it possible to work out genealogical links which, perhaps because of their remoteness, are not precisely known to the two parties concerned. None the less, in a "universal" system such people *will* use relationship terms to refer to each other. These may be collected systematically by asking every person in that universe what relationship term they use for every other person, and what term is used in return. Every answer is checked independently of course, when the other party is interviewed.

The method allows very distant "extensions" of the terminology to be investigated. This should ideally be done for all putative universal systems, given that their defining characteristic is taken to be the community-wide application of consistent, systematic principles of classification. The problem, though, is that such studies easily assume massive and daunting proportions. A population of N persons produces a matrix containing $1/2 \{(N)^2-N\}$ relationships, and double that number of relationship terms, every one of which must be collected twice. For a total population of 100 persons, no fewer than 4950 relationships would have to be enquired into, while for a universe of 1000 the figure would be 499,500! Collection is not even the major problem, for there follows the huge task of analysing these vast bodies of data. This is an area in which computerized techniques of analysis may well offer the most promising way forward (cf. Hackenberg 1967; Chagnon 1974). Such studies will have to be carried out eventually, if we are to be confident that these systems work as they are claimed to do.

In practice, the situation is not quite as bad as the above formula suggests. A substantial fraction of the population will be small children who cannot usefully be interviewed. Moreover, it may not be necessary (and almost certainly will not be possible) to interview even the entire adult population. None the less, it is hardly surprising that few such studies have been published so far. The most celebrated is Rose's investigation of the Groote Eylandt Aborigines (1960). He overcame the problem of having to describe un-ambiguously all 300 or so alters in his sample, in their absence and without appealing to genealogical referents, by the ingenious method of photograph-ing almost the entire population. Individuals were shown these pictures one by one, and asked to give the relevant terms of reference. Incidentally, Chagnon (1974: 228–229) used identification photographs for a somewhat different reason, namely to avoid using personal names in a society where this would cause offence.

3.4 Terminological identity and genealogical identity

We mentioned that the "genealogical" and "hypothetical question" methods, though both based upon an etically-defined genealogical grid, none the less yielded different kinds of information. In fact, the respective sets of data always differ in status even when, as usually happens, the answers are largely or even entirely the same. To understand this, we must draw a distinction between terminological and genealogical identity.

Kinship analysts are primarily interested in terminological equations relevant to the structure of the relationship terminology. For instance, a student of the English terminology might write:

$$uncle = FB = MB = FZH = MZH$$

This does not of course imply that a person's FB is also his MB and so on, but rather that the same relationship term is used for all these genealogical positions. In other words, this is a terminological identity.

On the other hand, consider the fact that Good's FB had married his MZ, so that his FB really is his MZH too. This is a purely contingent genealogical identity, not integral to the structure of the terminology but arising out of the peculiarities of Good's family history. No particular problem is posed in this case, because both genealogical positions are labelled *uncle* anyway. In the English system it is very rare for differently-labelled genealogical positions to coincide in a single individual, but this may be much more feasible elsewhere.

For instance, many South Indian groups practise marriage with the eZDy as an alternative to marriage with the MBDy, FZDy and their terminological equivalents. Such groups display the following distinctive terminological identity:

$$kol\underline{u}ndiy\bar{a}\underline{l} = \text{eZDy} = \text{MBDy} \doteq \text{FZDy}$$

In other words, the prescribed spouse (§6.3.2) comes from either ego's own genealogical level or that immediately following. There are several genealogical possibilities, according to the actual marriage choices made by ego and his ancestors. Figure 3.1 illustrates the cases where ego's F married (a) his own MBDy, and (b) his own eZDy. Relatives who would normally be terminologically distinct, as in case (a), become terminologically identical under the special conditions of case (b). In one locality at least, the convention

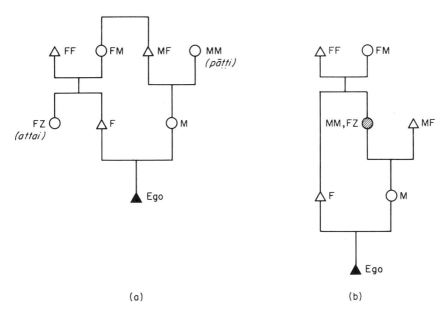

(a)   (b)

Fig. 3.1 *The genealogical situation when a Tamil ego's F marries (a) his own MBD and (b) his own ZD.*

is to refer to the shaded personage as *attai* rather than *pāṭṭi* (Good 1980: 491–495). This is a purely contingent genealogical identity, because men whose Fs did not marry in that way, and whose FZ and MM are therefore *not* one and the same person, use the two distinct relationship terms shown in case (a).

In this case, eZDy marriages are fairly common. Consequently, the situation shown in Fig. 3.1b, though not relevant to an understanding of the formal terminological structure, *is* commonly found when one examines kinship behaviour. Especially among closely inter-related groups of people, you may come across all sorts of cases like this, where two persons are linked in several different ways according to the etic genealogical grid. If, as here, that leads to the use of one particular relationship term rather than the others, you should always question people about the reasons for this choice. This helps you decide whether they recognize one relationship to the total or partial exclusion of the others, and why this should be so. Sometimes a given relationship term may be used in certain contexts but not others.

Systems of namesake equivalence pose a similar problem. The !Kung (Marshall 1976: 401–472) and Nharo Bushmen (Barnard 1978b) refer to relatives' namesakes by the same terms as they use for the relatives themselves. Among the Nharo, if a namesake link is closer than a consanguineous one, it takes precedence. Thus if the same individual is both FZD and ZN (Z's namesake) to ego, she will be termed a "sister" (*ki*, elder, or *!kwī*, younger), and not a "cross-cousin" (*tsxō*). In such cases it is essential to determine the emic as well as the etic notions of genealogy. In a sense, the Nharo and !Kung use "namesake" as a genealogical position.

As already indicated, you need for the purposes of formal analysis to be able to sort out the terminological identities, which *are* structurally significant, from the contingent genealogical or namesake identities, which are not. This is very difficult to do using the genealogical method alone, because that would require you not only to collect genealogies covering all desired genealogical positions in an unambiguous way, but also to obtain separate examples of all possible genealogical quirks. Moreover, this would have to be done with no prior knowledge of what was structural and what contingent. A much more simple solution here is to use the "hypothetical question" method too, since by its very nature this eliminates all contingencies and yields only the structurally significant, terminological identities required. The genealogical method should of course be used to check this information, with which it will presumably concur in most cases.

In short, the hypothetical question method, suitably checked, allows you to study the structure of terminological classification in a fairly abstract way.

The genealogical method shows you how that structure is applied in practice, and how ambiguities are dealt with. It is important to keep these matters distinct conceptually, even though most fieldworkers are ultimately concerned with both of them.

3.5. The data

When collecting terminological data by any of the methods described, what range of genealogical positions should you enquire into and in what order? The answers will again depend on which society is under investigation, and we shall confine ourselves to suggesting the bare minimum of information needed.

Notes and Queries (1951: 81–82) gives a list of basic relationships drawn from Rivers (1968 [1910]), and Fig. 3.2 displays the genealogical grid which these represent. Clearly, affinal relationships are more prominent here than in Rivers' instructions for collecting genealogies *per se* (§2.5; Fig. 2.1). There remain a few obvious omissions though. Patrilineal bias seems the only explanation for including the SWP but not the DHP: both should be enquired into, in our view. Further, the terms used for and by the spouses and children of ego's parallel and cross cousins are omitted, yet this information is often crucial to an understanding of how the system works.

We suggest that you investigate the entire grid shown in Table 2.1 and Fig. 2.3. The order in which this is done does not seem crucial theoretically, though particular strategies may suggest themselves in certain cases. It is necessary to be systematic, though, so as not to confuse your informants, or even yourself.

As drawn, Figs 2.3 and 3.2 may well be too simple, for they ignore several possible determinants of terminological usage. You should look out for, and fully investigate, the following.

(i) *Relative age.* Many terminologies distinguish relationships not merely in genealogical terms, but also (or instead) according to the relative ages of the two parties. This may happen in several ways. First (§3.3.3), relative age may be the prime determinant of terminological usage, overriding considerations of genealogical position in at least some cases. Secondly, and more commonly, individual genealogical positions may be sub-divided on the basis of relative age. Thus, many South Indian languages lack everyday words for "brothers" in general, and have only terms for Be and By. Thirdly, age relative to some person other than ego may be important. In South India,

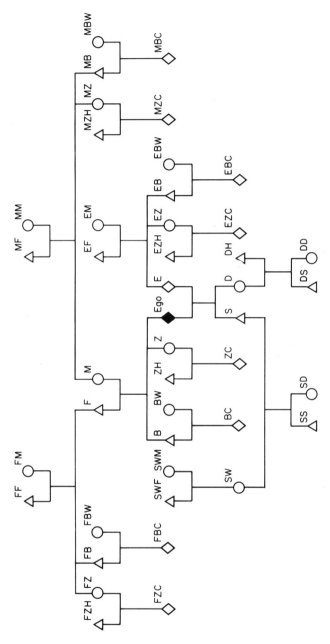

Fig. 3.2 *Genealogical grid for which terminological data are required, according to Notes and Queries (1951: 81–82). (For ease of preparation, the figure combines the affines of male and female egos. Moreover, considerations of relative age, relative rather than absolute sex of alter, and half-siblingship, have been avoided.)*

"father's brothers" are distinguished terminologically according to whether they are senior or junior to ego's father. Figure 3.5 contains examples of both the second and third of these possibilities.

(ii) *Absolute gender*. It goes almost without saying that the gender of alter is likely to be a major determinant of terminological usage. The gender of ego may also be important, though. Thus, Fig. 3.5 shows how among some South Indians, the junior MBS and MBD (for example) are termed *maccinan* and *kolundiyāl* respectively by male egos, but *kolundan* and *sammanti* by females. Unfamiliar though such features may be to English-speaking field-workers, they present few practical problems since both male and female egos are interviewed as a matter of course.

(iii) *Relative gender*. In many terminologies though, it is not absolute gender which is important, but alter's gender relative to that of ego. For instance, Trobrianders use the terms *tuwa* and *bwada* respectively to denote senior and junior siblings of the same gender as ego, and *luta* for siblings of opposite gender, irrespective of age (Malinowski 1932: 434; see also Fig. 4.3). All sorts of further complications may arise, and you should be on the lookout for them. Again, interviewing both men and women should allow you to sort out what is going on. Incidentally, we speak of "gender" rather than "sex" in these last two cases, because we are discussing social rather than biological identities (§8.7).

3.6 Making sense of the data

3.6.1 *Reciprocal sets*

Although it is convenient to draw a conceptual distinction between data-collection and analysis, these are never neatly separable in practice, nor should they be. All terminological data must be sorted out and arranged, in at least preliminary fashion, as soon as possible after being collected. Most of the time this simply involves checking their internal coherence and making sure that they conform to an already-set pattern. If they do not, you will have to decide whether a mistake was made, or whether something new and significant has been revealed. Obviously this checking is made much easier if the original discussion is still fresh in the memories of yourself and your informant. When a particular society, community or group is first investigated, however, no structural features can be assumed in advance and the terminology must be investigated from first principles. How is this best done?

One way to begin would be to tabulate the data, with the indigenous term in the left-hand column, and all its genealogical specifications (or the closest of them) to the right, as suggested in *Notes and Queries* (1951: 80). This will almost certainly prove the best way of presenting your comparatively raw data to the general anthropological audience, unless of course the terminology is so little based upon genealogy that to do so would seriously mislead. But in the preliminary stages of analysis this *a priori* assumption of the significance of genealogy seems unwise.

We recommend instead that you begin by arranging terms into *reciprocal sets*, without reference to genealogical denotata. Of course, the terms will always have been collected in reciprocal *pairs* whichever method has been followed, but reciprocal sets may be more complex than this. A reciprocal set is formed when all the terms ego might use for a particular, self-contained set of alters are arranged on one side of the equation, and all possible reciprocals on the other. Such sets are found in most terminologies, most (if not all) of the time, yet every structure is different. You will have to discover the principles whereby these self-contained sets are made up, and the nature of the relationship between the two sides of the equation. These two things are of course closely inter-connected.

The English terminology contains some common types of reciprocal set. First of all, the basic reciprocal pair may itself constitute a reciprocal set, as is the case with:

$$husband \; \langle -------- \rangle \; wife$$

Here the relationship is one between affines of the same terminological level, but opposite sex. Even simpler is the case where terms are self-reciprocal:

$$cousin \; \langle -------- \rangle \; cousin$$

Here the relationship involves ablineals (Fig. 3.3) or collaterals (Fig. 3.4) of the same level, irrespective of the gender of either party (we consider only first cousins here). A more complex case of reciprocity is:

$$brother, sister \; \langle -------- \rangle \; brother, sister$$

This concerns colineal (Fig. 3.3) or direct (Fig. 3.4) relatives of the same level, and usage depends upon the gender of alter but not of ego. English also contains several sets of the type:

$$father, mother \; \langle -------- \rangle \; son, daughter$$

This case involves lineal or direct relatives from adjacent levels. Again, the gender of alter is significant.

	lineal male	lineal female	co-lineal male	co-lineal female	ablineal
+2	grandfather	grandmother			
+1	father	mother	uncle	aunt	
0	(Ego)		brother	sister	cousin
−1	son	daughter	nephew	niece	
−2	grandson	granddaughter			

Fig. 3.3 *The English relationship terminology structure for close consanguines* (after Wallace and Atkins 1969 [1960]: 349).

This process could be carried out for all English relationship terms, producing not only an inventory of all the component reciprocal sets, but also a list of the principles differentiating and relating the two sides in every case. In English, as in most terminologies, certain principles (gender of alter, terminological level, and so on) recur in most if not all sets. These are the important structural features which your eventual analysis, however carried out, must take into account.

Sol Tax first explicitly stated the "rule of uniform reciprocals" (1955 [1937]: 19) which had long been implicit in the writing of Radcliffe-Brown and others. The use of reciprocal sets as an aid to formal analysis was pioneered by Goodenough (1967; §3.6.2, §8.6.1). Some have elevated the existence of such sets into a universal principle, going so far as to question the

	direct male	direct female	collateral male	collateral female
+2	grandfather	grandmother	uncle	aunt
+1	father	mother	uncle	aunt
0	brother	sister	cousin	cousin
−1	son	daughter	nephew	niece
−2	grandson	granddaughter	nephew	niece

Fig. 3.4 *The English relationship terminology structure for close consanguines* (after Romney and D'Andrade 1969 [1964]: 378).

accuracy of data which do not conform to it (Scheffler and Lounsbury 1971: 96n; Holston 1977; Scheffler 1978). Goodenough himself does not make such a claim (1967: 1208n), nor is it supported by the ethnographic evidence (R. H. Barnes 1977: 173; Good 1978: 129).

The "principle" can be saved only if one is willing to grant the distinction between "kinship terminologies" and "relationship terminologies" (§3.1) and, within the former, the existence of "verbally unrealised" superclasses (Scheffler and Lounsbury 1971: 9l; Scheffler 1977) containing several overlapping or individually incomplete sub-classes. For instance, in their analysis of the Siriono terminology, these authors report the reciprocal set:

ami (FF, MF), *ari* (FM, MM) ⟨– – – – – –⟩ *ake* (SS, SD, DS, DD)

This is not self-contained, however, because there is also a set:

ami (MB), *ari* (FZ) ⟨– – – – – –⟩ *akwani* (ZDms, BDws), *akwanindu* (ZSms, BSws)

Scheffler and Lounsbury therefore assume that there is an overall set:

ami, ari ⟨– – – – – –⟩ AK-

where "*Ak*- represents a hypothetical superclass from which are derived the subclasses *akwani* and *akwanindu* and the residue class *ake*" (1971: 91).

Three difficulties arise here. First, we have already questioned whether linguistic resemblances between relationship terms should be seen as significant (§3.2): there is probably no general answer. Secondly, the notion of the implicit superclass has already been mentioned. We do not wish to take up a dogmatic position on this issue, for although the introduction of superclasses smacks of sleight-of-hand, we recognize that not all relationship categories necessarily have corresponding terms (§3.6.2). Moreover, formal analyses aim to provide the best available abstract model of the terminology, that is, the model which comprises fewest variables and which is therefore most easily falsifiable (Popper 1972). Whether these variables are explicitly or implicitly recognized by members of the society concerned does not matter here, though it is of course crucial to the analysis of ideology and behaviour (Chapter 8). Thirdly, however, many of those who have adopted componential or transformational techniques borrowed from linguistics, reduce the various denotata of relationship terms to their alleged "primary foci" *before* arranging these terms into reciprocal sets (Scheffler and Lounsbury 1971; Carter 1974). These foci are usually taken to be their closest genealogical referents, etically defined: it is a kind of "extension of sentiments" argument (Radcliffe-Brown 1950: 25) applied in reverse. This procedure seems to us to pre-empt all possibility of analysis. *All* the recorded denotata of relationship terms must be taken into account when they are arranged into reciprocal sets.

To return to the question of the principle's universality, there are a number of reasons why terms should *not* form consistent, self-contained and mutually exclusive sets. Indeed, such anomalies often provide the most difficult, interesting, and revealing problems for analysis. First, suppose that a society is changing because of external influence or internal realignment. It is possible, though not inevitable, that this will cause a temporary or permanent breakdown of consistent reciprocal usages. For instance, the terminology of the Khumbu Sherpas includes the Nepali loan-word *samdhi* (CEF). This is partly self-reciprocal, but is also a possible reciprocal for the Bodic term *tsau* (DHF, ZH, ZDH, FZH). This in turn is a reciprocal of the set *uru* (MZ, MBD, WyZ) and *niermu* (WyZ), the first of which has yet other reciprocals not relevant here (Allen 1976: 571). Secondly, R. H. Barnes has pointed out that the principle does not apply when terms are arranged in a rank-order series, either (1978: 476). In Kédang, a male ego uses a series of terms for his male allies (wife-takers). Arranging these in ascending order, we find the following reciprocal usages (Barnes 1974: 266–273):

$$anaq\ maqing\ (FZSS, ZS, DH, BDH)\ \langle------\rangle\ epu\ (FMBS, MB, WF, WFB)$$
$$maqing\ (FZH, ZHF, FZS, ZH)\ \langle------\rangle\ epu\ (WBS, SWB, MBS, WB)$$
$$epu\ (FZHF, ZHFF, FFZH)\qquad (no\ reciprocal)$$

This by no means exhausts the genealogical referents of the term *epu*, nor the terms it may reciprocate, but is sufficient to show that self-contained reciprocal sets are not universal here.

Scheffler and Lounsbury (1971: 96n), like Holston (1977), argue that terminologies would not constitute *systems* if they did not display perfect reciprocity. This view seems much too static. Many terminologies are likely to be undergoing diachronic changes or, as in Kédang, simply to work in other ways. The arranging of terms into reciprocal sets is an extremely useful technique for the initial sorting of relationship terms, but there are cases in which this is not possible, and these are often of great analytical significance. It is time, therefore, to turn our attention to this question of analysis, a matter of which we present only a brief overview.

3.6.2 *Componential analysis: the logic of relationship terminologies*

Componential analysis came into being with Goodenough's famous analysis of Trukese kinship (1956). Since then it has become an integral part of general semantics (Lyons 1977: 317–335). In kinship, though, the over-enthusiastic formalism of many practitioners has led to various new approaches having little to do with the study of "meaning". Strictly speaking, many of these types of formal analysis are generative or transformational, and not componential at all. They are of little relevance for the fieldworker and so are not discussed here, but have recently been reviewed by Borland (1979).

We believe that the most useful aspects of componential analysis are those enabling the fieldworker, analyst or theorist to understand the *basis* (the components) of the structure being studied. In this sense it is difficult to imagine any such person who does not do at least some componential analysis, whether he calls it that or not. Our common-sense approach to the topic is far removed from most current work in formal analysis, and even from some aspects of Goodenough's original paper.

The essence of componential analysis is the study of *components*, also called "significata" or "distinctive features". The word "component" is used in a very different sense in Chomskyan linguistics, but here we are following the usage in semantics. Components are individual units of meaning which, when combined, define a category. Such a category will normally be labelled by an indigenous term (a "designatum"), e.g. a relationship term. Components or "significata" include such things as generation, gender and relative age. Those aspects of a category which are implied by it but do not formally define it, e.g. the behaviour associated with a particular category of relative, are called its "connotata". There is no conventional latinate term for the category itself, but it is useful to remember that the category and the term or "designatum" which designates it are conceptually different things. Hence the possibility of unnamed categories, such as marriageable people, or joking partners. Finally, any category, whether named or not, can be determined according to the genealogical points of reference or kin types making it up (the "denotata"). What is really of interest is why these particular points of reference are classified together.

Take for example the English word *uncle*, which is the designatum of a kin category. Its usual denotata are FB, MB, FZH and MZH. From these we can specify the following significata, or components: (1) male (this distinguishes it from *aunt*); (2) collateral (to distinguish *uncle* from *father*); and (3) first ascending generation (to distinguish it from *cousin* or *nephew*). Purists would insist that "first ascending generation" is more than one component, but we need not worry too much about that. Note that we have not signified *uncle* as either "consanguineous" or "affinal". These are problematic denotata, since "blood relatives" are defined differently in different societies. Moreover, although many English terms do make such a distinction, the category designated by *uncle* includes both consanguines (FB, MB) and affines (FZH,

MZH). The connotatum, by the way, would be uncle-like (or *avuncular*) behaviour, whatever that might entail. It is of course much less important to formalize the representation of connotata than of significata. The latter are, after all, the basis of componential analysis.

Always remember that the point of all this is to understand particular emic categories (those of the language and people you are studying), and their place in a system of such categories. Significata determine both the inclusion and exclusion of denotata from the category under consideration. This implies the existence of other categories, for which the given significata do not hold. In our example above, the rules do not allow the inclusion of, say, F or FZ in the category designated by the term *uncle*. English-speakers have other categories for these genealogical positions. Taking these into account, we can eventually build up the entire set of categories. In this case that set would be the English relationship terminology, though we could equally well be analysing Nuer time categories, Trobriand animal categories, Italian colour categories, or any other set of categories which constitutes a semantic (particularly a lexical) field. Colour and kin categories are particularly amenable to componential analysis because they are based upon etic principles. In colour classification, these are wavelength and brightness, while in kin classification, there is the genealogical grid.

Componential analysis is often useful in comparing relationship terminology structures too, either within an ethnographic region or language group, or between quite different systems. Box-type componential diagrams such as Fig. 3.5 illustrate the relations between categories and are particularly relevant for systems such as this Tamil one, which imply prescriptive marriage (§6.3.2). In relation to a given ego, all members of a Tamil ego's sub-caste can be classified into one or other of the categories. This is not the case with English, of course. Related to this is the major structural difference between the two terminologies: English distinguishes direct relatives from collaterals, while Tamil distinguishes parallel from cross relatives. The latter is far easier to represent diagrammatically, since ego can be structurally equated with his or her same-sex siblings (for example, same-sex sibling's children are termed as one's own). Note also that, strictly speaking, Tamil requires two diagrams, one for a male ego and one for a female. The structure is the same in each case, but the denotata are different. For English we give two diagrams, but merely to illustrate (with some modifications from the original) two different componential interpretations of the same system. Wallace and Atkins' (1969 [1960]) version (Fig. 3.3) is perhaps more formally precise, but Romney and D'Andrade's (1969 [1964]) (Fig. 3.4) seems intuitively more correct to native speakers of English (§8.6.1).

level	parallel		cross	
	Δ	O	O	Δ
+2	*tāttā*	*pāṭṭi*	*pāṭṭi*	*tāttā*
+1	*periyappā* *appā* *sittappā*	*attai*	*periyammāl* *ammāl* *sitti*	*māmaṉ*
+0	*aṇṇaṉ*	*akkāḷ*	*madiṉi*	*attāṉ*
−0	*tampi*	*taṅkai*	*koḻundiyāḷ* (m.s.) *sammaṇṭi* (w.s.)	*macciṉaṉ* (m.s.) *koḻundaṉ* (w.s.)
−1	*makaṉ*	*makaḷ*	*marumakaḷ*	*marumakaṉ*
−2	*pēraṉ*	*pētti*	*pētti*	*pēraṉ*

Fig. 3.5 *The Tamil relationship terminology structure, for an ego of Kondaiyankottai Maravar caste (Good 1981: 114).*

Finally, componential analysis can even be used to examine the usage of borrowed relationship terms. Barnard (1980a), writing on the use of Dutch terms as loan words in the Nama language, noted a structural similarity between these two otherwise quite different terminologies. The partial componential analysis of categories for close male consanguines in Fig. 3.6 illustrates this. Although Nama distinguish cross from parallel, and Dutch distinguish direct relatives from collaterals, the Nama term //*nurib* is used in a similar way to the nineteenth century Dutch term *neef* (contrast English *cousin, nephew,* and *grandson,* all of which can be translated by Dutch *neef*). If you encounter loan words, ask yourself how they are used: in the same sense as in the original language or (more likely) as loose translations for particular terms in the structure of the receptive relationship terminology? Above all, do not assume that English terms used by an English-speaking informant or interpreter abroad, are used in the same way as in Britain or America. For instance, many educated South Indians use the English word *uncle* in a much broader sense than Englishmen do.

Evans-Pritchard said that anthropology was ultimately concerned with the translation of culture. Getting to this stage, though, is the anthropologist's responsibility. Beware of the informant or interpreter who (mis-)translates

	NAMA		DUTCH	
	parallel	cross	direct	collateral
+2	//naob	////////	grootvader	////////
+1	//gub	//naob	vader	oom
0	!gàb	//nurib	broeder	neef
−1	/gòab		zoon	
−2	//nurib	////////	neef (kleinzoon)	////////

Fig. 3.6 *Nama and nineteenth century Dutch relationship terms for close male consanguines (Barnard 1980a: 30).*

his language and culture for you. On old maps of Gabon the names of rivers are variously recorded as Silo, Dilo and Sidilo. Apparently, in answer to the French fieldworker's question: *"Qu'est-ce que c'est?* (What's that?)", people replied *"C'est l'eau"* or *"C'est de l'eau* (That's water)". The fieldworkers wrote down what they heard, thinking that these were the indigenous names for the rivers! (Alexandre 1967: 38n). In kinship this kind of thing is a particular problem. Several ethnographers have made similar mistakes, recording personal names, entire sentences ("He is my – – – – –"), and literal translations ("his mother's brother") as relationship terms. Be aware not only of the social or behavioural context, but also of the linguistic context in which relationship terms are used. This is essential in order to ensure that they are correctly recorded.

4 *Relationship terminologies 2*

4.1 Caveat

In this chapter we discuss a number of *formal* typologies of terminological structures. In some cases though, the authors concerned have attached substantive and apparently ethnographically-derived labels such as "Dravidian" or "Sudanese" to each formal type. This seems an unfortunate practice. For instance, the term "Dravidian" is inherently ambiguous since it is used by Indians to refer to certain ethnic groups and by linguists to denote one particular language family. When it is also used to label a formally distinct type of relationship terminology, confusion is further compounded, especially as there is disagreement over precisely which formal features are diagnostic of "Dravidian-ness". Some Dravidian-speakers, such as the Nayar (Gough 1952) and groups practising eZDy marriage (Good 1980), do *not* have "Dravidian" terminologies according to any of these formal definitions, whereas some non-Dravidian speakers in the same region, such as the Kandyan Sinhalese, do (Yalman 1962). Similar problems arise with almost all such labels.

In short, the use of pseudo-ethnographic labels for formal types of terminological structure, inevitably produces a quite unnecessary ambiguity. None the less, such labels have been and still are widely used, particularly by some North American anthropologists. Consequently, despite our reservations, we feel it necessary to introduce into our discussion some of the most common of these labels. We shall however place them in inverted commas throughout. Thus, Dravidian refers to speakers of appropriate languages, and "Dravidian" to a particular formal type of terminology. Remember that whatever the labels used, the formal principles underlying the typology are our real concern.

4.2 Relationship term typology

In the history of kinship studies there have been several attempts to classify all the relationship terminologies of the world into two or more types. The first was by Lewis Henry Morgan, in his great *Systems of Consanguinity and Affinity of the Human Family* (1871). He classified such terminologies by language family, and then grouped the resulting six families into two basic types, "classificatory" and "descriptive". A number of writers have since used these terms in a loose sense, but for Morgan they were quite specific and referred essentially to one criterion alone. A "classificatory" terminology was one which merged lineals with collaterals, while a "descriptive" terminology was one which did not.

It is now known that this distinction alone is inadequate. It groups together numbers of systems which really have very little in common. Kroeber pointed this out in his famous article on "classificatory" systems (1909). He defined seven additional criteria intrinsic to relationship terminologies: generation, age (within a generation), sex of relative (alter), sex of ego, sex of connecting relative (this being the basis of "transformational analysis" today), consanguinity versus affinity, and whether the connecting relative was dead or alive. The last criterion is irrelevant in most cases, and Kroeber omitted one distinction now commonly regarded as important, namely the distinction of *relative* as opposed to *absolute* sex (cf. §3.5).

Kroeber never did formulate a typology on the basis of these distinctions. That was left to Lowie (1928, 1929) and Kirchhoff (1931). Their typology, which is still in use, classifies relationship terminologies according to usages in the first ascending genealogical level, and Kirchhoff also anticipates Murdock's (1949) typology by giving implied equations for relatives in ego's own level, too. Logically, for a given sex of alter, there are five possible ways of classifying relatives in the first ascending level. Of these, four are found to exist. These, as named by Lowie, are illustrated in Fig. 4.1. The fifth, very unlikely possibility, not mentioned by either of the two authors, would of course be:

$$MB = F \neq FB, \qquad FZ = M \neq MZ$$

Lowie's labels for the four types may require some explanation. "Bifurcate" refers to the bifurcation of the two sides of ego's family, so that relatives on the father's side are called by different terms from relatives on the mother's side. "Merging" refers to same-sex sibling equivalence, and "collateral" to the distinction between lineals and collaterals. It is important to

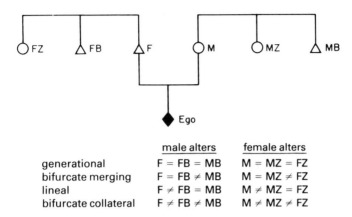

	male alters	female alters
generational	F = FB = MB	M = MZ = FZ
bifurcate merging	F = FB ≠ MB	M = MZ ≠ FZ
lineal	F ≠ FB = MB	M ≠ MZ = FZ
bifurcate collateral	F ≠ FB ≠ MB	M ≠ MZ ≠ FZ

Fig. 4.1 *The Lowie-Kirchhoff typology for first ascending genealogical level.*

note that the term "lineal" as used here has nothing whatever to do with unilineal descent (§5.1). If anything, "lineal" terminologies are found most frequently with non-unilineal (cognatic) descent systems. Such terminologies are simply those in which lineals are called by one term (e.g. English *father, mother* or French *père, mère*) and collaterals by another (*uncle, aunt* or *oncle, tante*).

Another way of classifying relationship terminology structures is by usage within ego's own generation. This now-familiar classification was probably the invention of L. Spier (1925). A number of writers, including Radcliffe-Brown (1952 [1941]) dabbled in such classification, but the classic attempt was that of Murdock (1949). His usages are commonplace in American anthropology, but one must be careful to distinguish the classification of terminology structure from that of social structure. Both kinds of typology are in fact found in the writings of Morgan (1871 and 1877, respectively), and they serve two different purposes. While it would indeed be nice to be able to classify social structures into neat types, all attempts at this, including Murdock's (1949: 224–259), are necessarily gross over-simplifications of little value to fieldworkers. Even so, a familiarity with Murdock's relationship terminology types may be worthwhile, not only because they have gained currency in American writing, but also because they do show some of the variety of terminology structures which can be expected. In this sense, relationship terminologies constitute what in semantics are known as "lexical fields" (like colour terms or plant taxonomy; cf. §3.6.2). Their study is a necessary part of the analysis of social organization, but it does not, in itself, predict social organization.

Murdock's six types are as follows. (1) The "*Hawaiian*" type of terminology is the simplest and logically derives from the same structural principles
as Lowie's "generational" type. It classifies siblings and cousins together by
the same terms (usually one for males and another for females). (2) The
"*Eskimo*" type, which includes the English-language terminology, distinguishes siblings from cousins, but does not distinguish cross-cousins from
parallel cousins. It derives logically from the principles of Lowie's "lineal"
type. (3) The "*Sudanese*" type distinguishes all cousins and siblings, giving
every genealogical position a distinct relationship term. A "Sudanese"
terminology in which the terms may be translated literally with possessives
like "mother's brother's daughter", is sometimes distinguished in Murdock's
writings by a different label, "descriptive". Notice that this is different from
Morgan's "descriptive" category, which would include "Eskimo" too.
"Sudanese" terminologies are often found in association with Lowie's
"bifurcate collateral" type. (4) "*Iroquois*" (or "*Dakota*") terminologies distinguish cross- from parallel cousins, and classify siblings either with parallel
cousins or by distinct terms. "Dravidian" terminologies closely resemble

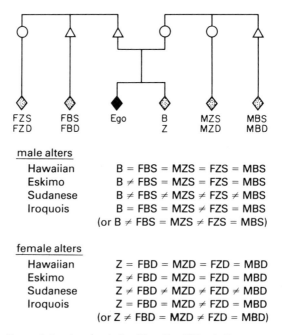

Fig. 4.2 *Murdock's cousin typology (excluding "Crow" and "Omaha").*

Murdock's "Iroquois" type, which is based upon the same principles as Lowie's "bifurcate merging". The equivalences for the four types mentioned so far are illustrated in Fig. 4.2.

The other types, (5) "*Crow*" (or "*Choctaw*") and (6) "*Omaha*", are also ideally found with "bifurcate merging" in the first ascending generation. These types are often troublesome for fieldworkers because they equate not only members of ego's own generation, but also members of ego's parents' generation, and often other generations too. By Murdock's definitions, "Crow" equates FZD with FZ, and "Omaha" equates MBS with MB. Yet the principles behind these equations, in an idealized "Crow" or "Omaha" terminology, may be expressed in many others:

"Crow": FZ = FZD = FZDD,   F = FB = FZS = FZDS, etc.
"Omaha": MB = MBS = MBSS,   M = MZ = MBD = MBSD, etc.

Consider a terminology of the "Crow" type, such as that found among the Trobriand Islanders (Malinowski 1932: 434–451; cf. Leach 1958). Relationship terms for some of the relevant genealogical positions are given in Fig. 4.3. The Trobrianders possess a matrilineal descent system, and in the figure matrilineages have been shaded for easy reference. Note that ego calls his own

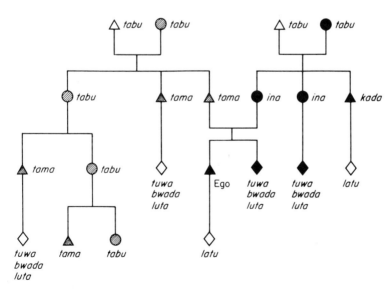

Fig. 4.3 *Trobriander relationship terminology (partial), for male ego. Matrilineages:* ■, *ego's;* ◆, *ego's father's;* ◇, *others.* Tuwa, *elder same-sex sibling, etc.;* bwada, *younger same-sex sibling, etc.;* luta, *opposite-sex sibling.*

matrilineal relatives by a variety of terms. However, he calls all his F's matrilineal kin by the same term: *tama* for males and *tabu* for females. Likewise, they will all call him by the respective reciprocals: *latu* (loosely, "child") or *tabu* (which is self-reciprocal), just as the male ego in the figure calls his own MBC *latu*, as the "child" of his matrilineage. To put it another way, a male ego equates himself with his MB and other male matrikin. A female ego would equate herself with her M and MZ, and other female matrikin. The general principle behind these equations is that an entire matrilineage may stand in a particular relationship to a given individual. Obviously, it is general principles such as this one, and not merely the configuration of the individual terms in the diagram, which are most likely to be important for the study of kinship behaviour and social organization. Moreover, it is these principles, rather than the genealogical details, which are most likely to be common to the various empirical instances of each ideal type.

Radcliffe-Brown's (1952 [1941]: 54–56; 75–79) discussion of Choctaw and Hopi is also relevant here. The Hopi, for example, call all members of the F's matrilineage *ina'a* (males) or *ikya'a* (females), and all members of the MF's matrilineage *ikwa'a* (males) or *iso'o* (females). These equivalences imply notions of kinship behaviour and (unlike the Trobriand ones) marriage probitions (Eggan 1950; §6.3.3). You should look for such patterns and enquire into their significance. If matrilineal clanship is found, a "Crow" type of system may be found with it, but in fact not all "Crow" systems by Murdock's definition are matrilineal. If you encounter such a terminology, see how far from ego the terms are extended, and find out its relationship (if any) to matrilineal organization.

"Omaha" systems are, of course, the mirror-image of "Crow" systems. Just as one can find an implicit matrilineal principle in "Crow" equivalences, so one can find a patrilineal principle implicit in "Omaha" equivalences: for example, MB = MBS or M = MZ = MBD (all these persons being patrilineally related).

According to some writers, an ideal "Omaha" system would be one which employed this patrilineal principle more widely, e.g. the Nyoro (Beattie 1957). An even further idealization might entail certain jural rules, particularly descent-defined marriage rules of the "Crow-Omaha" type (§6.3.3). Precisely what writers mean by "Crow" and "Omaha" then depends to a great extent upon their theoretical interests and perspectives, as we shall see: terminology specialists, descent theorists and alliance theorists all use the words differently. In the formal study of relationship terminologies, there have even been formulated so-called "Omaha" rules, such as the "Omaha III skewing rule" (MBC = ZCms) which go quite beyond Murdock's original typology. In some respects, even the real Omaha Indians of Nebraska may not be a good example of this clearly polythetic class known as the "Omaha" type (cf. Ackerman 1976). This should alert you to the dangers of using typologies not explicitly founded upon a small number of variables, and named with ethnographic as opposed to formal labels. In these respects, Lowie's and Kirchhoff's typology is better than Murdock's.

4.3 Typology and ideology

It is important to stress that the above discussion concerns the *formal* analysis of systems of classification. This does not necessarily yield any information concerning either systems of marital alliance or similar jural phenomena on the one hand, or kinship behaviour on the other (§1.3.2). These matters require separate investigation, and while it would be reasonable to assume that the ideological and behavioural features of a given kinship system would not directly conflict with each other or with the terminological structure, this does not mean that there cannot be a considerable degree of inconsistency among them (Good 1981).

This problem arises particularly for the comparative analyst faced with two terminologies of the same, formally or substantively defined type. Thus, both the Nuer and the Icelanders employ a "Sudanese" type terminology structure, but their kinship systems are very different with regard to ideology and practice. Furthermore, of course, not all Sudanese peoples have "Sudanese" terminologies.

One more example of the relation (or lack of it) between typology and ideology should be enough to illustrate the point. The Iglulikmiut, a Central Eskimo people, have an "Iroquois" terminology for same-sex siblings and an "Hawaiian" terminology for opposite-sex siblings. Curiously, its "Iroquois-ness" is not generated by a merging rule, but rather by the typically Eskimo notion of lineality and genealogical distance. For a man, links through males are believed to be closer than links through females. For a woman, the reverse is true. Thus an Iglulikmiut man terms and treats male members of his own generation as follows: his B is closest; his FBS (two male links) is next closest and termed similarly, though with a diminutive affix; his MZS (two female links) is the most distant of male first cousins, and is given a distinct term; and his FZS and MBS are classed together because these genealogical positions are reciprocal, and each involves one male and one female link. In proximity to ego, same-sex cross-cousins stand between the two types of same-sex parallel cousins, and are therefore called by the same term (Damas 1963: 34–57).

In cases like this, it is essential to find out *why* people classify relatives the way they do. Had the ethnographer merely given the terms, and misleadingly stamped his charts "Iroquois-type", few readers might have noticed, but his account would then have missed one of the terminology's most interesting features.

5 Descent and residence

5.1 Descent theory in historical context

At first glance, descent and residence seem reasonably clear-cut and simple notions which should present no great problems to the fieldworker. But appearances are once again deceptive.

From the 1920s, and particularly in the decade following the publication of Fortes' major monographs on the Tallensi (1945, 1949a), "British" social anthropology was preoccupied with the study of unilineal descent groups. Radcliffe-Brown had carried his message to Cape Town, Sydney, Chicago and back to Britain, and everywhere his students and students' students were finding descent groups on the "African" model. If the Nuer and Tallensi had corporate clans and lineages, so did the rest of Africa. If Africa had them, New Guinea might have them too. And even Australia had "underlying" descent lines.

Fortunately, if belatedly, scholars have now realized that there are drawbacks to the indiscriminate application of such models. Dumont (1966) successfully criticized the notion of "underlying" descent in Australia, and J. A. Barnes (1962) pointed out that "African models" really do not fit Melanesian ethnography (though La Fontaine (1973) takes a different view). Others have made more specific criticisms of the application of "African" and other models in Africa itself. One of the most interesting of these criticisms has emerged from the Lovedu debate. In a joint monograph, E. J. and J. D. Krige described this South African people as having "lineages", but noted that these were far less important than marriage or bilateral kin groups (1943: 86). Drawing on this monograph and an earlier paper by J. D. Krige (1939), Leach mistakenly interpreted the Lovedu system as "a kind of Kachin structure in reverse" (1961a: 97), comprising a system of patrilineal local descent groups which exchange women through repeated MBD marriage, sometimes hypergamously. As E. J. Krige points out (1975: 234–235), there are no ranked local groups in Lovedu society, and the rules of seniority and obligations relating to marital exchange are *individual-*, not group-oriented. In fact Lovedu practise obligatory marriage between genealogical rather than classificatory cross-cousins, and the exchange units are "houses" rather than lineages. This debate highlights the interplay between theory and comparison on the one hand, and ethnographic reporting on the other. It is easy to make mistakes like Leach's, even in the field, especially when in some societies with unilineal systems – such as the Tallensi (Fortes 1945: 33) – informants use the same word for both "lineage" and "house". Your understanding of your own data, and its comprehensibility for others, will be greatly enchanced if you take full account of polysemic usages of this kind.

Even as used by anthropologists, "descent" is sometimes a fuzzy concept. In her classic essay on the matrilineal societies of Central Africa, Richards (1950) notes great variety among the four examples she considers, and Leach (1961a: 4) suggests that in fact the very notion of "matrilineal societies" may here be as misleading as the class "blue butterflies" would be in zoology. Certainly the terms "line", "lineal", "lineage", etc., with or without the prefixes "patri-" and "matri-", have in the past been used in at least four different ways. First, they have been used to denote corporate descent groups, i.e. *lineages* proper. Secondly, they are often employed to denote the chosen *line* of inheritance, succession, etc., in a given society. Thirdly, in the study of relationship terminologies the expression "two-*line* prescription" has sometimes been used to refer to terminological structures consistent with "bilateral cross-cousin marriage". Finally, *lineal* (as opposed to collateral) relatives are ego's ascendants and descendants, regardless of which lines are favoured for the first three purposes (§4.2). Be aware of the different senses which these terms may take in the writings of others, but remember too that only the fourth usage is wholly unambiguous, for it only refers to purely formal, relational properties which can be defined independently of particular contexts.

Ironically, many relatively recent problems concerning the conceptualization of "*descent*" had been anticipated long ago by Rivers (1924: 85–88). He solved one major difficulty by confining the term to "membership of a group, and to this only". He distinguished descent from *inheritance*, "the transmission of property", and *succession*, "the transmission of office". Inheritance and succession have to do with rights and obligations ascribed to particular genealogical statuses. That is, they are egocentrically-defined, whereas "descent" can be defined sociocentrically. In classic descent-theory works like those of Richards (1950) and Fortes (1953), these distinctions are merely implied, whereas oddly enough, alliance theorists have sometimes been more careful to observe Rivers' precepts. Indeed, Dumont (1957: 4) went so far as to suggest that, to remove any remaining ambiguity, "descent" be used only in connection with recruitment to *exogamous* groups. Be that as it may, it seems clear that the second of our four usages is best avoided. Dumont suggests that instead of "patrilineal inheritance", we speak of "inheritance from father to son". Succession could also be characterized in this way. This precision is all the more desirable, given that the epithet "patrilineal descent" fails to distinguish, say: primogeniture and ultimogeniture (inheritance by the first or last born son, respectively); cases where a younger brother would inherit in preference to a son; and more complicated sets of rules, such as those governing "patrilineal" succession to the British throne.

Even in Rivers' or Dumont's senses, one cannot speak of, say, "a patrilineal society" without qualification. Not only must patrilineal descent be distinguished from inheritance and/or succession from father to son, but it must also be recognized that not all group memberships, types of property, and official positions in a given society are necessarily transmitted by the same route. This is true even if one adopts the narrow, Dumontian definition of "descent". For instance, the Kondaiyankottai Maravar of South India belong to matrilineally-constituted, exogamous *kiḷai* ("branches"). They cannot, however, be characterized as "a matrilineal society" since they worship family deities inherited from father to son, whose congregations are themselves exogamous (Good 1981). Maravar society thus contains both patrilineal and matrilineal "descent groups", though both are dispersed geographically and the latter are "groups" only in the one context of exogamy.

This notion of *group* has been the cause of many of the problems and confusions surrounding the notion of "descent", as we shall see (§5.4). To anticipate, we feel that Rivers' distinctions are still useful, but with two provisos. First, "descent" can be used not only with reference to groups of individuals with shared interests or property, but also to sociocentric *categories* or "descent constructs" (Scheffler 1966: 544), such as the *kiḷai*. Although the latter are "descent groups" in the strict sense for Dumont, and would be merely "descent constructs" for Scheffler, both authors are really saying the same thing, that entities which are non-corporate in the conventional sense, may none the less be regulated by principles of descent. Secondly, and of particular importance to the fieldworker, it may be necessary to make yet finer distinctions according to the character of your data.

Where encountered, related emic concepts must be used to supplement or modify Rivers' list. For the rest of this chapter, then, we shall be dealing with "descent" more-or-less in Rivers' sense, but with the caveats just stated.

5.2 Descent group organization

Formally speaking, there are six possible avenues for the transmission of descent group membership, or anything else, from parents to children (cf. Needham 1971b: 10):

1. patrilineal;
2. matrilineal;
3. double (duolineal or bilineal);
4. cognatic (bilateral or ambilineal);
5. parallel;
6. cross (alternating).

The first two are self-explanatory. Double descent, or more correctly, duolineal transmission, normally involves patrilineal transmission of one set of attributes and matrilineal transmission of another set. The Herero, for example, recognize two distinct sets of unilineal groups (Gibson 1956). Each person in Herero society belongs both to an *oruzo*, or patrilineal clan, and an *eanda*, or matrilineal clan. Each patrilineal clan is headed by a priest, who distributes property after the death of a member, and each clan shares food taboos, origin legends, ritual and other activities, and a sacred hearth. The matrilineal clans are less important, but share similar activities. Both types of clan are segmentary and exogamous. There are of course other examples of double descent in the ethnographic literature, the most famous being the Yakö (Forde 1950; §7.5.1).

In the cognatic or bilateral mode of descent, attributes are transmitted equally through both parents. No *unilineal* groups can be formed on a cognatic basis, but group structure can be cognatic, when membership is acquired through either the father or the mother. Over time this application of an ambilineal principle for descent group recruitment will generate cognatic descent groups. In Polynesia, for example, an individual often has the choice of joining either the father's or mother's group. The decision will depend on the advantages to be gained, and the more prestigous or higher-ranked group will probably be chosen (§7.5.4). A non-hierarchical form of cognatic organization occurs in societies which lack the ambilineal group principle. In Western societies, for instance, individuals typically recognize kinship equally through both sides of the family.

Societies in which kinship organization is based strongly on a bilateral principle pose special problems when it comes to defining the units of analysis. Firth, Hubert and Forge (1969: 290–291) use a plethora of heuristically-defined concepts – effective kin set, intimate kin set, extended family, kin group and kin network – to describe kinship in middle-class London. It is interesting that the authors deliberately avoid the term *kindred* because of its former wide use and consequent ambiguity (ibid: 281); each ethnographer and theorist has tended to use it in a different way (cf. Freeman 1961; W. E. Mitchell 1963). Yet what is important is not the label, but the concept you are trying to develop, or the ethnographic situation you wish to describe. It is pointless to seek universal, substantive definitions of such terms; usage will depend upon the particular point you are trying to make about the social organization of the people you are studying. In some cases it may be useful to include affines in your notion of "kindred"; in other cases it may not. It may also be useful to distinguish broadly, as Firth *et al.* do, between "*assemblies* of kin for specific social occasions" and "kin *units* of more regular nature" (1969: 266; orig. emphasis). Nuances such as these will often be relevant to the analysis of societies with unilineal descent as well, but they are of special importance in the study of cognatic societies because these may be the *only* kinds of descent groups or categories to be found there.

Parallel descent is a very rare form of transmission in which descent lines are sex-specific. Men transmit to their sons and women to their daughters (see, e.g. Maybury-Lewis 1960). Alternating or cross-descent, equally rare, is its opposite: i.e. men transmit to their daughters and women to their sons. Among both the Mundugamor (Mead 1939: 176–179) and the Nama (Hoernlé 1925: 9, 16; Barnard 1975), it occurs as a secondary form of descent. Political organization is in each case patrilineal, but cross-descent determines additional named, exogamous sociocentric categories.

In all these cases, the rule of descent (really a rule of recruitment) is but one of many considerations. Apart from their lineality, descent groups can also be characterized as either egalitarian or hierarchical. In a truly egalitarian system, all descent groups are of equal status. Individuals within the groups may hold particular status over others, but their status will be derived from age, rather than proximity to a senior descent line. The Nuer exemplify this type, which can be contrasted with a chiefly society or clan-based kingdom, such as Swaziland (H. Kuper 1947, 1963) or Bunyoro (Beattie 1960), as well as with hierarchical lineage systems such as the ambilineal "conical clan" societies of the Pacific (§7.5.4). Both the chiefly and conical types should be distinguished from systems in which hierarchy is purely relative or intransitive, as in a perfectly circulating connubium in which each lineage is ranked *individually* in relation to any other according to its wife-giving/wife-taking status, but in which no lineage or group of lineages can claim overall superiority (§6.4.1, §7.4.3).

In your ethnography you should make a particular effort to distinguish between emic and etic categorizations regarding descent groups. Fortes (1945: 33–38) distinguishes some five classes of lineage among the Tallensi, as indeed does Evans-Pritchard (1940: 193–203) for the Nuer. These classifications are useful heuristic devices for the study of kinship behaviour, but tell us nothing about ideology. It is important to note how the people themselves distinguish their kin groups, especially if, for instance, these are named or totemic.

You should also consider the distinction between the *order of segmentation* and the *span* of lineages (Fortes 1970: 37), and see whether the two coincide in your data. "Order" refers to the external relations of lineages, and a segment is any group within the lineage which is locally recognized as engaging in corporate action, in any context whatever. Thus a Tallensi primary lineage segment, that group of persons who unite to worship their common founding ancestor, may also comprise two or more secondary segments, who separately worship their own respective founders (ibid: 42–44). "Span" refers to the time depth of lineages, and is proportional to the number of generations separating living lineage members from their founding ancestor. Because segmentation is often a response to conflicts arising within the pre-existing segment of higher order, as in the Lugbara case (Middleton 1960: 214–215), it is not a purely automatic, structural concomitant of increasing lineage span, but a contingent event which may occur at different stages in the development of different lineages (§5.7). The relationship between order of segmentation and span is therefore not predictable in advance, but a matter for empirical investigation in every case.

You should also investigate the rights and duties that descent group members have over or towards each other, towards the group as a whole, and towards other kinds of relatives. Citing a distinction occurring in Roman law, Radcliffe-Brown (1952: 32–33) identifies two kinds of rights one may have in relation to other individuals, rights *in rem* and rights *in personam*. Rights *in rem* include those over an individual "as a thing", i.e. rights over that individual which no other person or group holds, such as, in many societies, the right of a married person to exclusive sexual access to their spouse. Rights *in personam* require the person in question to perform certain duties towards the holder of the rights, as when, for example, a father-in-law has the right to demand labour as "bride-service" from his daughter's husband. It is worthwhile codifying such rights as stated in ideal form by your informants, as well as observing the extent to which they apply in practice.

5.3 Complementary filiation

It is most unlikely, as stated above (§5.1), that all such rights should be structured according to a single descent principle, even in the most unilineal societies. After all, even in these cases "filiation . . . is normally bilateral" (Fortes 1970 [1959]: 106). This fact led Fortes to develop the somewhat controversial notion of "complementary filiation". Its existence should not be taken to imply double descent (§5.2) however, for whereas *filiation* in French does indeed mean "descent" (Dumont 1971: 48), in English the two terms are distinguished, and "filiation" means merely "the fact of being the legitimate child of [both] one's parents" (Fortes *loc. cit.*, gloss added). *Complementary filiation* is then the relationship which an individual has towards that side of his family through which descent is *not* traced. Thus where matrilineal organization is found, complementary filiation is patrilateral, and vice versa. Certain rights and duties may not operate within ego's own, say patrilineal, descent group, but may link ego to the natal patrilineal group of his mother. These duties may include rituals to honour maternal ancestors, economic obligations of particular kinds, and specially close personal ties towards maternal grandparents or mother's brothers.

For Fortes, filiation is primarily a phenomenon of the domestic or familial domain, and is therefore an aspect of "kinship" in his restricted sense of that term. On the other hand, descent is

> fundamentally a jural concept [and forms] the connecting link between the external, that is political and legal, aspect of . . . unilineal descent groups, and the internal or domestic aspect. (1970 [1953]: 84)

Moreover, whereas filiation links ego with his parents alone, descent is transitive, and extends step-by-step through ego's lineal ancestors to form his *pedigree* (1970 [1959]: 107–108; §2.3.1). So in a patrilineal system, for example, a man is linked by filiation alone with his mother and her relatives, whereas he is linked by both filiation and descent with his F and FF. This is essentially what Radcliffe-Brown was also saying in his famous discussion of the avunculate (1952 [1924]: 29), and indeed Fortes (*loc. cit.*) illustrates his own distinction with reference to Tallensi joking relationships. A Tale man is on joking terms with both his FF and his MF when they meet in the domestic context, as befits members of alternate generations. But when ego interacts with his FF in the jural domain, at a funeral rite for instance, then ego is under his FF's authority and cannot possibly joke with him. Such situations never arise in the case of the MF.

Fortes' position involves three propositions (cf. Dumont 1971: 76): (1) unilineal descent is not an aspect of kinship but of the politico-jural domain; this matter is discussed further elsewhere (§2.4, §7.5.1); (2) descent is more important than kinship in the social structure as a whole, because it links the external and internal domains specified above, whereas filiation is confined to the latter; (3) the total social system is primarily a politico-jural entity, in which the corporate descent groups constitute both the moral and legal elements. Other social institutions merely ensure the proper functioning of the system. For instance, rules of exogamy and other marriage regulations have the function of "fixing lineage membership for legitimate offspring" (Fortes 1970 [1955]: 269).

Kinship – that is, the ego-centred sphere of domestic life and marriage – is here treated as merely the "functional by-product" (*sous-produit fonctionnel*, Dumont 1971: 77) of the descent system. Affinal links are egocentric, ephemeral, and therefore structurally unimportant. Criticism of the notion of "complementary filiation" has focused upon this last point in particular. Leach argues that this stress upon "descent" as the organizing principle in society, has led to the genuinely structural ties resulting from marriage, particularly in societies with positive marriage rules, being ignored, or rather, disguised, under the name of "complementary filiation".

> The essence of this concept . . . is that any Ego is related to the kinsmen of his two parents because he is the descendant of both parents and not because his parents were married. (Leach 1961a [1957]: 122)

With this proposition, Leach strongly disagrees. Figure 5.1 shows the three relationships in question for the patrilineal case, while Fig. 5.2 depicts the situation among the Kachin, Leach's counter-example. In the case of the "Ordinary Jinghpaw", the relationship between wife-givers and wife-takers (*mayu* and *dama*) is "a crucial part of the *continuing* structure of the system" (ibid; orig. emphasis).

So for Leach, marriage may both create and maintain structural relations between lineages, a point to which we shall return (§6.3). In his view, the error in the "complementary filiation" argument stems from its acceptance of Radcliffe-Brown's generalization that there are three types of elementary or "first-order" kinship link:

> viz., the relation of parent and child, that of husband and wife, and that between siblings. (Radcliffe-Brown 1950: 6)

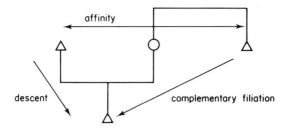

Fig. 5.1 *Descent, complementary filiation and affinity (patrilineal case).*

This is a fallacy, says Leach, encouraged by the existence of the English term "parent". Its use implies:

that the relationship between father and child is in some major respect the same as [that] between mother and child. (1960: 9)

But this is by no means so in every society. In other words, filiation is *not* universally bilateral. Clearly, every fieldworker needs to ascertain whether parent–child relationships are explicitly or implicitly equated or differentiated.

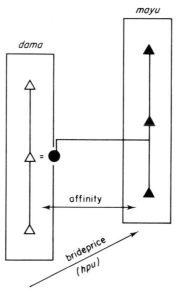

Fig. 5.2 *The structural importance of alliance among the "Ordinary Jinghpaw" Kachin (after Leach 1961a [1957]: 121).*

5.4 Corporateness

There has also been a major debate within descent theory over the concept of "corporateness". Ethnographers sometimes report the existence of "corporate descent groups" without saying exactly what this phrase implies, or use very broad and hence ambiguous definitions intended to apply to a wide range of societies. Radcliffe-Brown, for example (1950: 41), used the word to cover collective actions such as: the performance of clan rituals – here he follows Durkheim (1915); common allegiance to a chief or council, implying Weber's *Verband* (1964: 145); and the collective ownership of property, Maine's (1861) distinctive feature. We feel it best to separate these factors, for which J. Goody (1969: 95–97) suggests the labels "assembling or convening groups" (not necessarily localized), "pyramidal groups", and "corporate groups", respectively. But the labels themselves are less important than making the context clear.

More fundamental is the question of whether "descent" need in fact be a matter of "corporateness" at all. Both Fortes and Leach, despite their differences, assume the existence of behavioural entities called "descent groups". It is simply that whereas for Fortes these alone form the enduring structural framework around which individuals weave their ephemeral, marital webs, Leach adds the permanent cross-beams of repeated inter-group alliance. Two kinds of criticism have been made here. The first, exemplified by Dumont (1953; 1957) and Leach (1961a [1951]), this time with his alliance-theory false nose on, tends to dispense wholly or partly with "descent" as a *structural* principle, in order to focus even more upon alliance relationships. Postponing consideration of this until later (§6.2.3), we consider here another, not-unrelated view which prefers to see "descent" as a possible emic ideological principle, rather than as an objectively observable socio-structural feature.

As briefly mentioned in §5.1, Scheffler distinguishes *descent groups*, as empirically observable entities, from "descent constructs" or, as we prefer, *descent categories*. The latter are, first, the components of a system of classification and, secondly, vehicles for the expression of jural rules assigning rights and duties to those subsumed under the various headings. Now, and this is the crux of the matter:

> Groups and categories designated by the same term may show relatively little correspondence in their personnel. (Scheffler 1966: 550)

In other words, we must distinguish situations where groups are in practice recruited on the basis of one or other of the six forms of descent (§5.2), from those in which people speak of those groups *as if* they were recruited on such a basis. In some cases, both (or neither) of these situations will arise, but in others one may be found to the exclusion of the other. For instance, any agricultural society with patri-virilocal residence after marriage (§5.5), and inheritance from father to son, is bound to develop local communities whose male members are recruited largely by means of patrilineal descent, whether this is explicitly recognized or not.

The reverse situation is perhaps more interesting. Here people subscribe to a particular ideological view of descent which is, as it were, prescriptive, in the sense that it structures rather than reflects the local situation on the ground. The case of the Nuer is famous in this regard:

> it may be partly just because the agnatic principle is unchallenged in Nuer society that the tracing of descent through women is so prominent and matrilocality so frequent. (Evans-Pritchard 1951: 28)

Nuer villages are by no means composed entirely, or even largely, of lineage mates and their wives, though in external relations villagers often behave as if this were so (ibid: 23). The same matter has been treated more systematically by Sahlins, who shows how the same, fixed genealogical links among a set of local residence-groups, may be reinterpreted so as to correspond to a variety of emic idioms. He redraws his specimen genealogy so that it appears to depict straightforward agnatic descent groups, cognatic descent groups, segmentary lineages, non-local clans, and so forth (1965: 106). In general, there need be "no particular relation between the descent ideology and group composition" (ibid: 104). The latter is partly a product of extra-social factors to do with demography and ecology, and partly the result of political self-interest (ibid: 106; Scheffler 1966: 550).

The very concept of "group membership" may itself be emically problematic. As Firth (1963: 36) has suggested, there will not always be a clear-cut "full, exclusive and unitary set of rights and obligations", but rather "a considerable degree of permitted ambiguity" in determining who is a member of a unilineal or cognatic "corporate" group. These ambiguities should of course be investigated.

In the most radical criticism so far, Adam Kuper (1982a) attacks the very idea of "the lineage model", and particularly the related notion of segmentary patrilineal organization touched on in §5.2. His grounds are that these ideas do not conform to folk-models, and appear to bear no relation to the ways in which political and economic activities are actually organized in the paradigm cases (cf. Holy 1979; Verdon 1982). His arguments may seem overstated, but they are none the less worth serious thought.

To conclude, you will need to consider "descent" from at least three points of view, though not all may prove relevant in any given case. First, do people classify themselves and others, in sociocentric rather than egocentric fashion, according to "descent" criteria, however expressed in local idiom? Secondly, do rules allocating rights and duties make use of such classifications, in any context whatever? Thirdly, are any actual local groupings, again in any context, composed wholly or in part of persons linked by one, or a fixed combination, of the formally possible rules of descent? You will then need to compare your answers to these three questions, decide whether and to what extent they correspond or diverge, to try to account for these correspondences and divergences.

In this section we have dealt with what Sahlins (1965: 106) terms "the supposed confusion between kinship and descent". We must now turn to what he calls "the more egregious confusion between descent and residence" (ibid).

5.5 Residence rules and norms

There exist some five to seven (or more) forms of post-marital residence, depending on how they are counted. The most common, worldwide, is *virilocality*, residence in the husband's natal home. Its opposite is *uxorilocality*, or residence in the wife's natal home. These terms are preferable to the more usual but misleading "patrilocality" and "matrilocality" (Adam 1948). Murdock (1967: 48) prefers to make a fine distinction between virilocality and "patrilocality", and between uxorilocality and "matrilocality", on the basis of the tendency for such rules to create unilineal kin group residential units. However, we feel that what is important, particularly for fieldworkers, is an accurate description of the procedure for taking up residence after marriage, rather than the pinning of a particular label on the process. See whether the couple move to the same household or homestead in the same ward or village. Here we are distinguishing *households*, the separate units in the domestic economy and often most conveniently distinguished by possession of distinct cooking facilities, from *homesteads*, or physically distinct living quarters (cf. Kopytoff 1977). Ask if this residence is temporary or permanent, and find out *why* such a rule (if there is one) occurs. Is there a discrepancy between the jural rule and the behavioural norm? Do some individuals or social classes favour one rule over another? And who benefits from such practices?

Residence is often closely related to descent group structure. Lowie (1920:

passim) and Murdock (1949: 201–218) believed that residence rules *determined* group formation in an evolutionary sense. This may or may not be the case, but there do exist logical relations between residence rules and descent group structure.

Repeated virilocality in a patrilineal society serves to keep the men of a group in the same place (see Fig. 5.3). Among the Tiv, for example, young men generally bring their wives to live with them in the compound of their father. They remain there even after the father's death, which keeps male agnates together over several generations. This agnatic unit is the focus of many of their social and economic activities (Bohannan and Bohannan 1968).

Virilocal residence is found in matrilineal societies too, but there it is of course less likely to fulfil such functions. The two residence rules which maintain kin group structure in matrilineal societies are uxorilocality and avunculocality (residence with the man's MB). The former keeps the women together and disperses the men of the matrilineal kin group (Fig. 5.4). This pattern is found, for example, among the Bemba (Richards 1934, 1961: 111–117). Its disadvantage, given that men generally control property – one

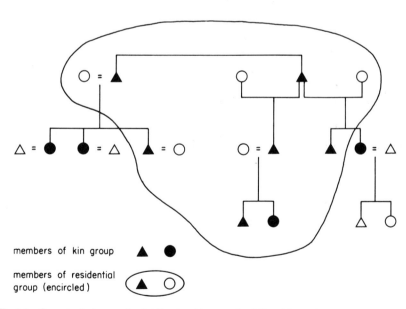

members of kin group ▲ ●

members of residential group (encircled) (▲ ○)

Fig. 5.3 *Genealogical example of virilocal residence and patrilineal descent.*

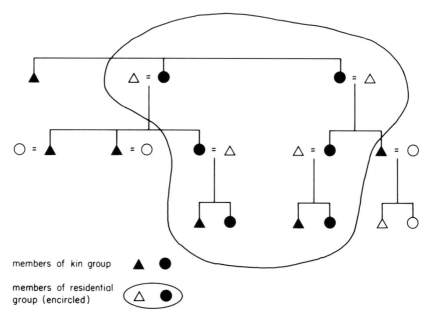

Fig. 5.4 *Genealogical example of uxorilocal residence and matrilineal descent.*

of Fox's "four principles" (1967: 31; §1.1) – is that the adult men are separated from that property.

Avunculocality, in contrast, keeps matrilineally related adult men together but disperses the women through whom they trace their descent (Fig. 5.5). The classic case is that of the Trobriand Islanders (Malinowski 1932). A Trobriand boy grows up in the village of his father's sub-clan, where he is forever taunted and told that he does not belong. His own matrilineal sub-clan village is that of his MB, and he moves there for the first time after this marriage. A woman *never* normally lives in her own sub-clan village. Having grown up in her father's village, she eventually takes up residence in that of her husband. There are exceptions, but these involve the deliberate breaking of the rule of avunculocality, when a powerful chief succeeds in keeping his S and SW with him after the son's marriage, normally to the latter's FZD (who would belong to the chief's sub-clan). In your fieldwork, watch for such exceptions and seek the reasons behind them.

A fourth rule of residence, common in Western societies, is *neolocality*. This occurs when young married couples go to live in new places of residence, which are the natal homes of neither party. Obviously, this breaks apart any

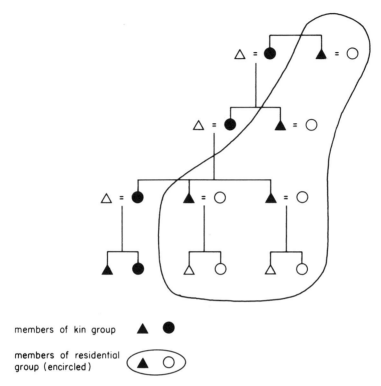

members of kin group ▲ ●

members of residential group (encircled) (▲ ○)

Fig. 5.5 *Genealogical example of avunculocal residence and matrilineal descent.*

potential unilinear kin groupings. Its opposite, in a sense, is the very rare form of residence known as *duolocality*. In duolocal or *natolocal* residence the husband and wife live separately, in their natal homes. As a regular practice it would keep kin groups together, but at the expense of the marital bond. True duolocality is virtually non-existent as a long-term practice, but it does occur in some West African societies as an *initial* stage of post-marital residence. It is worthwhile distinguishing this type of residence, both from that in which men live in a "men's house" and women live separately, and from such typologically-aberrant cases as the Nayar *taravād* (Gough 1959) or West Indian matrifocal family (Smith 1973).

The last two types of post-marital residence are *ambilocality* (or bilocality) and *uxori-virilocality*. Ambilocality permits a couple to reside either uxorilocally or virilocally, and is typically found in small-scale hunting-and-gathering or herding societies with migratory band organization. Uxori-virilocality is often found in societies which practice bride-service. Among the !Kung Bushmen (Marshall 1976: 168–172) for example, a couple normally resides with the wife's parents for several years following their marriage. The husband hunts game for his parents-in-law and proves to them that he is capable of taking care of his wife and children. After this period he is free to return with his wife to his own band.

Notice that this entire system of classifying and distinguishing residence patterns takes for granted that the most significant variable is the place of post-marital residence of the *married couple*. But is this necessarily so? Meillassoux, in his concern to emphasize the mechanisms of social reproduction (§7.3.2), argues that it is more important to consider the residential rules regarding the couple's *children*. He therefore contrasts *gynecostatic* societies, which are generally associated with matrilineality, or at least an emphasis upon matrilocality, with *gynecomobile* ones, which are generally also patrilocal and patrilineal (1981: 24). Of the two, gynecostatic systems tend to be the more inflexible and unstable (ibid: 31). They are, he argues, characteristic of certain types of "planting agriculture" (ibid: 25n), whereas gynecomobility is particularly associated with cereal-producers (ibid: 26).

These, then, are the basic types of residence. It is of course likely that even when there exist jural rules specifying one particular type, not everyone will follow them. It is equally possible that people practise certain types of post-marital residence *without* formulating explicit rules, and without being aware of their consequences for social group formation. There are several more complex possibilities, too.

First, careful study of actual residential patterns may reveal that whereas one rule is stated as the ideal, other forms of residence are the behavioural norm. Secondly, alternative forms of residence may be recognized, but unequally ranked. The well-known case of the Sinhalese illustrates both points. For them, *dīga* (virilocal) residence after marriage is widely regarded as superior to *binna* (uxorilocal) residence. The latter is associated with impoverished husbands and/or heiresses without brothers, and carries connotations of the subordination of the husband to his father-in-law. Yet in practice the two forms occur with comparable frequency (Leach 1961b: 81–85; Yalman 1967: 122–130).

Not only may more than one type exist in the same society, but so may various combinations or extensions of the basic ones. Here, above all, one realizes how inadequate and unwieldy are the terms at our disposal. As an admittedly extreme example, consider the matrilineal Tamils of south-eastern Sri Lanka, where parents and unmarried siblings move out of the family home when the eldest daughter marries, so that she may reside there with her husband. The rest of the family move into a new home which eventually becomes the dowry house of the second daughter, and so on. Clearly this pattern conforms to none of the straightforward forms in our paradigm. With tongue somewhat in cheek, McGilvray (1980) elects to call it "successive matri-uxorilocal dotation".

5.6 The structure of the residential group

Knowledge of the local rule of post-marital residence does not in itself tell us anything about the size and structure of the residential grouping in which the married couple will live. The possibilities here are endless, and although we shall try in this section to codify them, our attempt cannot pretend to be complete. One of the best and most comprehensive typologies is that of Kolenda, who points out that there are two questions that must be answered by any account of family types:

> First, *what* is shared by the family unit referred to, and, second, *who* shares it. (1968: 344; orig. emphasis)

Most writers use *commensality*, in particular the use of a common cooking hearth, as the defining criterion of the family unit, which is then a household according to our earlier definition (§5.5). Others emphasize *co-residence* in the same homestead or house site. You will have to decide which approach best suits your observations.

Turning now to the composition of this commensal or co-residential unit, 12 situations have been distinguished by Kolenda (ibid: 346–347). We list these below, though in some cases the definitions are reworded to make them less specific to the Indian context for which they were first devised.

(1) *Nuclear family*: a couple with or without their unmarried children.
(2) *Supplemented nuclear family*: type (1) plus one or more extra unmarried, separated, divorced, or widowed relatives of the couple.
(3) *Subnuclear family*: a fragment of a former unit of type (1).
(4) *Single person family*.
(5) *Supplemented sub-nuclear family*: a unit of type (3), plus one or more extra unmarried, separated, divorced, or widowed relatives.
(6) *Collateral joint family*: two or more married siblings with their spouses and unmarried children.
(7) *Supplemented collateral joint family*: a type (6) unit plus one or more extra unmarried, separated, divorced, or widowed relatives.
(8) *Lineal joint family*: two lineally related persons, their spouses and

unmarried children. "Lineal" is here used in the fourth of the senses distinguished in §5.1, and not with reference to *rules* of descent.

(9) *Supplemented lineal joint family*: a type (8) unit, plus one or more unmarried, separated, divorced, or widowed relatives belonging to neither of the constituent nuclear families.

(10) *Lineal-collateral joint family*: three or more persons linked lineally and collaterally, together with their spouses and unmarried children. Typically, this might comprise a couple and two or more of their married children, plus the spouses and offspring.

(11) *Supplemented lineal-collateral joint family*: a type (10) unit, plus one or more unmarried, separated, divorced, or widowed relatives belonging to none of the constituent nuclear families.

(12) *Other family types*: not included in the above list.

Several points arise here. First, the existence of the residual type (12) indicates that the list is not exhaustive, and does not claim to be. Secondly, the way it is drawn up, described and inter-related is clearly biased in favour of the nuclear family and, even more, the married *couple*, as basic building blocks. For instance, no fragments of type (10) are independently listed, and it is presumably assumed that the various possibilities are covered by types (7) and (9). Yet what of the famous Nayar *taravād*? It could certainly be said to involve three or more persons related matrilineally and collaterally, but spouses would of course be lacking in every case (Gough 1955: 47). Thirdly, the list does not distinguish clearly between distinct structural types of family on the one hand, and different stages in the developmental cycle of a single family type on the other (§5.7). For instance, the sequence

$$\text{type (2)} ---\rangle \text{ type (1)} ---\rangle \text{ type (3)} ---\rangle \text{ type (2), etc.}$$

must be quite common in modern British society. Lastly, and in partial explanation of the third point, the typology is a purely *behavioural* one, designed to classify observed residential or commensal units. Every society will presumably have explicit *ideal* forms of family structure, which you will have to discover. But every substantive typology is bound to present difficulties of these kinds, and Kolenda's is as satisfactory as any for the purposes of ordering your data and comparing them with the findings of others.

5.7 The developmental cycle

Closely tied to studies of residence is the notion of the developmental cycle of domestic groups. The developmental cycle is the regular pattern which emerges as residential groups change composition over time, due to births, deaths, marriages, and ensuing changes of residence. In principle, an ethnographer could witness an entire developmental cycle by staying at the fieldwork site for, say, 40–60 years. In practice, of course, you will only be there for one or two years, and you will therefore have to infer this diachronic aspect of group composition from synchronic data. The principle, first enunciated by Fortes (1949a, b; cf. Goody 1958), is best illustrated by example. The classic cases of Tallensi, Ashanti, LoDagaba, etc., are well known, so we shall draw here on complementary and more diverse data from our own fieldwork regions.

Bushman bands aggregate and disperse seasonally, but also expand, contract, and change composition over longer periods of time. One writer (Yellen 1977: 43) has described !Kung territorial organization as an "almost random" movement of individuals from camp to camp, or band to band. However, as Yellen notes, the !Kung do not see things that way. They recognize a person's permanent membership in a band, even when he is visiting for months elsewhere, and further recognize his rights to join a new band to which he is linked by appropriate ties of kinship. Changes in band membership which appear random to a short-term observer often involve a *return* to bands in which individuals grew up or previously resided. This has been borne out recently by both the explicit statements of informants and long-term census data collected by the many ethnographers of the !Kung (see, e.g. Lee 1979: 54–76).

Census data on other Bushman societies are inevitably less complete. One early ethnographer reports a preference among the Hai-//'om for childhood residence with one's grandparents (Bleek ms.). Whether these are the paternal or maternal grandparents is not made clear, but post-marital residence is virilocal (ibid; Fourie 1928: 92). If adhered to, such preferences might well have detectable effects on the generation structures of bands. The relative sizes and age compositions could then be seen not as random, but as products of this unusual rule of residence. A full study of Hai-//'om band organization has yet to be made.

Somewhat more straightforward is the case of the North Indian "joint family". Ideally, this corresponds to Kolenda's tenth type (§5.6), and comprises a man, his sons, and sons' sons, together with their respective spouses and unmarried children, all resident in a single homestead. Incomes are pooled and form part of the joint estate, out of which each constituent nuclear family draws whatever it needs for subsistence. Sometimes there is a single, joint cooking hearth, in which case it would be more precise to speak of the residence group as a "joint household".

Clearly this arrangement is consistent with the existence of a landed estate in which all members of the patrilineal segment are co-parceners. Indeed, many anthropologists and most casual observers have viewed the joint family as incompatible with the "modern" cash economy or urban living (Bailey 1957: 92). Yet not only is there evidence that joint households are as common in some rural areas now as they were 150 years ago (Kolenda 1970), but they seem *more* prevalent now in the metropolis of Calcutta than they may ever have been in rural areas (Sarma 1964).

Why, then, should it have been assumed for so long that joint families were on the point of disappearing? One answer seems to be that the dissolution, which forms an inevitable part of their growth cycle, tends to be sudden, visible and rancorous, whereas the expansion of the resulting nuclear fragments into new joint families is a slow and undramatic process. Not only that, but Indians often speak of a past "golden age" in which the joint family was universal. This would clearly have been impossible, for demographic reasons alone. Beware of accepting at face value the glorifications of the past with which you are likely to be regaled in many contexts. They are certain to reveal more about contemporary ideology, than about historical practice.

How are you to assess what is really going on, given the limited time-scale of most fieldwork? The obvious answer is a combination of "extended case" and "life history" methods (see the discussions by J. C. Mitchell 1984; du Boulay and Williams 1984). The former may be applied whenever you are able to observe significant changes taking place in the structures of particular families during your stay. In each case, you should not merely observe *what* happens, but discuss with as many of the principal actors as possible just *why* it happened, and what they and others are likely to do next. The "life history" method may be used to supplement this information (as well as being applied to persons in less transitional situations), because the origins of what you actually observe almost certainly lie far in the past, before your arrival. Asking individuals in detail what sizes and kinds of households they have lived in during their own lifetimes, is likely to yield much more precise and accurate results than questions about general trends.

A recent study of North Indian Rajputs by Parry (1979), allows him to distinguish three "levels of causation" operating in the partition of domestic groups such as Indian joint families. The model seems generally applicable, at least in outline.

(1) There are first of all the *underlying* causes of partition, which have to do with the structural contradictions inherent in the growth of the family itself. In the Indian case, the pre-eminent factor here is the conflict between a man's

loyalty to his brothers and parallel cousins on the one hand, and that to his wife and children on the other. The more generations the group endures, the weaker become the former loyalties in comparison to the latter.

(2) The *predisposing* causes of partition arise out of contingent economic and demographic circumstances, which suddenly make partition of the estate an attractive proposition for one particular family segment. For instance, a man with only two children may see advantages in taking his own half-share of the land, and splitting off from a brother who has seven or eight mouths to feed. The mere existence of such predispositions does not make partition inevitable, however.

(3) There must also be *immediate* causes of partition, incidents even of a trivial nature which none the less lead to, or serve as pretexts for, the actual breach. Among the Rajputs these are often quarrels between brothers' wives, so that the incoming women carry the can for this rather shameful act on the part of their husbands (Parry 1979: 193–194). See whether a model of this kind, suitably modified to allow for cultural differences, makes sense of your own observations.

6 *Marriage and alliance*

6.1 Problems of definition

There are always problems involved in taking a term out of ethnographic context, and assigning to it a definition of would-be universal applicability. In fact, there is a strong case for arguing that advances in anthropological understanding generally take the form of a recognition, with one such concept after another, that this "substantialist fallacy" (Dumont 1964: 83) does not work. This certainly seems the conclusion to be drawn from a celebrated anthropological controversy concerning the definition of "marriage". The debate focused upon various South Asian societies, notably the Nayar of Kerala, but the issues raised are quite general.

For Leach (1961a [1955]: 107–108), the phenomenon commonly labelled "marriage" comprised "bundles of rights", including for instance: legitimation of offspring; access to the spouse's sexuality, labour and property; and the setting-up of affinal alliances between persons and between groups. No single case of "marriage" involves all possible types of right, nor is any one feature common to all forms of "marriage". Moreover, other features can be added to the list without compromising it in any way.

Gough (1959: 23) seized on this last point as an apparent logical flaw, which would enable any ethnographer to "define marriage in any way he pleased". This might be adequate within a given ethnographic context, but for purposes of cross-cultural comparison we needed a single, precise definition so as to be sure we were comparing the same kinds of thing. However, she recognized the inadequacy of the *Notes and Queries* definition, which read:

> Marriage is a union between a man and a woman such that children born to the woman are the recognized legitimate offspring of both partners. (1951: 110)

This failed to take into account such institutions as Nuer woman–woman marriage (Evans-Pritchard 1951: 108–109); leviratic unions in which the child is the legitimate offspring of a man other than its genitor; and the institutions with which Gough herself was most directly concerned, namely unions among Nayar, or between Nayar girls and Nambudiri Brahman men. She therefore proposed the following modified definition:

> Marriage is a relationship established between a woman and one or more other persons, which provides that a child born to the woman under circumstances not prohibited by the rules of the relationship, is accorded full birth-status rights common to normal members of his society or social stratum. (1959: 32)

This copes successfully with the three cases just cited, though not with certain others, such as the homosexual unions of Western Egypt (Cline 1936; cf. Leach 1982: 210). Moreover, one obvious argument against making legitimation of offspring the universal concomitant of marriage, is that "marriages" to which children have not (yet) been born are not thereby automatically invalidated. In such cases, "marriage" is clearly felt to involve more than mere procreation, and can exist in the absence of the latter. As Laura Bohannan (1949) has pointed out on the basis of evidence from Dahomey, rights over a woman as a wife (rights *in uxorem*) must be distinguished from rights over any children she may bear (rights *in genetricem*).

More fundamentally, this approach begs the question of whether there is in fact a definable, cross-cultural phenomenon in the first place. This is precisely Leach's point in his comment that "all universal definitions of marriage are vain" (1961a: 105). As Needham has pointed out, "marriage" considered cross-culturally is a class based upon serial likenesses rather than some common structural feature (1971b: 6, 30). Any characterization of "marriage" can therefore only be polythetic, an open-ended checklist rather than a "parsimonious definition" (Gough 1959: 23). That, at least, is the position we take up here.

That being so, why retain the word "marriage" at all, to the extent of including it in the title of this chapter? We feel that the term does have utility, provided it is defined in Nominal rather than Real terms. A "Nominal definition" (see Southwold 1978: 369) is: "a declaration of the signification of a word or phrase". Thus, words may be nominally defined with reference to the contexts in which they are actually used. The class of phenomena to which each word refers "is merely the totality of things to which people have applied [the] word" (ibid: 370). "Marriage", then, is first and foremost a word used by English-speakers to specify a certain range of phenomena in their own societies. In this context, it has at least four inter-related but none the less discriminable senses (cf. Leach 1982: 82–83): (1) the mutal, legal rights and duties of the spouses *vis-à-vis* each other and their children; (2) the personal relationship between the spouses, as in the idea of "a happy marriage"; (3) the wedding ceremony; (4) relationships of alliance set up thereby, as in the phrase "making a good marriage".

When used by anthropologists attempting cross-cultural comparison, on the other hand, the term "marriage" may serve to *translate* appropriate words in other languages. This procedure is adopted here, and our use of the term does not even imply that the institution thus labelled displays any of the features just listed, nor any of the nine rights in Leach's original "bundle". We use the word purely for convenience, to orient the reader without resort to tedious circumlocutions. What is really of interest, after all, is not the institution itself, abstracted from context, labelled, and thereby over-reified, but rather its place in the entire conceptual and socio-structural framework within which it occurs.

6.2 Rules governing sexual intercourse and marriage

Every society regulates sexual intercourse in one way or another. First, there are criteria for determining those who may not have sexual relations: these are the *rules of incest*. Then there are the positive and negative *marriage rules* which demarcate, respectively, the *unit of endogamy* within which ego should marry, and the *unit of exogamy* within which he should not. We use "unit" here to encompass both sociocentric "groups" and ego-centred "categories" (cf. Dumont 1957: 4), either or both of which may be involved in each case. These are not the only kinds of rule to be considered. For instance, sexual access to those who are already married is generally restricted, both negatively by *rules of adultery*, and positively, by means of polygamy, the levirate or sororate, or Islamic *mut'a* (short-term) marriage (cf. Leach 1982: 210). None of these sets of rules is unproblematic, and all have given rise to more debate than we can possibly deal with here. Instead, we provide a synthesis of what seem to us the more important points.

6.2.1 *Sexual prohibitions*

Anthropologists have perhaps spilt more ink on the topic of incest than on any other subject in the field of kinship. The search for a universal explanation of the phenomenon has produced all kinds of mutually contradictory conclusions, many of which are ably summarized by Fox (1967: Ch. 2). He tries to explain the origins of the prohibition in terms of the presumed living conditions and demography of early hominids, a matter upon which you may form your own judgement. We wish here to take up and extend another of his points, that incest is not always abhorred or prohibited, and is not even universal in form or extent (ibid: 63).

The first point to be made is that "incest" in British society refers not to one phenomenon, but three: sexual liaisons between F and D, M and S, and B and Z. In other societies, the range of prohibitions is often very different. It must have been narrower in the Egypt of the Roman Empire, whose census returns indicate that around 15–20% of marriages were between full brothers and sisters (Hopkins 1980: 304). By contrast, the Nuer concept *rual* – translated by Evans-Pritchard as "incest" – leads them to prohibit not only F/D and B/Z liaisons but all those involving members of the same clan, and not only M/S liaisons but all between cognates within six generations (1951: 30–31). Clearly, Needham is right to point out that:

> All that is common to incest prohibitions is the feature of prohibition itself. (1971b: 29)

Even that is not the end of the matter. Other usages of the Nuer term *rual* refer to activities that would be classed in English, assuming both parties to be single, not as "incest" but as "fornication". Moreover, *rual*, is also used of sexual relations between a man and his lineage kinsmen's wives (Evans-Pritchard 1951: 37), which in English would be "adultery". Given the inadequacy of treating terms like *rual* as local synonyms for "incest", Jack Goody suggests a more precise, structural typology of heterosexual offences generally (1971: 73). A version of this is shown in Fig. 6.1. The neologism "incestuous adultery" refers to an offence which, among the patrilineal LoDagaa, is more serious than mere incest, since the sexuality of the woman in question has by then "been alienated to . . . another clan" (ibid: 74). Throughout, in fact, Goody assumes the existence of unilineal descent

| | offences with: | |
	unmarried person	married person
intra-unit offences	incest	incestuous adultery
extra-unit offences	fornication	adultery

Fig. 6.1 *Typology of heterosexual offences (after Goody 1971: 73).*

groups, a bias we have tried to remedy by substituting "unit" for "group" in our figure.

Having clarified the issue by demarcating this entire, structured field of "heterosexual offences", you are then in a position to investigate such matters systematically. What groups and/or categories of person are prohibited as sexual partners for a given ego? Is intercourse with such persons regarded with horror or comparative equanimity? What penalties, legal or supernatural (if that distinction is meaningful) follow upon breach of these rules? How are these offences classified locally? What, bearing in mind Gough's stress upon legitimacy, is the status of children both outwith marriage, particularly as a consequence of incestuous or otherwise forbidden sexual liaisons?

6.2.2 *Rules of exogamy and endogamy*

So far we have discussed only rules which can be breached by individual fiat. The rules of exogamy and endogamy, by contrast, regulate *marriage* between particular groups or categories. As marriage (whatever else it may be) is by definition a socially recognized relationship, such rules are upheld by social pressures operating before (to forbid) the event, rather than afterwards (to punish it). This is not to say that such rules cannot be bent or broken, but that when this is done there will generally be recourse to some face-saving legal formula to justify the union. For instance, the Nuer ban on sex, and hence *a fortiori* on marriage, with quite distant cognates (§6.2.1), can be overcome in borderline cases by the performance of a rite whereby the prospective spouses publicly "split kinship" (Evans-Pritchard 1951: 31).

At first sight, exogamy and endogamy are straightforward matters: *exogamy* is the requirement that one marry outside a particular unit, *endogamy* the requirement to marry within another, obviously larger unit. Neither is quite so easy to deal with in practice, however.

In the first place, there is the usual need to distinguish categories, rules and behaviour (§1.3.2). Every society categorizes its members, and some of these conceptual distinctions are used to express exogamic and endogamic rules. This need not be their only, or prime purpose, however. Thus, every Nuer clan has a set of spear names used during sacrificial invocations (Evans-Pritchard 1956: 231). Those of the bride and groom are shouted out during weddings, and must differ to some degree if the marriage is to conform to the requirements of clan exogamy (Evans-Pritchard 1951: 30). Similarly, the Kondaiyankottai Maravar of South India worship patrilineally inherited family deities, and as persons sharing such a deity may not marry, these congregations constitute *de facto* exogamous groups (Good 1981; §5.1). We cannot anticipate all cultural possibilities here: the important thing is to recognize exogamic and endogamic rules *whatever* form they take. They need not, of course, be genealogically based even in the implicit fashion of our two examples. They may, for instance, reflect physical contiguity, as in the case of village exogamy.

The behavioural situation may be different again. For instance, the *de facto* units of exogamy and endogamy may be, respectively, larger or smaller than those defined jurally. Only detailed analysis of demographic, genealogical and residential patterns (§2.2, §2.5) is likely to reveal such discrepancies. For example, although it is usually correct to describe Indian castes as endogamous, this is often misleading since their component sub-castes may also be endogamous. The *de facto* endogamous unit may, moreover, be an even smaller entity than this, unnamed locally but called by Mayer (1960: 4) the "kindred of recognition".

6.2.3 *Other marriage rules*

Marriage rules run the whole gamut from the formal requirements considered so far, which are frequently supported by legal or moral sanctions, to mere norms, conventions, and ideas of "appropriateness". These more diffuse notions may interact with the formal requirements concerning incest, endogamy, etc., in a variety of ways. For example, exogamy and endogamy place limits upon the choice of spouse, but do not in themselves positively determine his or her identity. Other factors come into operation here, such as political and economic considerations, sexual attraction, and even – in a few, highly aberrant cases (Little 1966) – romantic love.

Moreover, as always when dealing with rules, we must take into account the possibility of them being broken. A special, and very interesting case of this arises when two or more normative requirements conflict. For instance, suppose a ban on marriage with distant agnates threatens a less precise, but none the less normative desire to make as politically advantageous a match as possible. You may well find that within limits such strategic considerations outweigh those of exogamy among the political élite, as Trautmann shows for Sinhalese royalty (1981: 416; §7.4.2). Clearly then, it is not enough merely to state the marriage rules operative in the society concerned. You need also to give some indication of their strength. Case studies of jural breaches and conflicts will be invaluable here, but it is just as important to study cases in which rules are "obeyed" (§8.3).

In short, you will need to ascertain the rules governing marriageability in the society under study. These need to be reported and understood both in their local forms, and using standard anthropological vocabulary. This of course demands knowledge of local systems of classification. You then need to examine the extent to which each rule is obeyed; the penalties entailed, in both theory and practice, by their violation; and the outcomes of situations in which jural or normative principles conflict.

6.3 Positive marriage requirements: alliance theory

The points made in §6.2 are of general applicability. Another type of marriage requirement is found only in certain types of society, but has nevertheless been central to the development of kinship theory over the past 30 years. We refer to the phenomenon conventionally, though misleadingly, as "prescription" or "prescriptive alliance". To explain why this issue is so important, and why the terminology is unsatisfactory, we shall have to summarize the development of the ideas involved. Our arguments in the next two sections are both tendentious and polemical. Neither characteristic is at all desirable in a book of this kind, but there is, alas, no generally-agreed view on the matters with which we have to deal.

6.3.1 *The elementary structures*

As we saw in §5.4, some writers have accorded great, even predominant, structural importance to the marriage bond. One of the earliest and most famous was Lévi-Strauss, whose *Les Structures élémentaires de la parenté* was first published in 1949: the revised 1967 edition appeared in English translation in 1969. Lévi-Strauss was concerned with "elementary structures", namely those kinship systems which do not merely prohibit certain forms of marriage, but also "prescribe [*prescrivent*] marriage with a certain type of relative" (1949: ix, 1969: xxiii): systems, in other words, with positive as well as negative marriage requirements. The broader implications of Lévi-Strauss's theory are well brought out by Dumont (1971: 89–120), and we confine ourselves to summarizing those aspects directly relevant to the matter in hand. In this exposition, we take temporarily for granted some notions, particularly the fundamental one of "exchange", which we shall later argue are irrelevant in this particular context (§6.3.2).

For Lévi-Strauss, though, the essential feature of elementary structures is the systematic *exchange* of women in an explicitly Maussian sense. This may take several forms. First, there is *restricted exchange*, which involves "pairs of exchange-units so that, for any one pair X–Y there is a reciprocal exchange relationship", i.e. X ⟨– – – –⟩ Y (1969: 146). The simplest form involves units which are patri- or matrilineal exogamous moieties, and the system is formally equivalent to one of sister-exchange. This in turn, if repeated in succeeding generations, is formally equivalent to bilateral cross-cousin marriage, as Fig. 6.2 demonstrates.

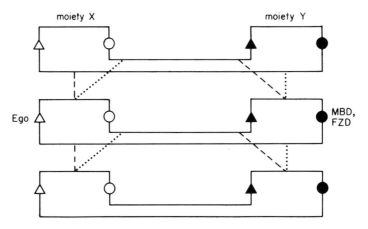

Fig. 6.2 *Restricted exchange: bilateral cross-cousin marriage.* – – –, *patrilineal case;* . . . ., *matrilineal case.*

Exchange may also occur asymmetrically, a procedure which necessitates a minimum of three exchange-units (A – – –⟩ B – – –⟩ C – – –⟩ A) and which Lévi-Strauss terms *generalized exchange*. If, in the simplest case, an *A* man gives his Z in marriage to *B*, who in turn gives his Z to *C*, and so on, and if this is repeated by their lineal descendants, it gives rise to matrilateral cross-cousin marriage between a man and his MBD. Figure 6.3 shows that this arrangement, too, is compatible with both patri- and matrilineally constituted exogamous units, but whereas the symmetry of restricted exchange implies equality between the exchange-units, the asymmetry of generalized exchange makes status differences possible, though not inevitable (§6.4).

According to Lévi-Strauss, matrilateral marriage constitutes "the most lucid and fruitful of the simplest forms of reciprocity" (1969: 451), and is superior to restricted exchange by virtue of its ability to integrate an indefinite number of units into long cycles of exchange. The other possible form of

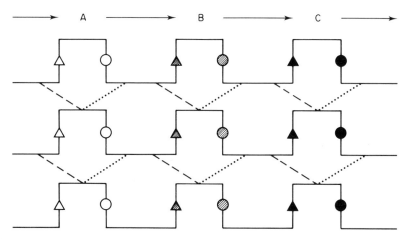

Fig. 6.3 *Generalized exchange: matrilateral cross-cousin marriage. – – –, patrilineal case; . . . . . .,
matrilineal case.*

generalized exchange, namely patrilateral cross-cousin marriage, is however
"its poorest and most elementary application" (ibid). As Fig. 6.4 shows,
exchanges are again symmetric but reverse their direction with each succeeding generation. This is less socially cohesive than the matrilateral form,
because the exchange cycles are short. The bond of endebtedness is redeemed
by the return of a woman after one generation. From the viewpoint of the

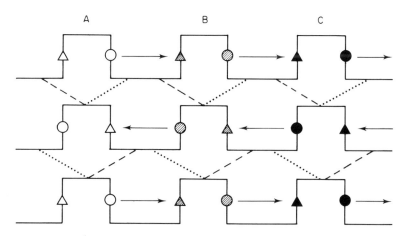

Fig. 6.4 *Generalized exchange: patrilateral form. – – –, patrilineal case; . . . . . ., matrilineal case.*

individual, though, it represents less of a "risk", since the return for a woman given is much more direct. This psychologistic idiom is doubly unfortunate, since it helped spark Homans and Schneider's (1955) "explanation" of cross-cousin marriage in terms of individual sentiments, a view which Lévi-Strauss himself unequivocally repudiates (1963: 322; cf. also Needham 1962).

Finally there is "avuncular" marriage between a man and his "sister's daughter", which is in Lévi-Strauss's view an "oblique" sub-type of patri-lateral marriage (1969: 451). The resemblance lies in the regular alternation of the direction of exchange, which this time seems to occur every "half-generation", as shown in Fig. 6.5a (see also Rivière 1966: 738).

Lévi-Strauss never examined *repeated* ZD marriage. Had he done so, two difficulties might have become apparent. First, while the alternating direction of exchange evident in Fig. 6.5a might indeed seem to indicate a formal resemblance to marriage with the FZD, the same system can be portrayed as in Fig. 6.5b, as an apparent form of symmetrical, restricted exchange (see also Leach 1961a [1951]: 60). After all, only two exchange-units are involved. Secondly, *both* forms of the figure reveal that repeated ZD marriage is, simultaneously and inevitably, a form of marriage not with the FZD but with the MBD! In short, Lévi-Strauss's distinctions between restricted and gener-alized exchange, and between the matrilateral (long cycle) and patrilateral (short cycle) forms of the latter, completely break down in this instance. The matter is far from purely academic, because several indigenous societies in Latin America (Rivière 1969: 272–283; Boremanse 1981: 29–30) and South India display just these features. In the latter area, moreover, the equivalence of MBD and ZD marriage is explicitly recognized (Aiyappan 1934; Good 1980).

This system cannot be diagrammed in conjunction with matrilineal descent, since MB and ZD belong to the same matrilineal unit. There would, of course, be nothing to stop members of matrilineal societies marrying other members of the categories to which MB and ZD belong, but the fact that we cannot depict such systems using the genealogical format of Figs 6.2 to 6.5, inevitably throws doubt on the utility of such diagrams (§1.2.3). All these figures portray the systematic links between alliance units as if they were close genealogical links between lineages of individual persons (cf. Leach 1961a [1951]: 61–64). This is never the true situation, of course. First, although Lévi-Strauss believed that most "primitive" societies had systems of unilineal descent, this is far from true (Leach 1970: 105). The exchange-units need not even be lineages at the conceptual or jural, still less the behavioural level: they may be formed on the basis of co-residence, for example. Secondly, even when there *are* lineages, these are never really made up of one male and one

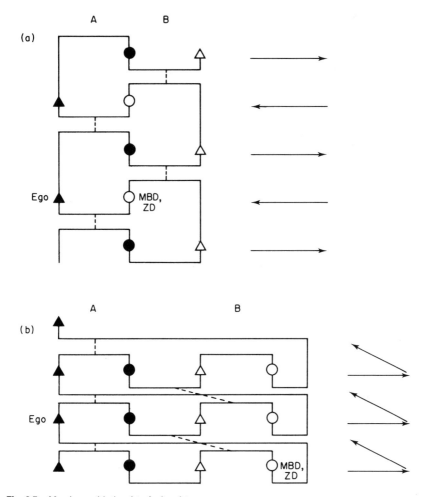

Fig. 6.5 *Marriage with the sister's daughter.*

female in each generation. Systems in which every male marries his MBD, or FZD, or bilateral first cousin, are impossible demographically. The alliances portrayed in the figures link, in reality, members of groups or categories rather than genealogically close relatives: hence, presumably, Lévi-Strauss's use (not, unfortunately, throughout) of the neutral phrase "exchange-units" (*unites échangistes*).

The problem is more acute for the patrilateral case represented in Fig. 6.4, because the distinctiveness of this supposed type rests largely on the formal characteristics of the diagram, rather than of the social system it allegedly portrays. The need to distinguish alternate generations requires us to assume that all individuals in every generation marry at more-or-less the same time. This would be unlikely demographically even if the figure were indeed the close genealogy it appears to be: in reality, there is not one man and one woman in each generation of each exchange-unit, but an indeterminate larger number with, inevitably, a considerable age spread. The younger A.2 men will still be receiving brides *from* B at the same time as the older A.3 women are being given as brides *to* B. In short, once one recognizes exchange as a group affair rather than an individual, genealogical one, it becomes clear that the patrilateral form of exchange must inevitably lose, in practice, any semblance of asymmetry. An ego-centred *rule* of FZD marriage is perfectly possible and does occur, but "short-cycle", asymmetric, generalized exchange as envisaged by Lévi-Strauss cannot, and does not, exist (cf. Needham 1958). For this reason, Fox (1967: 204, 222) describes both bilateral and patrilateral cross-cousin marriage as forms of *direct exchange*, the only difference being that exchange is "immediate" in the first case but "delayed" in the second. Even this is open to question though, because the latter distinction still seems to take too literally the spurious genealogical format of Figs 6.2 to 6.4.

To sum up the argument so far, Lévi-Strauss's original four types of exchange have since been reduced to two, as depicted in Fig. 6.6: symmetric (equivalent to Fox's "direct") and asymmetric. The apparent subdivision of the latter into long and short cycles of exchange, and the further discrimination of oblique exchange within the second of these forms, are, we have argued, chimeras produced by the genealogical format of the relevant diagrams. Contrary to appearances, both forms of "short-cycle" asymmetry must give rise to symmetrical exchange in practice. Even the association between matrilateral marriage and asymmetry is not absolute, as the case of avuncular marriage shows.

6.3.2 *Prescription and preference*

The last section seemed to create more difficulties than it resolved. This was inevitable, for Lévi-Strauss's great book was based upon much inadequate ethnography and was, moreover, confused or confusing in many theoretical respects (cf. Leach 1970: 105; Needham 1971a: xciii). One very basic confusion concerned the notion of "prescription" with which his book began.

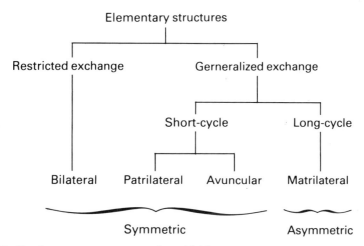

Fig. 6.6 *The elementary structures according to Lévi-Strauss.*

This has since been clarified, though not to the satisfaction of Lévi-Strauss himself, as we shall see.

We have repeatedly stressed the usefulness of making an analytical distinction between categorical, jural and behavioural data. The question then arises, to which level(s) do Lévi-Strauss's models apply? In particular, it is not clear from his text whether the elementary structures of exchange are categorical or jural in character, largely because he himself did not, and does not, agree to distinguish the two.

For Needham, rules cannot be viewed unequivocally as prescriptive (as opposed to merely preferential) because of the many cultural variations which may arise. Marriage rules may be phrased in terms of "genealogical connexion, relationship category, locality, descent group, social class, prior affinal alliance", and so on (1973a: 173). How could the "prescriptive" character of such varied cultural formulations be defined and compared? How might they be distinguished from the preferential rules phrased in similar terms, which operate in complex systems? Behaviour, for its part, cannot usefully be labelled "prescriptive" either. Just because, at a certain moment, 100% of all marriages in a given society happen to be, say, matrilateral in form, that does not automatically mean that it has a prescriptive system. Any

> sudden change in people's marrying habits would presumably alter any institutional alignments [e.g. of exchange-units] based on statistical trends, whereas in a

prescriptive system this would be irrelevant. (Maybury-Lewis 1965: 226; gloss added)

So, rejecting both these options, Needham sees prescription as "a formal property of a system of categories of social classification" (1973a: 174); in short, as a feature of the relationship terminology. In societies of this type, the terminology is based upon the requirement that ego marry a person in one particular relationship category. Consider, for instance, the Maravar terminology in Fig. 3.5. In that case, there is a prescriptive requirement that a male ego marry a junior cross relative of his own terminological level, in other words a *kolundiyāl*. Clearly, a woman has to marry a senior cross relative of that same level, an *attān*. It is important to realize that this requirement is *not* a marriage rule, but a self-fulfilling prophecy. If the spouse is a previously unrelated person, or if (as in rare cases) a terminologically wrong marriage is contracted, then the couple and their relatives thenceforth adopt usages which treat the marriage as if it *had* been between an *attān* and a *kolundiyāl* (Good 1981: 126). This ability to redefine "wrong" marriages retrospectively is diagnostic of prescription. To speak of prescription as "a rule" is therefore incorrect: the statement that "the woman you marry shall be a marriageable woman" is jurally a pure tautology.

Prescription, then, is a terminological phenomenon, and there is no necessary correlation between this "categorical imperative" (Needham 1973a: 175) and any institutionalized preferences which may exist in the same society. Nor does the prescription positively *determine* the choice of spouse, genealogically or even categorically, though it would be surprising if it did not exert a strong influence upon choice. Any consideration of marriageability in a given society must therefore investigate separately, and compare: the terminological prescriptions (if any); the institutionalized exchange preferences; and the behavioural practices of that society. The collection of the necessary terminological data has already been discussed (§3.3), and the information on behaviour may be acquired from your consolidated genealogies (§2.5). As usual, the preferential rules present more of a problem. Because of their cultural variability you cannot seek them by means of standardized procedures. Moreover, their status is unclear (cf. Chapter 8).

In these two sections we have cut a swathe through one of the most vitriolic debates in recent anthropological history, and inevitably many people will disagree with the conclusions we have reached. One line of criticism demands less cavalier dismissal, for it comes from Lévi-Strauss himself in his preface to the second edition of *Elementary Structures*. He argues that Needham has interpreted his use of "prescription" too narrowly. The phenomenon differs only relatively from preference, because a preferential system is prescriptive at the model level; a prescriptive system must be preferential [e.g. for demographic reasons] when envisaged at the level of reality. (1969: xxxiii; gloss added)

Here, the second proposition sets up a false dichotomy, as our Maravar example demonstrates, because reality is interpreted *in terms of* the prescription. As for the first, Lévi-Strauss explains that in his view:

the sole difference between prescriptive marriage and preferential marriage is at the level of the model. It corresponds to the difference . . . between . . . a '*mechanical model*' [one whose elements are in one-to-one correspondence with the thing modelled, like the symbols of a true genealogy] and a '*statistical model*' [involving distributions and probabilities]. (ibid: xxxv; glosses and emphases added)

A jural rule *is* prescriptive, he argues, "since it says what must be done" (ibid: xxxiii).

Figure 6.7 summarizes the conflicting usages of Lévi-Strauss and Needham. Clearly, we are more sympathetic to the latter. The mechanical/ statistical distinction merely introduces yet another source of confusion,

Fig. 6.7 *Contrasting views of prescription and preference.*

because the apparently mechanical, "genealogical" format of Figs 6.2–6.5 masks, as we saw, a more complex, possibly statistical, reality. It must be admitted, though, that Needham's position is not without its unhappy terminological consequences. First, the literal meaning of "prescription" explicitly invokes rules rather than categories. Needham retains it (with misgivings) because of its long pedigree (1973a: 177), and we shall do likewise. Secondly, however, "prescriptive alliance" seems a doubly unfortunate usage. The epithet "alliance" is best reserved for jural relationships between persons or groups: the same goes for "exchange", as the means whereby this alliance occurs. We prefer to speak of symmetric or asymmetric "prescription" at the categorical level, on the one hand, and of symmetric or asymmetric "exchange" or "alliance" at the jural level, on the other. Neither feature entails the other, nor does either necessarily determine or reflect all observed marriage behaviour. The distinction between the two seems to us the essential starting point for an adequate understanding of both elementary exchange structures, and prescriptive terminologies.

In view of the complexity and importance of these issues, let us summarize our position. We see several confusions in Lévi-Strauss's formulation of "alliance theory". These stem principally from his conflation of categorical and jural factors, in the forms of "prescription" and "exchange", respectively. Prescription is a terminological feature, whereby ego's potential spouses are drawn from a particular, ego-centred category of persons, and where, conversely, actual spouses may if necessary be assimilated retrospectively to that same category. This feature has no necessary connection with any of the possible types of "exchange". The latter are jural phenomena involving the systematic linkage, by means of preferential marriage, of particular individuals, families, lineages, or other exchange-units. One may have elementary structures in both the categorical and jural senses, but the existence of one in no way requires the presence of the other.

This concludes our discussion of the elementary structures of kinship. Before proceeding, however, we must consider briefly a type of system which appears to lie midway between "elementary" and "complex".

6.3.3 "Crow–Omaha" systems and marriage prohibitions

We have already met "Crow" and "Omaha" systems above (§4.2). It is worth recalling that not all anthropologists who use such terms agree on what they are to mean. There are three common usages.

(1) Murdock and his followers employ "Crow" and "Omaha" for relationship terminologies which have at least the equations FZ = FZD (Crow) or MB = MBS (Omaha). (One would also expect the respective reciprocals: BCws = MBCws and ZCms = FZCms.) We might call this the "terminology theory" viewpoint.

(2) Radcliffe-Brown (1952 [1941]: 54–56, 75–79) took account of the fact that the terminological equations are often much more extensive. He noted that the Choctaw terminology ("Crow"-type) equated a number of members of ego's F's matrilineage, and that the Omaha terminology available to him equated male members of ego's M's patrilineage. This "descent theory" view is also pursued by Murdock (1949: 239–248), though it is quite distinct from usage (1) above. An ideal "descent theory" system would be one in which many members of the parental lineage through which ego does *not* trace

descent group membership were all called by the same pair of terms, one for females and another for males. In this sense the Trobrianders are a very good example of the "Crow" type. A Trobriander male ego calls all members of his F's matrilineage *tama* (males) or *tabu* (females). Thus, the Trobrianders are "Crow"-type on both "terminology theory" (FZ = FZD, *tabu*) and "descent theory" (FZ = FZD = FZDD, etc.; F = FB = FZS = FZDS, etc.) grounds. As Leach (1958) shows, such terminological equations can also be related to rules of residence. In fact, this "residence theory" view may come closer to the Trobrianders' own understanding of the system.

(3) The third viewpoint (if we count "residence theory" as an aspect of "descent theory") is that of Lévi-Strauss and some of his French colleagues, whose "alliance theory" definition is of particular interest in the study of marriage. It would exclude the Trobrianders on the grounds that they have preferred marriage to the actual FZD. The Lévi-Straussian "Crow–Omaha" system is precisely one which prohibits such marriages.

To illustrate this viewpoint, let us take a society which *does* work more-or-less according to prediction. The Hopi, according to Eggan (1950: 20–21), call members of closely related lineages by egocentric relationship terms. Male ego, for example, calls his FZ, FZD, FZDD, etc., *ikya'a*, and is forbidden to marry members of this cateogry. He is also forbidden to marry within his own lineage or clan (the females here being called by a variety of terms) and, in fact, within his own phratry. In short, the terminological equations generally follow matrilineal descent lines, and marriage is forbidden to members of lines in which such egocentric equations occur (1950: *passim*). In patrilineal "Crow–Omaha" systems, according to this view, similar marriage prohibitions would hold for patrilines (certainly those of MBD, MBSD, etc., who might be equated with M and MZ, and perhaps other lines too). In formal terms, the descent-defined extention of kin categories prohibits marriage to persons in such categories, and so these extensive prohibitions allow marriage to relatively few individuals. This process eliminates the possibility of repeated intermarriage between lineages, and is thus the reverse of that entailed by generalized exchange. This reduction in the range of choice of spouse would tend to make "Crow–Omaha" systems empirically-defined (if not ideologically defined) elementary structures (Barnard 1978a: 73–74). In Lévi-Strauss's view, they stand between true elementary structures and true complex structures, since they contain elements of both.

Perhaps the most successful example of this approach has been Héritier's (1979, 1981) study of the relations between the ideological models and the statistics of marriages among the Samo of Upper Volta and other West African peoples. These groups employ "Omaha" terminologies, with terms applied throughout the lineages of close relatives, and they forbid marriage to members of these lineages, and to other close relatives. Anglophone alliance theorists, however, have found Lévi-Strauss's contribution of little help, on the grounds that far from generating marriage prohibitions, "Omaha" terminologies (as defined by Murdock) are not uncommonly associated with prescriptive MBD marriage (e.g. Ackerman 1976; R. H. Barnes 1976).

Finally, as if there were not enough confusion to contend with, one proponent of Lévi-Strauss's view (M. Godelier, pers. comm. to Barnard) has further suggested that the !Kung Bushman kinship system (Marshall 1976) exhibits "Crow–Omaha"-like marriage rules without either extension through lineages or any other aspect of "Crow" or "Omaha" terminology. He referred instead to the extension of marriage prohibitions through rules of namesake equivalence. Names are transmitted from second ascending generation lineals or first ascending generation collaterals, and *namesakes* of close relatives are forbidden as spouses (even if not otherwise traceably related). Godelier's ingenious comparison, if read as a definition, would make the category "Crow–Omaha" fully polythetic, as the "terminology theory" definition shares *no* common feature with this new and more radical "alliance theory" one!

The first moral of this salutary example is that substantive types of this kind tend to create, rather than solve analytical problems (see also §4.1). Secondly, some authors define "Crow–Omaha" systems with reference to terminological structure: they are then intermediate between "elementary" and "complex" because although, like the latter, they lack terminological prescriptions, they do *proscribe* marriage with whole classes of persons, on the basis of terminology rather than genealogy (e.g. Trobrianders). Others define these systems with reference to their patterns of inter-group alliance. Here again they resemble elementary structures in proscribing marriage with entire lineage groups, but do not positively prescribe marriage into any particular group or groups. In short, they have the negative rules of an elementary structure, and the positive rules of a complex one (e.g. Samo).

6.4 Marriage and status

6.4.1 *Isogamy and Anisogamy*

In most societies, marriages reflect the statuses or status aspirations of the respective exchange-units, but if they do not involve status differences of any regular or systematic kind, they are said to be *isogamous*. Conventionally, "isogamy" has meant simply "marriage between equals", but in some circumstances it may be preferable to employ the alternative, stricter definition, "marriage without prescriptive status implications". There are two kinds of *anisogamy*: *hypergamy*, in which the natal family, lineage, clan or exchange unit of the H is always, or ideally, higher in status than that of the W; and *hypogamy*, in which the reverse is true. Put another way, in hypergamous systems wife-takers rank above wife-givers, and in hypogamous systems wife-givers are superior.

As usual, matters cannot be left at this straightforward level. For Dumont the essence of anisogamy is "normative neutralization" (1980: 117). Hypergamy occurs only when:

> between recognized limits . . . the inferior status of the wife's natal group does not bring any inferiority to the status of the children. (1964: 86)

One could make a similar stipulation for hypogamy, of course, by simply substituting "husband" or "wife" in the quoted passage. It is also necessary to broaden Dumont's definition to recognize that normative neutralization must result in the child being of the F's status in strongly patrilineal systems, and of the M's status in matrilineal ones. The four logical possibilities are displayed in Fig. 6.8, which also indicates societies corresponding to three of these ideals. The matrilineal, hypogamous case seems intrinsically unlikely.

Parry (1979: 196) finds a looser definition more in tune with his own, North Indian field situation:

> The minimum requirement of [hypergamous] systems is that a woman should preferably be married to a man of higher rank but may be married to an equal.

In our view, either kind of definition may be adopted, depending upon the particularities of the local situation. Unlike Parry, though, we feel that it may sometimes be meaningful to distinguish "prescriptive" and "preferential" anisogamy. The prescriptive form arises when an appropriate status difference is assumed to exist by definition, merely as a consequence of the marriage having taken place. In preferential anisogamy, on the other hand, such unions are recommended, but equals who happen to form alliances remain equal thereafter. Let us be clear, though, that the systematic status-differentiation of exchange-units has no necessary connection with the kinds of *terminological* prescription discussed above (§6.3.2). Moreover, anisogamy, even of a prescriptive kind, can occur in conjunction with both elementary and complex kinship systems.

Cross-cutting this distinction between "prescriptive" and "preferential"

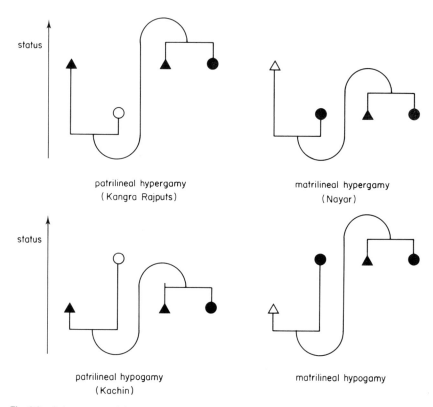

status

patrilineal hypergamy
(Kangra Rajputs)

matrilineal hypergamy
(Nayar)

status

patrilineal hypogamy
(Kachin)

matrilineal hypogamy

Fig. 6.8 *Anisogamy and descent.*

forms of anisogamy, is another based upon the nature of the status unit involved. Three ideal cases can be distinguished analytically: the status differences which regulate or result from marriage may be ego-centred, unit-centred, or society-centred. *Ego-centred anisogamy* arises when, for instance, the groom and/or his F are in some sense superior or inferior to the bride's B and/or F, but this status difference does not extend to cover all members of their exchange-units. The Bengalis described by Inden and Nicholas (1977: 43–44) seem to exemplify this situation. The bride's F demonstrates his inferiority both ritually and in the pattern of gift-giving, but affinal relationships are confined within the genealogically-defined *kuṭumba*, or "relatives by marriage' (ibid: 15–17; §8.5.2). *Unit-centred anisogamy* arises when, to give the simplest possible case, unit A is superior to its wife-givers or -takers B, who are superior to C, who are in turn superior to A.

The hypogamous Kachin of Burma provide the best-known example of such a situation: ideally, their circles contain five units (Leach 1961a [1951]: 82). Whereas in both these cases status differences are intransitive, some societies have *society-centred anisogamy* whereby, for instance, my wife-takers' wife-takers are my wife-takers too, and perhaps all the more desirable as such since the putative status difference is even greater. The hypergamous Kangra Rajputs typify this situation. The required size of their dowry (§6.5.2) increases as the status gap between givers and takers widens (Parry 1979: 241), and those who successfully marry their daughters far up the scale can hope thereby to "leapfrog" over erstwhile wife-takers whose status is closer to their own.

Transitive anisogamy presents certain structural problems. It must give rise to a surplus of marriageable women at one end of the status hierarchy, and a corresponding dearth at the other. High-ranking Kangra Rajputs, for instance, formerly resorted to female infanticide to resolve the first of these difficulties, but nowadays give daughters in marriage far away to the west. Those of low rank acquire brides from the east, or from the caste immediately below themselves in status. The existence of this "geographical hypergamy" serves as a salutory reminder that cultural forms are, as ever, highly variable. In the case of the matrilineal, hypergamous Nayar of South India, "closure" of the system at the upper end is helped by demographic factors, since the higher the status of the group the fewer tend to be its members. The process is completed by the contracting of alliances with younger sons of the otherwise patrilineal, isogamous Nambudiri Brahmans, as shown in Fig. 6.9. These are perfectly regular unions from the (admittedly idiosyncratic) traditional Nayar viewpoint, and are even prestigious because of the high status of the male party, but they constitute mere concubinage in the eyes of Nambudiri (§6.4.2). Low-status Nayar permit liaisons between equals, although hypergamy carries greater prestige. Given the demographic situation, and the absence of monogamy, there is no overall shortage of acceptable sexual partners at this end of the scale.

In view of all this, several necessary lines of questioning suggest themselves. Are status differences structurally or systematically significant for the regulation of marriage? If so, does this happen prescriptively or preferentially? How is status defined and expressed, and what kinds of status-unit are there? If there is anisogamy, is it transitive or intransitive? Does the status of offspring depend upon that of one parent only, or upon both? How do transitive systems cope with the uneven availability of spouses?

In the discussion, two things have been taken temporarily for granted. First, all the societies referred to are assumed to have "marriage" in at least a

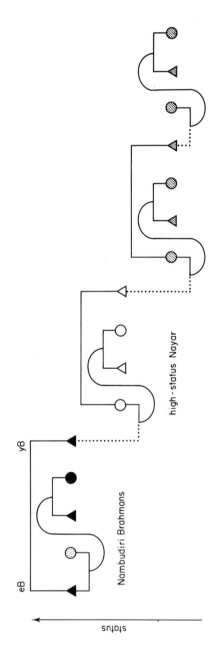

Fig. 6.9 *Transitive hypergamy among the Nayar.*

Nominal sense (§6.1). Secondly, we have ignored the possibility that there may be alternative forms of recognized sexual union, with different status requirements and implications, even within a given society. It is to this possibility that we now turn.

6.4.2 *Hierarchy of conjugal unions*

Many societies contain conjugal unions of different types, which differ in desirability, legitimacy and status. For instance, the following general paradigm of South Asian conjugal relationships has been proposed by Dumont (1964, 1980). First, such relationships may be "legitimate" or "illegitimate", as in the widespread distinction between wives and concubines. Legitimate unions are further sub-divided according to status. From the male viewpoint, "principal" (senior or first) wives are distinguished from "subsidiary" (or subsequent) ones. But whereas men can often undergo several weddings with full rites, it is almost always the case in South Asia that women can be married in the strictest or "primary" sense, by means of the full ritual, only once in their lives (1980: 114). For them, subsequent unions, even if legitimate, involve only truncated wedding rites, and are in this respect at least, inferior or "secondary". A marriage which is both the "principal" union of the man and the "primary" one of the woman, is subject to the strictest regulation *vis-à-vis* the identities of the spouses. "Subsidiary" and/or "secondary" marriages are less rigidly circumscribed, and concubinage is the least regulated of all.

Although these details are culture-specific, some general lessons may be drawn. It is always necessary to ascertain whether more than one form of "marriage" is recognized, whether these forms are differently ranked and subject to regulations of differing stringency, and whether distinctions like that between "wife" and "concubine" are made. Variations in these matters are almost certain to correlate with variations in the phenomena discussed in the rest of this chapter, such as plural marriage (§6.4.3); the degree of elaboration of wedding ritual (§6.5.1); the kinds and sizes of marriage prestations (§6.5.2); and the possibility of divorce and remarriage (§6.6).

6.4.3 *Plural unions*

The existence of distinct, ranked forms of conjugal union is particularly likely where there is the possibility of plural relationships, as the South Asian example suggests. There are two possible forms of *polygamy*: *polygyny*, whereby a man is permitted more than one recognized or legitimate partner, and *polyandry*, whereby that freedom is permitted to women.

Fischer (1952) distinguishes polygamy, or plural marriage, from *polykoity*, where there is merely plural sexual access. This distinction may be useful in particular contexts but cannot be drawn in general for the very reason that "marriage" itself cannot be universally defined (§6.1). Again, Fischer recognizes polygamy only when the relationship between each pair of partners is inaugurated by its own, distinct ritual. In these terms, many apparent cases of *adelphic polyandry*, in which the male partners are brothers, and *adelphic* or *sororal polygyny*, in which the female partners are sisters, would not count as "true" polygamy because only one wedding rite is performed, generally involving the senior sibling. These, too, are matters upon which fieldworkers must decide for themselves. Finally, *disparate polygamy* arises when one of the spouses is superior in status to the others of the same gender (*Notes and Queries* 1951: 112–113).

6.5 The wedding

6.5.1 *The ceremonial cycle*

Marriage is almost everywhere instituted by some kind of wedding ceremony. This need not be an elaborate event, though it frequently is. Clearly, the study of ritual *qua* ritual is outside the scope of this book, but some very broad comments do need to be made. In general, you should beware of concentrating too much upon events on the day(s) of the main ceremony itself, at the expense of activities which precede and follow it. Leach distinguishes "secular time", which is sequential and quantized, from the more elastic "ritual time", and comments that in ritual, "the message is transmitted as if everything happened simultaneously" (1976: 44). For instance, the wedding may not be completed all at once, but may be spread out over a lengthy period in secular time. In the Nuer case, the betrothal (*larcieng*), wedding proper (*ngut*), and consummation (*mut*) may be spread over several weeks, and even then matters are not really finalized until the girl has borne and weaned a child (Evans-Pritchard 1951: 59, 72). The widespread incidence of this gradualist approach to marriage is hardly surprising, given the anthropological truism that marriage is normally not an affective bond between two individuals, but a politico-legal alliance contracted by two exchange-units. In the circumstances, every alliance is entered step-by-step, with plenty of opportunity for second thoughts, and for checking the *bona fides* of the prospective allies (§7.4.2).

Looking at things rather more broadly, a wedding is merely one rite of passage in the kinship careers of the bride and groom. Jack Goody suggests that the extent to which a given rite of passage is ceremonialized, depends upon the amount of "work" that has to be accomplished, in the form of transference of rights, duties and property (1976: 9). Moreover, the form and degree of elaboration of a rite of passage, will depend upon the natures of the new statuses instituted thereby, and upon their places in the overall social structure. Although the number and nature of the ritual steps through which every individual must pass varies from culture to culture, the socio-structural purposes which these rituals serve are much more constant. In the case of marriage, one major concern is almost certain to be the legitimation of offspring, as we saw, but although the wedding may be a necessary step towards this, it is by no means always a sufficient one. The status of the groom may need to be clarified first, especially in patrilineal societies where he will become the status-transmitting parent, by means of puberty rites or initiations of some kind. The same may be true of the bride's status, particularly in matrilineal societies. Finally, the status of each child may need to be individually secured by performance of appropriate birth and childhood rituals.

In short, the wedding must be understood in a much broader overall context, as part of a cycle which, to a greater or lesser extent, was foreshadowed by events in previous generations and will exert its influence upon rituals and generations still to come. For instance, the very varied South Asian practices associated with female sexuality, can all be assimilated into a single framework:

> Girl –(puberty rite)–⟩ Woman –(wedding)–⟩ Wife –(birth rite)–⟩
> Mother –(H's funeral)–⟩ Widow

For the matrilineal, matri-avunculocal Nayar, the main emphasis falls upon assuring the statuses of girls and their offspring, *vis-à-vis* their natal matrilineages. For this reason, the *tāli*-tying rite (in terms of our paradigm, the "puberty rite") is given much greater importance than the ritual inaugurations of the same girl's *sambandham* liaisons, or "weddings" (Gough 1955, 1959; Fuller 1976). For the patrilineal, patri-virilocal Nambudiri Brahmans, on the other hand, the statuses of girls *vis-à-vis* their husbands' lineages are crucial, so much so that there is no separate female puberty rite, and ritual emphasis falls almost exclusively upon the "wedding". Quite logically, such patrilineal groups tend instead to place more ritual emphasis upon male sexuality, as evidenced by Brahmanic thread-tying initiations.

Generally, the need to control female sexuality is satisfied by rites which either transfer responsibility before puberty to her H's family; or incorporate her into her natal family, at least temporarily. Other things being equal, the former situation is likely to be associated with patriliny; inheritance and succession from F to S; dowries for women (§6.5.2); and virilocal residence. The latter is likely to go along with matriliny; inheritance and succession from MB to ZS; stronger rights for females in family property; and avuncu-local, uxorilocal, or even natolocal residence. The Nambudiri Brahmans and Nayar approach the first and second of these poles, respectively. The South Asian stress upon caste status and individual purity has obvious effects upon ritual form in these cases (Yalman 1963), but the socio-structural con-gruences just mentioned may well be far more widespread. You should at least bear in mind, when considering the varied ritual practices of societies *within* a given culture area, the need to look at the overall context of general kinship practice in every case.

6.5.2 *Marriage prestations*

In many societies, wedding prestations form the major economic transactions in a person's lifetime. Even when less pre-eminently important, they almost invariably reveal much about the structure of the society concerned. In all cases, therefore, these prestations demand detailed and careful study.

Two particularly widespread configurations of marriage prestations are *bridewealth* (or *brideprice*) and *dowry*, the ideal forms of which are shown in Fig. 6.10. They are opposites only in the very abstract sense that women and material goods pass in opposite directions in the former case, and in the same direction in the latter. At a more substantive level, the opposite of brideprice is *groomprice*, whereby wealth is transferred from the bride's F or exchange-unit to that of the groom and/or his F. One variant of brideprice is *bride-service*, whereby a man works for his father-in-law for a specified period, before returning home with his bride (§7.4.1).

Early observers saw bridewealth as indicating marriage by purchase, but in most cases the woman herself is not regarded as a commodity to be bought and sold. More commonly, certain rights (to her labour, sexual services, or offspring, for instance) are transferred, and the bridewealth compensates her natal group for the loss of these. This helps explain such phenomena as Nuer "ghost" and woman–woman marriage, as well as their practice of the

(a) Bridewealth

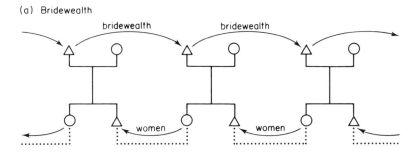

(b) Dowry

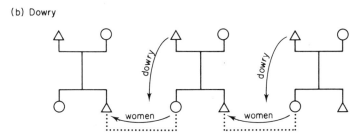

Fig. 6.10 *Bridewealth and dowry.*

levirate. Whoever its genitor may be, the pater or socially-recognized "father" of a Nuer child is the man or woman who paid its mother's bridewealth cattle. Hence, Mair (1971: 61) argues, Nuer cattle transfers might be better termed "child-price".

Bridewealth also provides the bride's family with the wherewithal to obtain brides for their own sons, a fact most explicitly recognized in the "cattle complex" prevailing in many parts of southern and eastern Africa. Here a man often has a special relationship with that sister whose bridewealth cattle were used to pay his own bridewealth. Among the Lovedu, the ideal spouse is a "cattle-linked cross-cousin", namely the D of male ego's M's cattle-linked B (Krige and Krige 1943: 142–145). Reference to Fig. 6.3 will show that, ideally, bridewealth therefore passes in the same direction every generation, between the same pairs of patrilineal exchange-units. The Lovedu themselves say that the sister "builds her brother's house", and that it "has a gate which the [bridewealth] cattle seek" in the next generation. You will of course need to investigate your own informants' views on the meaning and purpose of marriage prestations.

Mair (1971: 50) prefers to restrict use of the term "bridewealth" to this type of African context, and calls all other forms "brideprice". She does not mean to imply thereby that all other cases necessarily involve true marriage by purchase, although that does seem to be the situation in parts of North India, for example (Sharma 1980: 175n). Goody (1976: 8) draws a similar distinction, and also proposes that *both* terms be reserved for prestations exchanged not by the bride and groom themselves, but by the exchange-units from which they come. When property passes from the groom (or, presumably, other members of his family) to the bride herself, whether or not this involves her own F as intermediary as in South India (Tambiah 1973a: 104), Goody terms this *indirect dowry* (1973b: 2, 1976: 11). As he notes, ethnographers have often referred to such prestations as "brideprice", so his proposed new usage raises practical difficulties for comparativists. Despite this, he is clearly right to distinguish such prestations from bridewealth proper.

Direct dowry involves the transfer of valuables from the bride's F or unit to the couple, or, defining the term more strictly, to the bride herself. In both cases though, *de facto* management of this property may lie with the groom's natal family. Brides in North-West India do not even have a formal say in its disposal (Sharma 1980: 50), but even here dowries received by brothers cannot readily be used in the same transitive fashion as bridewealth, to furnish dowries for their sisters (Tambiah 1973a: 62). Where such practices *are* permitted, the initial prestation is perhaps better termed "groomprice" rather than "dowry", though it is not possible to draw an absolute distinction between the two.

Despite the impression which may have been created so far, it is very rarely the case that weddings involve only a single exchange of wealth, or its transfer in one direction only. Even hypergamous unions involving enormous dowries, as a consequence of which the families of bride and groom will have almost no direct social contact thereafter, none the less display a limited degree of reciprocity during the wedding cycle itself (ibid: 96, for North India). So the terms "bridewealth" and "dowry" imply at most a high degree of imbalance in the prestational exchanges. Moreover, some anthropologists (ibid: 92) use them as purely analytical concepts: whatever is given by the groom's side to the bride's side is termed "brideprice", and whatever passes from the bride's side to the couple is classed as "dowry". A single wedding can then be said to involve *both* forms of prestation, and the two may even be comparable in size. While it is, as usual, dangerous to seek over-precise definitions, it does seem preferable to restrict use of these terms to cases resembling the polar extremes with which we began. The often complex web of partly reciprocal prestations observed in a given society are best referred to, in the first instance, by their indigenous titles, since these provide some indication of how they are seen and classified by the participants themselves.

When we take "brideprice" and "dowry" to be (admittedly polythetic) ideal types in this way, we are able to draw attention to all sorts of institutional regularities and correlations with which they are associated. For instance, dowry can readily be associated with hypergamy, and brideprice with hypogamy, but the reverse seems rather unlikely (ibid: 67; Leach 1961a [1951]: 102). The bride's F, in an hypogamous milieu, or the groom's F, in an hypergamous one, are scarcely likely to make large prestations merely to solicit affines of acknowledgedly inferior status. Moreover, dowry can be seen as a form of pre-mortem inheritance. It is likely to co-exist with a distinction between male (often immovable) and female (usually movable) property (Goody 1976: 6); with the existence of distinct economic strata within the society (ibid: 23); with in-marriage (ibid: 106); and with patri-virilocal residence after marriage (Tambiah 1973a: 109). Dowry is likely to correlate with delayed marriages, at least for women, because their families need time to accumulate the large amounts of wealth involved: by contrast, women are likely to be married at an early age where bridewealth is involved, since this brings the family the immediate economic return needed for the marriages of its sons (Goody 1973b: 10).

In sum, the study of wedding prestations must be set into broader context. You need to ask who gives what to whom, not only at the wedding itself, but in the entire cycle of life-crisis events of which the wedding forms part. Bear in mind, too, that although the main donors and recipients are usually the bridal couple and their immediate families, a *group* of relatives is usually involved in each case (cf. Evans-Pritchard's account of the distribution of Nuer bridewealth, 1951: 74–89). As usual, you should look not only at the jural ideals, but at who exerts *de facto* control over the transferred wealth; at what happens when the ideal is not adhered to for any reason; and at local explanations of both the rules and their expectations. Case studies of individual weddings, both typical and atypical, are essential here. Finally, and most broadly of all, you will not understand such prestations fully without taking into account the complete set of rules and practices governing the ownership, control and inheritance of property.

6.5.3 *Participants and functionaries*

As with all collective events, it is essential to obtain precise information on the social identities of wedding participants, both ideally and in practice. If the term "prestation" is defined so as to cover not merely material gifts, but exchanges of rights, duties, and obligations of all kinds, then you are interested in all who make or receive prestations on these occasions, even those whose obligations are limited to mere attendance as guests or spectators. You need to know the social identities, *vis-à-vis* the bridal couple, of all such personages, particularly of course the main participants in both the ritual and economic senses.

Sometimes the perspective may have to be even broader. As we saw, birth, puberty, marriage, death, and all other life crises recognized by the society concerned, are likely to be inter-related in all kinds of ways, not only in the ritual symbolism employed, but also in the kinship or other social indentities of the main ritual participants. The MB is in many societies a key ritual functionary or maker of gifts, not only at weddings, but at all other rituals undergone by his ZC. To give a more specific instance, the women who officiate at a Tirunelveli Tamil girl's puberty rite, wedding, and first confinement, all stand in the same terminological category relative to her, and may even be the same person (ideally her MZ or FBW; Good 1982). Ultimately, of course, the importance of such key functionaries must be related to the total socio-structural context in which the events occur. Given that one virtually universal aspect of life crisis ritual is the dramatization of significant social relationships, the study of such rituals yields very valuable information about that wider context.

Rather than give an example which could only be highly specific and, given the amount of detail we are advocating, extremely lengthy, let us re-emphasize here the general, and very important point. For every life crisis rite or similar collective event you attend, you should obtain the most complete information possible about the participants and functionaries, including their contextually relevant social identities, and the natures and extents of their duties and responsibilities. You will of course need to discuss the ideal situation with as many people as possible, but it is also vital to observe actual cases directly. Your consolidated genealogies (§2.5) should be of considerable help in working out the relevant interpersonal relationships, but unrelated functionaries or officials of the local community or state may also be involved.

6.6. The dissolution of marriage

6.6.1 *Divorce*

Logically, only those who are married can undergo divorce. As "marriage" cannot be defined with precision (§6.1), it follows that divorce, too, cannot be unequivocally defined. Further problems arise when marital alliances are contracted in stages (§6.5.1), with both parties having a degree of choice at every stage, over whether to proceed further or back out. In such cases, you will have to decide whether to reserve the term "divorce" for the regularized fission of an hitherto fully-established union, or extend its meaning to cover breakdown at some or all of these intermediate stages.

Whatever your decision, you will need to ascertain the circumstances under which divorce is permitted, whether it involves prescribed ceremonial, and if so, what form this takes and who participates in it. Is the subsequent marriageability of a divorced person restricted in any way (see §6.4.2, for instance)? Finally, and often most crucially of all, what arrangements are made for the disposal of any wealth transferred as part of the original ceremony, or subsequently acquired by the couple, jointly or individually? This includes, of course, arrangements made for the upbringing and property entitlement of the offspring.

The answers to these questions will of course depend upon other aspects of social structure. For instance, comparative evidence allows us to draw certain general conclusions concerning the relationship between marriage stability, "genetricial rights" over offspring, and the form of descent (J. C. Mitchell 1961: 323). All things being equal, marriages should be stable and of long duration in patrilineal societies where such rights are vested in corporate descent groups; of medium duration and stability in unilineal societies where-in these rights are held by individuals rather than corporate groups; and of short duration and low stability in matrilineal societies where geneticial rights are never transferred outwith corporate groups, and in "bilateral societies" where such rights are irrelevant. You should examine your data on divorce, separation, and marriage stability with such general perspectives in mind.

6.6.2 *Widowhood*

Death involves, among other things, a rearrangement of kinship, economic and other links among the living. In particular, the death of a married person introduces the surviving partner willy-nilly into a new social state, that of widowhood. You will need to examine the rights, privileges, restrictions and responsibilities of this state, for both men and women. Sometimes, widowhood restricts a person's economic activities or rights over property. Thus, Brahman widowers can no longer work as temple priests (Fuller 1979: 463), while in parts of North India property may, in fact if not strictly according to current law, pass back to a man's natal family when he dies, especially if his widow has no children for whom to hold it in trust (Sharma 1980: 53–54). Widowed persons may find their social status diminished in all sorts of ways: they may for instance be barred from attending religious or other events associated with fertility, auspiciousness, or vitality.

The existence of such sanctions may be an encouragement to remarry. On the other hand, remarriage may be forbidden, as in many parts of India, or strictly regulated, as in the *widow inheritance* of the Mayombe: here the deceased's B may have children by the widow, on payment of a small supplementary bridewealth (Richards 1950: 217). This practice must be distinguished from the *levirate*, in which the woman continues to be married to her dead H, who remains the pater of any children subsequently engendered by his agnates. A looser form of this is *widow concubinage*, in which a dead man is the pater of his widow's children regardless of the identity of the genitor (Evans-Pritchard 1951: 116). All these practices are clearly consistent with bridewealth systems, in which the group making the initial prestation retains rights over a woman's offspring even after the demise of the individual in whose name it was initially paid.

6.6.3 *Step relatives*

Wherever divorced or widowed people can remarry, step relationships are bound to arise. Your genealogical investigations (§2.5) should provide information about such cases, and you will also need to discover whether there are distinct relationship terms, as there are (for reference) in English. Assuming that unions are not ranked in status (§6.4.2), *half*-siblings in polygamous marriages may all have equal claims upon the property of their co-parent. *Step*-siblings, though, are bound to have different inheritance expectations (J. Goody 1976: 52–55), and may be particularly vulnerable to the manipulation of property by their step-parent. You should therefore establish the legal and practical position with regard to the control and inheritance of property in such cases, and should also find out how such unions are viewed. The wicked step-mother is a figure not confined to European folklore.

6.7 Mathematical approaches

Some aspects of marriage can be investigated only by means of quantitative or other mathematical procedures (cf. J. C. Mitchell 1967). The techniques used can generally be kept very simple. Indeed, sophisticated forms of statistical analysis would be widely inappropriate given the scope and nature of the data collected by the typical fieldworker. Samples are generally too small, the time-scale too narrow, dates of birth, marriage, and death too imprecisely known for it to be otherwise.

Still, much can be done on the basis of the consolidated genealogies and census returns discussed in Chapter 2. These can be used to calculate the percentages of marriages involving persons in specific genealogical, terminological, social, geographical and economic positions with respect to each other. One can also investigate the ages at which men and women marry and have children, the mean family size, the age-spacing of siblings, and so on. These statistical "bulk properties" of the society must be compared with the opinions explicitly put forward on these matters by its members. It is by no means always the case that societies conform at all closely to their own ideals.

Significant statistical correlations, as well as the concordances and discrepancies between ideals and practices, may then need further investigation. The initial calculations should therefore be carried out while you are still in the field. Nothing mentioned above is beyond a simple pocket calculator, or even a book of log tables, though use of the latter may be rather laborious if standard deviations, least-squares, or chi-squared calculations are required. We cannot go into these statistical methods in any detail here (but see, for example, Anderson and Zelditch 1975), and we shall confine ourselves to two *very* elementary comments. First, it is often important and revealing to work out both the *mean* and *median* values of the variables under consideration. Assuming a normal distribution, these two values should be more or less equal. If they differ widely, this indicates a skewed or distorted distribution which may bear further investigation. Secondly, even more basically, try to avoid the most common failing among those anthropologists who venture occasionally and half-heartedly into quantification, which is to give results whose apparent accuracy far surpasses that of the data upon which they are based. If you know the ages of a group of husbands and wives to within a couple of years or so, then it is quite fatuous to calculate the mean age difference between spouses down to two places of decimals.

We now turn to a couple of specific points of particular interest. The first concerns the demographic modelling of specific marriage systems, particularly elementary structures. This gives rise to predictions which can be tested using the kinds of data which every fieldworker collects. For example, Hajnal (1963: 134) has argued that a man is likely to be slightly older than his MBD but slightly younger than his FZD. Given the common situation in which men are normally older than their wives, this would make FZD marriage the less likely of the two on purely demographic grounds (Reid 1974: 272). Some authors come close to arguing that such factors account for observed matrilateral practices, preferences, or even prescriptions, where these occur (ibid; Martin 1981: 401), but this is to confuse genealogical MBD marriage with categorically prescribed or jurally preferred "matrilateral" marriage systems (cf. Barnard's comment in Martin 1981: 407). None the less, it is worth investigating whether your own data bear out any models which may have been developed in connection with that kind of system. With regard to the above case, Good (1980: 485) found that, not only were MBDy and FZDy marriages equally frequent in his sample, but the age differences between the spouses in the two cases did not differ significantly. These results are from a small sample, and one would not be justified in saying more than that they do not conform to Hajnal's or Reid's predictions.

Secondly, a brief comment on the so-called "rates" of marriage, divorce, natality, mortality, and so on, which figure so prominently in demographic literature (cf. Pollard *et al.* 1981). At the risk of seeming iconoclastic, we must point out that the "marriage rate" in a given society is simply the number of marriages occurring there in a given unit of time. This is a matter for observation, not calculation. What demographers seek to determine is not, as they commonly describe it, the *rate* of marriage but what would in chemical kinetics be termed the *rate constant*; namely, the number of marriages per unit of population per unit of time. Thus J. A. Barnes (1967b), in a paper aimed specifically at anthropologists, deals not, as he states throughout, with the calculation of divorce rates, but with divorce rate constants.

Pursuing the chemical analogy a little further, it can be argued that a marriage is like a second-order chemical reaction, in which two molecules combine to form a single product (in this case, a "married couple") (Benson 1960: 8). Consequently, the desired parameter (k), the "rate constant" in our terminology, is given by the formula:

$$\text{Marriage rate} = k \, [\text{marriageable men}] \, [\text{marriageable women}]$$

where $[X]$ represents the marriageable population at the relevant time. Likewise, divorce resembles a first-order chemical reaction, in which a single molecule splits up into two components (ibid: 14). The divorce rate is simply the number of divorces actually occurring per unit time, and the rate constant (k') may be calculated by the formual:

$$\text{Divorce rate} = k' \text{ [married couples]}$$

In both cases, it is possible to calculate rate constants for the entire society or for particular age-cohorts, social categories, etc., of persons, simply by putting the figures for the desired population into these equations and carrying out the necessary integration. The advantages of this approach are its simplicity, and the fact that it treats getting married or divorced as kinetic, dynamic processes.

7 *Kinship in economics, politics and religion*

7.1 Introduction

It need hardly be said that there is a close relation between kinship and other aspects of social organization. Descent, residence and marriage are key factors in many societies, and so are often inseparable from political and economic institutions. Every ethnographer has to gain a comprehensive understanding of the place of kinship in society as a whole, so in this chapter we consider ways in which data on economics and politics can be brought to bear on problems in kinship. We shall also look briefly at the relation between kinship structures and cosmological ones. Kinship always bears some relation to the ways in which people perceive the world around them, whether this be in the form of ancestor worship, "totemism", origin myths, or symbolic associations between kinship categories and other indigenous concepts.

Writings on economics and politics inevitably reflect the theoretical orientations of their authors. Yet the data you collect should be generally understandable, comparable with that collected by others, and usable by anthropologists with different theoretical interests. We cannot discuss all relevant theoretical issues in detail, but concentrate instead upon some practical and pan-theoretical problems relevant to ethnographers of all persuasions.

7.2 The collection of economic data

Scarlett Epstein (1967) has described a means of collecting data on various aspects of economic activity, which she employed during her studies in South India and New Britain. She devised five schedules, to be filled in during formal interviews and later checked by spot-observations. Many of the suggestions which follow derive from points raised in her useful article.

Even in a non-monetary economy, goods and activities have a "cost" in terms of labour time, exchange value, or use value (a point made by both Marxists and formalists). Such costs may or may not be appreciated by the people being studied, but they can usually be ascertained by a diligent ethnographer. In non-monetary economies, for instance, this may require the collection of information on the sizes of fields, crop yields, labour time, number of possessions, and so on. Even in foraging societies, economic data can be collected with accuracy, as demonstrated by Lee's study of subsistence and work (1979), and Wiessner's (1977, 1982) study of gift-giving partnerships, which cross-cut the kinship domain, among !Kung Bushmen (§7.8).

Epstein's five schedules are designed to measure the time spent on various activities, input and output in farming, household expenditure, property ownership, and so on. When the emphasis is upon kinship, such schedules should also take into account dowry or bridewealth transactions, bride-service labour, tribute paid to affines, gift exchanges, and so on. It might be important to distinguish property owned by lineages or other corporate groups, from that owned by households, and by individuals. Also note whether gift giving and food sharing ties are kinship-based or not, which relatives stand to benefit from particular kinds of economic transactions, and who gives what to whom in every specific case.

Include as much information as you can on each schedule, and aim whenever possible at the verbatim recording of informants' remarks. No questionnaire is ever remotely perfect, and in the long run such explanatory material could prove even more useful than your statistics. Gathering such basic data from a sample population or, if possible, from the entire community, should enable you to formulate generalizations. It will also provide the background information needed to understand many events during your fieldwork (disputes, for example). Obviously, then, it would be useful to obtain such data early on in fieldwork, perhaps while collecting census data or genealogies. But as we mentioned in that regard, it may not be easy to obtain sensitive economic data until you have become more fully accepted into the local community. In any event, use the same system of cross-referencing for both economic and genealogical material, and assign individuals and households the same code number (§2.2) in both contexts.

Just as one should not ask an Englishman the size of his bank account, so it is impolite to ask a Nuer how many cattle he owns or how many children he has (Evans-Pritchard 1956: 14). People may boast of their possessions, or undervalue them for fear of greedy kinsfolk or tax collectors. It goes without saying that you must always be polite, and protect confidential or potentially harmful information. At the same time, you need to collect accurate and meaningful data. *How* this is done and how well it is done, depend above all upon your skill and sensitivity.

If people understand your aims, they may be much more willing to co-operate. Just as you begin asking about genealogy with the F, not say the FFZSD, so you should begin discussion of economic matters with things they are likely to think important, and to volunteer immediately. This helps build up the rapport needed for dealing with more difficult issues. A general question is therefore probably a better beginning than a specific one. For instance, you might first ask: "Is bridewealth today the same as it was in the past?" Later, you can ask what was given in connection with your informant's own marriage, from whom it was obtained, and to whom given. Clearly, genealogical knowledge (§2.5) is an essential pre-requisite here, if you are not to be constantly interrupting the flow of the answer with questions about the precise identities of all the persons mentioned. Finally, ask in detail about each element of the transaction, and find out whether it is thought to have been typical or not.

Questions which would be impolite if posed in isolation, may be less offensive as the natural follow-up to a series of less sensitive questions and answers. It is worth adding here that you will often find the tables turned, with local people inquiring into certain matters which are taboo for *you*. For instance, Indians ask openly about one's salary, and enquire the price of all one's possessions. This gives you some idea of what you are able to ask freely in return. But people may even deliberately ask you questions which they would not expect a member of their own society to answer. Their attitude to your impertinent questions may well depend upon how you respond to theirs.

Some local people will become your friends, in which case your interest in what they say can be taken for granted. But other informants, too, may lead conversations or interviews down paths far removed from your original intention. If certain aspects of, say, bridewealth or household finance, are important to them, then they must be important to you also. Never be afraid to change preconceived lines of questioning to meet unforeseen circumstances. There is no such thing as "complete" data; what is important is the degree to which you gain in understanding. Opinions and theories expounded to you, even those which seem half-baked or which you have heard many times before, are as important at the *nth* time of asking as they were at first. The ultimate sociological question, after all, is "*who* knows *what*?" (§8.2.1).

To sum up, you should collect economic data systematically and efficiently, but without causing offence, and with a flexibility which allows you to pursue any new interests which emerge during your survey. Although it may be possible to collect the necessary data along with your genealogies, you will probably find it better to collect such information either throughout fieldwork, perhaps during lulls in the seasonal work cycle when informants enjoy greater leisure, or near the end, when you know them well and understand their sensibilities better. This does not apply to studies of household budgeting (§7.3.3), which should cover as long a period as possible to take account of seasonal or other variations.

More precise guidance would carry us beyond the intended scope of the present book. In any case, there are several more detailed accounts of methods in economic anthropology *per se*. For instance, in addition to Epstein's (1967) article already mentioned, Colson (1967: 11–12) summarizes the very extensive census form which she used during her fieldwork among the Tonga. J. C. Mitchell (1967) and Pelto and Pelto (1978: 123–176), both provide useful overviews of problems in sampling, and in analysing quantitative data.

7.3 The domestic economy

Data of the kinds just discussed provide you, in the first instance, primarily with information about the domestic economy. What is the relevance of such data to the wider economy, to the social system as a whole, and, above all in the present context, to kinship? The role of the domestic unit (typically, the household) in the productive process varies from one type of society to another. Much more constant is its role in social *reproduction*. We shall now consider these two points, before dealing briefly with the household as a consumption unit.

7.3.1 *The domestic mode of production*

Most agricultural and pre-agricultural societies are significantly under-productive, according to Sahlins, not merely in relation to modern industrial society, but in terms of their own productive potential.

Labor power is underused, technological means are not fully engaged, natural resources are left untapped. (1974: 41)

Such underproduction, he argues, arises from the characteristics of the economic systems in such societies. Typically, these are organized on the basis of kinship relations, and founded upon domestic groups as the primary productive units.

This "domestic mode of production" has three main features:

(i) A division of labour based on sex constitutes the dominant form of economic specialization. Hence marriage serves, among other things, to bring into being a basic productive group (ibid: 79).

(ii) There is a simple technology which can be operated by a single individual and which does not require unduly high degrees of skill. The tools merely serve to amplify the human body's own capabilities (ibid: 80).

(iii) Production is carried out to the extent necessary to provide members of the domestic unit with their livelihoods, not to produce a surplus. Even when exchanged for other, similarly produced commodities their produce has primarily a "use value" rather than an "exchange value" (ibid: 83).

As Sahlins points out (ibid: 82), these points, and especially the last, are entirely consistent with "Chayanov's rule". Chayanov (1966 [1925]) studied Russian peasant farmers of the immediate pre-revolutionary period, and concluded that the higher the ratio of producers to consumers in a household, the less each individual producer worked. In other words, work levels depended primarily upon needs. He demonstrated this by calculating the average number of days worked per year by each *working* member of the household, and showed that this increased more or less lineally with an increase in the consumer/worker ratio (cf. Sahlins 1974: 91). Numbers of anthropologists have collected data of just this kind, of course, often with much greater detail and precision (cf. Richards (1961) for the Bemba, and Lee (1979) on the !Kung).

If you collect accurate data, it ought to be possible to test hypotheses such as "Chayanov's law", or even to demonstrate other kinds of statistical correlation between features of the process of domestic production on the one hand, and the kinship structure of the domestic unit on the other. It need hardly be added, though, that such studies demand systematic, painstaking, and protracted observations of a "scientific" kind, which some ethnographers (in our view, wrongly) have traditionally found unpalatable. Do not imagine that you can make meaningful general statements about household economics without some recourse to numbers. But equally, use only such numbers as are necessary to further your own understanding and that of your readers. Quantification can all too easily become an end in itself, and an analytical blind alley.

Meillassoux has criticized the notion of the "domestic mode of production" on two counts. First, Sahlins does not specify "the historical period" to which this mode of production belongs (1981: 7). By this, Meillassoux apparently means the historical *stage* according to a Marxist evolutionary framework. Secondly, Sahlins' characterization of the "domestic mode" applies interchangably to, and so does not distinguish between, a whole range of *different* types of economic exploitation, including fishing, pastoralism and agriculture, as well as hunting and gathering (ibid). This is clearly so, but whereas Meillassoux sees this lack of precision as a drawback, it appears to us a positive advantage. If the notion of the "domestic mode of production" can indeed be applied, *mutatis mutandis*, to Bushmen on the one hand and Russian peasants on the other, then its practical utility to the fieldworker is greatly increased. At the very least, whatever type of economy you work within, you will have to determine the extent to which the family or household unit constitutes a productive entity, and evaluate its contribution to the overall process of commodity production. You need to look at who produces, what they produce, and who receives or "owns" the products. Look also at mechanisms for redistributing agricultural and other goods. Find out who controls these redistributions, both in theory and practice. You may witness disputes bearing upon these issues.

7.3.2 *Production and reproduction*

Meillassoux has attacked the "illusion . . . that kinship was the key to social anthropology" (1981: 49). Even a Marxist like Godelier (1973) was so taken in that he saw kinship in simple societies as not merely a superstructural phenomenon, but also an infrastructural one. That is, kinship was not merely jural and/or ideological in nature, but also formed an integral part of the "relations of production" (see also Friedman 1974: 445). Against this view, Meillassoux argues that in economies based upon domestic production:

> power . . . rests on control over *the means of human reproduction* – subsistence goods and wives – and not over the means of material production. (1981: 49; our emphasis)

Domestic relations of reproduction have been, in one form or another, common to all modes of production up to the present (ibid: xiv). But their role has been misunderstood, or more precisely, the emphasis has been wrongly placed. Thus:

> The Elementary Structures of Kinship is entirely devoted to the problem of the choice of a spouse . . . without considering the central problem of kinship, which is *the destination of the offspring*. (ibid: 20; orig. emphasis)

As we saw in §5.5, Meillassoux differentiates kinship systems according to their rules governing the place of residence of the *offspring*, not of the spouses themselves. Similarly, he interprets marital exchanges of women, the material prestations with which these may be associated, the general position of women in society, and so on, all in terms of their contribution to the relations of *re*production (1981: 42–49). The argument is perhaps overstated and over-simplified, but it is an hypothesis which you should bear in mind, no matter where you do fieldwork.

Interestingly, the importance of social reproduction has recently been independently emphasized in a very different way, taking little or no account of Marxist assumptions. Instead, Jack Goody stands in the tradition of Fortes (1958: 1–2) and Radcliffe-Brown, in so far as he stresses the jural functions of kinship in regulating rights and duties (1976: 9). Inheritance is accorded particular importance here, the main contrast being drawn between: (i) "homogeneous" inheritance of property by a man from the same clan or lineage as the previous holder; and (ii) "diverging devolution", whereby property passes to heirs of both sexes, and so diffuses outside the lineage (ibid: 7). Within each of these broad possibilities there may be other differences, depending for instance upon the stage in the life-cycle at which transmission of property takes place. Thus, women may receive male property at the death of the previous holder, or as direct or indirect dowry (§6.5.2) when they get married. This in turn has other consequences, for example, in the degree of elaboration in life-crisis rituals.

> Where marriage establishes a conjugal fund (as in dowry systems) the wedding ceremonial will be more elaborate than when it does not; where funerals redistribute the dead man's property, they will be more elaborate than where a holder divests himself of his property during his lifetime. (ibid: 9)

Moreover, the mode of property transmission is, in the last analysis, related to the mode of agricultural production. Systems of diverging devolution seem to be linked to advanced agriculture (ibid: 118–119).

So Meillassoux emphasizes allocation of offspring, and Goody the transmission of property, but both grant some degree of causal status to the prevailing mode of production. To this extent, their initial premises at least are clearly not incompatible. Either or both of these perspectives may prove suggestive in almost any fieldwork situation.

7.3.3 *Domestic consumption*

So far we have dealt with the role of the domestic unit in production, reproduction, and (briefly) in exchange and redistribution. Most ethnographic work has focused upon these aspects, and patterns of consumption (and *internal* distribution) have been largely ignored. These very distinctions are themselves somewhat artificial, but they are necessary for purposes of analysis, especially as production units and consumption units do not necessarily correspond (Forde and Douglas 1971: 407). The individual hunter may share his kill with the entire band (§7.4.1), whereas workers in multinational companies spend the bulk of their net incomes on subsistence and "consumer" items for their own spouses and children. The household (§5.5) is the most important (though not the only) consumption unit in many societies (LeClair 1968 [1962]: 200), and requires study from this point of view.

You need to know, what exactly *is* consumed by each household, or other domestic unit? Moreover, can these goods be divided into different categories, according to their respective values? The first question can only be answered by painstaking, detailed observation over long periods of time, covering households of differing social compositions and economic standings, and taking account of seasonal or other regular changes in consumption patterns.

Scarlett Epstein (1967: 174–179) and Rosemary Firth (1934: 56–60) have discussed some of the practical problems which such studies present. These are especially acute for items outwith the cash economy, or in societies lacking standardized units of measurement. Moreover, it is extremely difficult to remember every single act of consumption, purchase, or other domestic transaction in which one has been involved: you can easily check this for yourself, by trying to account for every penny you have spent over, say, the past week. So it is up to the fieldworker to take the initiative by asking specifically about every kind of item household members might conceivably have consumed during the period in queston. Yet it may not be immediately evident to you, as an outsider, what items need to be included in your household budget schedule: to take a few examples at random, Epstein's list for South India (1967: 167) takes account of expenditure on domestic worship, snuff and cinema attendance. Clearly, you need some broad knowledge of what people are likely to spend money on, before you can get down to studying your chosen households in detail. That, coupled with the prolonged and intimate nature of the questioning required, suggests that such studies cannot usually be carried out in the very early stages of fieldwork.

As we just hinted, you cannot assume that local definitions of "subsistence" or essential expenditure will necessarily coincide with your own intuitions. In any case, it is important to see how informants themselves classify the various commodities they consume, according to their comparative utility, or *value*. Tikopia, for instance, distinguish "weighty" items like bonito hooks and shark fishing lines, from "light" ones such as bows or mats, though these categories are neither mutually exclusive nor rigidly defined independently of context (Firth 1965: 338–339). The estimation of value, so as to quantify observations on exchange and consumption, is complicated where you have distinct *spheres of exchange* (ibid: 340–344; Barth 1967). In the Trobriands, for instance, not only do *kula* exchanges, *gimwali* barter of utilitarian items, and ceremonial *wasi* exchanges of fish and yams, involve different sets of commodities, but each has its own distinct ethos, and its characteristic, distinct contexts and social relationships (Malinowski 1922: 176–194). Always be on the look-out for such regularities. This kind of thing is by no means unknown in cash economies where – at least in theory – every item can ultimately be assessed in terms of its cash value. Thus, Barth (1967: 167) reports that men in Darfur were willing to do a day's work house building or in the fields, in return for five litres of beer, yet refused a Forestry Department cash wage worth 12 times that. Similar situations arise even in modern industrial economies. For instance, one cannot adequately reciprocate a relative's Christmas card by buying its sender a drink or meal, although the value of the latter may be much greater purely in cash terms. Such cases can only be understood in terms of local ideology.

Finally, you should examine the ways in which the roles of various household members are differentiated within the domestic sphere. What kinds of household expenditure or consumption are specific to adults and what to children? What are the domestic activities and responsibilities of the husband and wife? For example, studies of the allocation of "housekeeping money" among various British working class communities reveal interesting differences. A working husband may hand his entire wage packet over to his wife, receiving "pocket money" back from her. Alternatively, he may deduct his own allowance before giving her the rest. He may, however, assume personal responsibility for certain kinds of expenditure, on large consumer items or recurrent fuel bills for example, in which case the wife's housekeeping allowance will be a smaller proportion of his total earnings (Gray 1979: 191). But whether there is a cash economy or not, it is necessary to establish local norms concerning such matters, and to look for variations in practice.

Much more could be said on all the topics reviewed in this section, but that would take us beyond the scope of the present book. In particular, we have barely mentioned the significance of exchange in the domestic economy. The next section partly remedies this omission, albeit for the limited context of marriage.

7.4. Economic and political aspects of marriage

7.4.1 *Bride-service, bestowal, and the uxorilocal son-in-law*

Marriage prestations normally involve the transmission of property, as in the cases of dowry and bridewealth (§6.5.2). As we have just seen, such exchanges are vital elements in the social reproduction of the domestic economy. But as Leach pointed out (§6.1), marriage often involves the transfer of labour rights too, a fact emphasized by certain types of marriage prestation.

For example, bride-service is one of the most protracted forms of marriage prestation. Though occasionally found among herders such as the Nama of Namibia, it is more characteristic of foraging and small-scale horticultural societies, particularly in South America, which lack the anthropologically classical medium of exchange, livestock. Knight (1978) drew attention to the "own kill rule" often found, in one form or another, among peoples practising bride-service. The principle behind this rule is that eating the products of one's own labour, particularly game animals, is likened to incest, or otherwise condemned. One therefore hunts or produces food for one's affines, and may receive food in return. According to Knight, even where such rules are neither strictly observed nor explicitly used as incest metaphors, they can sometimes be observed in the practice of obligatory meat sharing. For example, !xõ, !Kung and Nharo Bushmen stipulate that the best thigh meat of large game animals should go to the parents-in-law of the owner of the killing arrow (Bushmen do not normally shoot their own arrows, but lend them to others). Interestingly, the !xõ (Heinz 1966: 206–208) and !Kung (Marshall 1976: 266–270; Lee 1979: 240–242) practise bride-service, while the Nharo operate this rule as a supplement to bridewealth and childbirth gifts, which are very sharply distinguished from meat sharing and other forms of exchange (Barnard 1980c: 120–122).

Bride-service is frequently required until after the first child of the marriage has been born, but this is not always the case. Among the Piaroa of Venezuela, bride-service lasts for six months only. During this time the couple lives with the parents of the bride, and the groom is required to work solely for the bride's father. Ideally, both parents come from the same "house", but if they do not, then the couple has the option of living with either set of parents once bride-service has been completed (Kaplan 1975: 83, 122–123). In addition, the groom must give small gifts to his father-in-law throughout his lifetime, and if he comes from outside Piaroa territory, he must also pay bridewealth before the wedding ceremony can take place (ibid: 135). Hence bridewealth and bride-service are not mutually exclusive. Take note of any such variations and seek the principles which lie behind them.

An emphasis on bestowal often accompanies bride-service. The practice of "giving away" the bride, is of course found in many societies, but may have particular political and economic significance when she is given in exchange for services to her natal household. In the case of the Tiwi, a pregnant woman's husband has the right to bestow her unborn daughter upon a chosen friend or protégé. This power allows Tiwi elders to occupy a dominant political position, which the superior physical strength of the young men might otherwise wrest from them (Hart and Pilling 1960: 14–16, 77, 82). Bestowal is not always performed by the bride's father. Maddock (1972: 47–54) describes four patterns of bestowal found in Aboriginal Australia: a man may bestow his D, his ZD, his Z, or (in the case of her remarriage) his M. It is important to be clear about the inter-relationships of bestower, bestowed and recipient. For example, a Dalabon girl may be bestowed by her M and/or MB, both of whom in fact use the same relationship term for her. (Her father, on the other hand, uses a different term.) Maddock calls this "niece bestowal", to distinguish it from "daughter bestowal" in which a man gives away his D (1972: 48–49). Because "niece bestowal" involves three clans rather than two, Maddock argues that it is worthwhile to distinguish three "marriage functions": wife-yielding, wife-receiving and wife-bestowing, as opposed to the more conventional pair, wife-giving and wife-taking.

Bride-service and bestowal have been much neglected in theoretical writings. Their significance varies greatly *vis-à-vis* other aspects of exchange, such as bridewealth and dowry. In the same limited sense that bridewealth is the inverse of dowry (§6.5.2), so bestowal can be seen as the inverse of bride-service. Thus, bestowal confers upon the husband rights in his wife's labour, whereas bride-service grants rights in the husband's labour to his wife's relatives.

Prolonged bride-service merges imperceptibly into the phenomenon of the uxorilocally-resident son-in-law. In Sinhalese *binna* marriages (§5.5), a man goes to live in his father-in-law's house and, in effect, works for him. Ultimately, he becomes the mere manager of an estate which actually belongs to his wife. This is said to be humiliating, yet in practice such unions are as frequent as *dīga* (patri-virilocal) ones (Leach 1961b: 84). There are economic reasons for this. *Binna* marriages are contracted by heiresses without brothers, and by men who are landless, or whose family has been ostracized for infringing caste rules. *Binna* marriage carries slightly less stigma when a man marries his MBD, so that his father-in-law is also his MB (ibid: 85). Least demeaning of all is the case of a man who himself has inheritance rights in his wife's village. This can easily happen, as children inherit land from both their father and their mother (ibid: 137), and these two estates are usually in different villages. If a man marrying into his M's native village has land of his own there, then his ability to manage his wife's estate, *as well as* his own, may actually enhance his wealth and influence. This of course depends upon how much land he receives from each parent; how much land his wife receives from her parents; the productivity of these various plots; how well he gets on with his F and father-in-law; and so on. Clearly, cases of this kind can only be understood after detailed analysis of the particular factors involved. It is not enough simply to state the alternative "residence rules" and indicate the degree to which each is obeyed.

7.4.2 The politics of marriage

Marriage rules are not purely theoretical constructs or arbitrary cultural preferences; often they are expressions of political and economic ideology. In bridewealth systems, marriage itself is a political act regardless of who is married, as long as bridewealth is exchanged.

In studying this aspect of marriage you need to ask: what sort of category of person would make a good spouse, and why? Pay special attention to the way these questions are answered. Do people have to think about the problem, or are answers easily forthcoming and stereotyped? For instance, marriage rules may be expressed in symbolic or proverbial ways, rather than as mere prosaic statements of the advantages to be gained by the groom, bride, matchmaker, or other interested party. Consider for example these three African sayings:

Lozi: "Cattle beget children." (Gluckman 1950: 184)
Lovedu: A woman may "pull down the house she built at her brother's." (Krige and Krige 1943: 143)
Tswana: "Child of my father's younger brother, marry me, so that the cattle may return to our kraal." (Schapera 1950: 151)

The Lozi proverb explains the simple economic facts of bridewealth payments, emphasizing their role in legitimating children of the lineage. The

Lovedu saying alludes to a woman's claim over the labour of her cattle-linked brother's daughter and so to MBD marriage on the part of the woman's son (§6.5.2). A man's marriage depends upon that of his sister, and the sister whose own bridewealth cattle pay for her brother's marriage, can demand that her brother marry his daughter to her son, so that her daughter-in-law comes to work for her in her household (see Fig. 7.1). If her brother is unwilling or unable to meet this obligation, she may "pull down his house" by taking back her cattle and giving them to a more amenable relative elsewhere. This may set off a chain reaction of demands for the return of cattle, especially if her brother has already used some of the animals involved in exchanges with his WB. The ramifications, if left unchecked, may be so great that the entire country is "spoilt" (Krige and Krige 1943: 143). Finally, the Tswana proverb expresses directly the real political and economic concerns of close agnates. The Tswana talk about ideal marriage preferences in terms of a ranked series: for a man, marriage with the MBD is best, then with FZD, FBD, and finally MZD (A. Kuper 1975a: 78). In practice though, Tswana nobles prefer the FBD option, and members of royal houses are even more likely to favour such marriages, since they transform competitive relations into supportive ones (ibid: 79).

Trautmann (1981: 406) explains in similar vein the (terminologically) highly irregular tendency of Sinhalese royalty to contract parallel cousin marriages. Hereditary rulers can adopt two distinct kinds of politically or strategically inspired marriage policies. A policy of "extensive alliance" (ibid: 425), in which marriages are contracted with distant relatives, or members of unrelated ruling families from elsewhere, increases the number of one's allies,

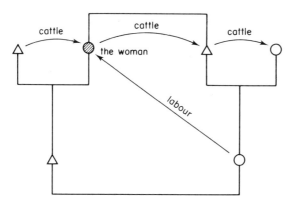

Fig. 7.1 *The politics of Lovedu MBD marriage.*

but the "closeness" of the affinal relationship is likely to be reduced. Conversely, "intensive alliance" (ibid), or close intermarriage within the ruling family, produces fewer allies with very close inter-relationships. Historical evidence suggests that Indian rulers usually favoured the latter practice, to such a degree that, as in the Sinhalese case, normal rules governing marriageability were often ignored. Similar considerations may apply to the inheritance of wealth, and succession to hereditary office, too. In practice, of course, both alliance strategies can be combined together in varying proportions, and you will need to examine marriage behaviour with both the political and economic circumstances of the participants very much in mind.

In general, preferences for close-kin marriage have political implications. For instance, FBD marriage is practised in a number of societies, particularly in West African and Arab countries (§8.3). In these cases, there is often the added sanction of Islamic relgion, yet its quasi-religious representation, as well as its political functions, may well differ from one ethnic group, social class, or individual to another. These subtle differences can tell us a great deal about the structure of political power. Similarities resulting from the influence of Islamic culture may be superficial, and hide deeper and more varied political and economic motifs.

A synchronic regional approach, such as Adam Kuper (1982b) has applied to southern Africa, would be well suited to highlighting such variations. Kuper's thesis is that Southern Bantu systems of kinship and marriage possess a characteristic underlying structure, that differences among the various Southern Bantu kinship systems can be seen as transformations of that structure, and that the essence of these transformations is to be found in the politics and economics of marriage. Although the detailed marriage preferences vary radically among the systems, higher status individuals in all of them are able to perpetuate their power and wealth through bridewealth transactions. The Tswana tend to marry hypergamously, and bridewealth is relatively low. Southern Sotho tend to marry hypogamously, and bridewealth is high. Swazi men who marry lower status women tend to pay less bridewealth than those Swazi man who marry higher status women (ibid: 160). In every case, preferences for close kin marriages of various kinds operate in conjunction with the control over people and cattle.

In other types of society, of course, particularly those lacking "universal" relationship terminologies (§3.3.3) and/or "elementary" structures of jural alliance (§6.3.2), marriages between non-relatives may be the politically important ones. For instance, Tsonga commoners, who are forbidden to marry first cousins and many other classes of kin, "apparently scatter their marriage links" (ibid: 123). The closely related Chopi do the same, thereby ensuring "that no one group monopolises power and status" (Webster 1977: 202). Consequently, the Tsonga and Chopi systems represent egalitarian versions of the Southern Bantu structure mentioned above.

Kuper's argument illustrates the importance of setting your own findings into their regional, ethnographic context. His understanding of each of the systems just mentioned is greatly enhanced by his awareness of the existence of the others. In the same way, the very varied marriage systems of southern India and Sri Lanka become much more fully intelligible when they are all considered together (§6.5.1; Good 1982). For instance, hypergamous marriages in which the children acquire their father's status (cf. Fig. 6.8), are seen to be associated with patrilineality, patri-virilocal residence after marriage, weak or non-existent female rights over landed property, and the payment of large dowries. Uxorilocal residence, on the other hand, indicates a far more even distribution of property rights among male and female children, as in the case of the Sinhalese (§7.4.1). The interpretation of your field data may prove very much easier if you have a regional framework of this kind within which to set your results, or against which to oppose them.

To sum up, marriage is a standard means for converting actual or potential enemies into allies (Mair 1971: 78). Hence the widespread incidence of statements such as "We marry those whom we fight", which are reported from Africa (Gluckman 1955: 13), New Guinea (Meggitt 1965: 101) and other places. In such cases, some kind of balance has to be struck, in practice and maybe jurally too, between strengthening one's links with old and trusted allies of proven respectability, and widening one's range of affinal contracts by arranging marriages with "strangers" or "enemies". Lest all this gives too Machiavellian an impression, let us add at once that, by and large, people also seek what is best for their children, in terms of wealth, position, or personal happiness. It may be analytically convenient to separate strategic considerations from personal ones, but it is obvious that both come simultaneously into play whenever the actual marriage of a particular child is under discussion.

In every type of case, therefore, it is important to collect really full data both on the jural rules regulating marriageability, and on behaviour in particular kinds of strategic situation. As we have indicated, the rules need not be explicitly stated as such. They may take proverbial or mythical forms, for instance. On the other hand, societies with long literary traditions may even have documents dealing with marriageability. The Indian *Arthaśāstras* actually discuss the very kinds of strategic consideration to which we have referred (Trautmann 1981: 360–361). If at all possible, work out marriage patterns while you are still in the field. This should help you ask the right questions about: (a) the varying degrees of jural preference accorded to marriages with individuals of different economic and social statuses, or standing in certain types of terminological relationship to ego; and (b) the reasons for actual marriage choices, both in cases which conform to stated preferences and in cases which do not (§8.3).

It will sometimes be possible to look at diachronic data on marriage practice, using either the work of previous ethnographers or official records. Conté (1979) has argued that marriage preferences and practices, especially those entailing endogamy (such as FBD marriage), should never be viewed as structural constants. Instead, they are meaningful only in so far as they can be defined in terms of the *evolution* of a group's economic and political organization. As we shall see in §8.3.2, it is possible to go even further and see such preferences in the light of the personal circumstances of *individual* members of such groups. Both these approaches can productively be fitted into a Marxist, transactionalist, or other dynamic theoretical framework.

7.4.3 *Marriage and hierarchy*

In the course of the previous section we looked at some of the political implications of contracting marriages with particular categories of close kin. Another, more simple way in which marriage can relate to political hierarchy, is found in systems of "asymmetric prescriptive alliance" (§6.3). There are three possibilities in such systems, namely isogamy, hypergamy and hypo-gamy, all of which have been discussed in general terms in §6.4.1. Because asymmetric alliance entails by definition a distinction between wife-giving and wife-taking exchange units, isogamy is rare. There will normally be an ideology of hypergamy or hypogamy, to which you will need to pay particular attention whenever (as is very likely) both the social and cosmological notions of the society are expressed in similar hierarchical terms. For instance, Hindu societies in both India itself and South East Asia, tend to be hyper-gamous, as the Kangra Rajput case (§6.4.1) illustrates. Throughout this region, hypergamy is seen as "natural". For Indians, it reflects the necessary primacy of the male "seed" over the female "field", and the inherent superior-ity of receivers over givers of gifts (Tambiah 1973b: 198–199). For the Hindu Balinese, hypergamy fits neatly into their general cosmological idiom, in which status is expressed in terms of geographical altitude: thus, hyper-gamy is appropriate because, like water, semen does not flow uphill (Hobart 1978: 21).

Natural or not, hypergamy is certainly not a universal, as Lévi-Strauss seems sometimes to assume (1969: 474). Empirically, hypogamy is actually more common in systems of "generalized exchange" (Leach 1970: 109). These are found over much of Asia, and perhaps the best-known instance is that of the Kachin of highland Burma (Leach 1954, 1969).

This society oscillates between an egalitarian (*gumlao*) form of social organization, and a stratified (*gumsa*) form. Both forms are hypogamous, though the neighbouring Shan Chinese, whom Kachin chiefs seek to emulate, possess an hypergamous ideology. *Gumsa* Kachin are divided into three social classes: chiefs, aristocrats and commoners. Lineages stand in wife-giving (*mayu*) or wife-taking (*dama*) relationships with each other, both within each class and across class boundaries. Wives pass down the social hierarchy, while goods, in the form of bridewealth, tribute, etc., pass up. Every lineage stands in wife-giving or wife-taking relationships with more than one other lineage, so the flow of goods and wives is not, strictly speaking, simply up and down the hierarchy, respectively. It takes more of a spiral form, with circular or "horizontal" exchange within classes, as well as "vertical" exchange between them (Leach 1961a [1951]: 86). So hypogamy, especially when coupled with bridewealth passing to the high-status wife-givers, is clearly consistent with stratified forms of lineage organization, though rather less so than hypergamy, in which both wives and dowry can pass in the same direction, from low-class to high (Tambiah 1973: 64; §6.5.2).

Yet hypogamy need not be associated with *absolute* or transitive hierarchy, of either group-centred or ego-centred kind. Some societies display a circular form of hypogamy, associated with only a *relative* or intransitive hierarchical distinction, which in the simplest case takes the form:

$$A ----\rangle B ----\rangle C ----\rangle A$$

In some cases, there are in fact no lineages nor any other corporate exchange units other than cognatically defined families. Each lineage or family stands in either a wife-giving or wife-taking relationship (but not in both) with every other lineage or family with whom it has ever intermarried. The first marriage between any pair of lineages between whom no marital union has previously occurred, sets the precedent and establishes both the direction of any subsequent marriages, and the relative or absolute hierarchical distinction between the two exchange-units. The classic systems of this type are the Purum (Das 1945; Needham 1962), the "circulating connubium" found in parts of eastern Indonesia (van Wouden 1968 [1935]) and, once again, the Kachin, this time in their *gumlao* form (Leach 1954).

This should not necessarily be taken to mean that *gumsa* and *gumlao* are straightforwardly stratified and egalitarian social forms, respectively. As Friedman (1975) shows, the relationship between wealth, prestige and marriage among the Kachin and their neighbours is an immensely complicated one. In both *gumsa* and *gumlao* systems, prestige is converted into rank. This leads to a structure of ranked, hereditary lineage groups in the former case, and to a "big man" society in the latter (Friedman 1974: 467). Both ecological and sociological factors govern the potential for transformation of the system from *gumsa* to *gumlao*, and vice versa. There is a complex feedback loop, linking the exchange of women, brideprice, inputs of land and labour, the production of a material surplus, the giving of feasts, and personal or group status (ibid: 454).

This highly abstract style of analysis is far removed from the initial collection and interpretation of the data, and you would hardly expect to develop models of this sophistication while still in the field. None the less, this example is a salutary one, and underlines the importance of looking for interconnections between ostensibly diverse areas of social life. You simply cannot afford to compartmentalize your observations too rigidly into "kinship", "economics", "politics", and so on (§1.4, §8.8).

7.5. Cross-cutting ties

In every society individuals have rights, jural obligations, and moral responsibilities towards persons related to them by ties other than descent ones. In fact, they will probably have *different* obligations towards members of their descent group (if any), local group, immediate family, senior kin, and so on. These conflicting rights and obligations are known as "cross-cutting ties", and they play a vital part in resolving conflicts and maintaining social order, particularly in acephalous societies. Thus:

> men quarrel in terms of certain of their customary allegiances, but are restrained from violence through other conflicting allegiances which are also enjoined on them by custom. (Gluckman 1955: 2)

This process has both positive and negative aspects. That is, cross-cutting ties not only link individuals with groups other than their own, but also, by so doing, create divided loyalties *within* groups that prevent them becoming too distinct from the community at large. This point underlies Gluckman's famous analyses of "the peace in the feud" and "the bonds in the colour bar" (ibid: *passim*), and it is clearly of very wide applicability.

Although the phrase "cross-cutting ties" is often taken to refer to an individual's obligations towards the different *groups* with which he is connected, it is equally appropriate, and often more accurate, to apply it also to his conflicting rights and responsibilities *vis-à-vis* persons falling into different *social categories*. This not only includes sociocentric categories, but also categories defined egocentrically, such as "close kin", "matrilateral relatives", or "in-laws". Every society has cross-cutting ties of these kinds. Some are kinship based (e.g. ties of descent or filiation (§5.3)), while others are based upon non-kinship factors such as local group membership or age-set membership. Some are a combination of both, as where kinship ties coincide with membership in local groups. The examples which follow are by no means exhaustive, but illustrate the kinds of things you should be looking for.

7.5.1 *Descent, filiation and politics*

Among the most striking forms of kinship-based cross-cutting ties are those involving double descent, as in the Herero case discussed briefly in §5.2. "Double descent" societies are defined by Radcliffe-Brown as those "in which there are both patrilineal and matrilineal corporate kin groups" (1950: 41). Every individual is then reckoned to belong to a particular, patrilineally constituted descent group for some purposes, and to another, matrilineally constituted descent group for others.

Although double descent usually implies conflicting loyalties for the individual, it can also involve conflicts between entire groups, such as those between Yakö villages. In this classic case, the tendency towards village endogamy, coupled with the village-centred kinship organization, creates large and strongly independent settlements. Villages (average size, 4000 people; Forde 1950: 286) are grouped into wards, each ward being associated with a particular set of patrilineal clans or *yepun* (ibid: 302), and although the matrilineal clans (*yajima*) are dispersed, close uterine relatives usually live in different wards of the same village (ibid: 306). Thus kinship ties in both lines exist mainly within one's own village, and do not lead to the peaceful cooperation between villages which is found in double descent systems where villages are smaller.

But whatever the form, double descent can provide a complex but very effective means of organizing a small-scale society, without the need for either strong leadership or a principle of lineage segmentation. Leach (1962) has drawn attention to the fact that filiation (in Fortes' sense) can apply just as well in a double descent system as in a unilineal one. Among the Yakö, since land rights are held in the patrilineal groups, an individual can exploit his ties to his mother's or wife's patrilineages (1962: 133). Similarly, since rights to certain ritual offices are held matrilineally, a Yakö can exert influence in these

matters through his ties with his father's matrilineage or his wife's matrilineage (ibid).

If you work in a similar society, observe as carefully as you can how far the
generalizations made by individuals about corporate property, the transmission of rights, and so on, match what they actually do. Find out where
loyalties lie, and discover what kinds of moral, as well as jural responsibilities
are due to each of the two descent groups to which every individual belongs.
Are there differences in these regards between the positions of males and
females, chiefs and commoners, elders and juniors, or locally-resident and
non-resident members of the kin group?

Cross-cutting ties are not, as we said, found only in connection with
overlapping membership in different *corporate* groups. Such ties can arise in
ego-centred fashion, and are indeed implicit in any society recognizing
bilateral filiation. *Complementary* filiation, though, is frequently a more
delicate and subtle matter, as we saw in §5.3. In Fortes' terms, filiation is in
practice often embedded more in the "domestic" domain than in the "politico-
jural" one (1970 [1959]: 110). Its analysis therefore presents different
problems and raises different issues than does the study of more formal types
of organization. This is particularly true when compared to the jural rights
and duties associated with clan and lineage membership.

In the domestic domain, those difficult but interesting questions of love and
affection, joking relationships, and mutual aid in times of stress, may come
into play. In many societies, individuals will have very different attitudes
towards clan members on the one hand, and close relatives from other clans
on the other. These should be closely examined, as should the extent to which
such idealized attitudes are realized in practice. They can shed light on a host
of problems, particularly in the realms of sex roles, and seniority or age
differentiation.

7.5.2 *The politics of lineage organization*

In a lineage-based society you must ascertain the jural functions of each kind
of descent grouping. For the Iroquois, Morgan (1877: 70–85) lists ten
privileges and obligations conferred and imposed by the "gens" (plural,
gentes; Latin for "patrilineal clan") upon its members. These include the
rights to elect and depose clan chiefs, collective rights of inheritance,
reciprocal obligations of help and defence, and the rights to bestow names
and adopt strangers into the clan. In other societies, there may also be rights
in common clan territory or other property, religious shrines, and ancestral

spirits, as well as rights and obligations connected with marriage (including rules of exogamy, or of preferential endogamy).

In segmentary systems, you will have to distinguish the respective rights and duties associated with every level of segmentation. These levels need not all be recognized locally, or at least may not have distinguishing titles. For instance, the Bemba have matrilineal clans (*imikoa*). These are exogamous, have their own myths of origin, and the succession to certain hereditary offices passes through them. But there are also smaller, un-named descent groups which are the important units in relation to ancestor spirits, and within which the succession to certain other offices is restricted (Richards 1940: 87–88). The levels of segmentation may be much more numerous than this, of course.

Bridewealth and dowry transactions are generally not the concern of large lineages as such, but of smaller lineage segments, or of those lineage members most closely related to the bride or groom. In the case of the eastern Nuer, bridewealth consists ideally of 40 head of cattle, and these are distributed among certain relatives of the bride, as follows: ten go to the bride's own F and her half-brothers, and another ten to her FB, FZ and F(half)B; ten go to the bride's M and uterine B, and the remaining ten to her MB, MZ and M(half)B. The bride's four grandparents are in fact entitled to one beast each if they are still alive, though it is assumed that they will normally not be. There is also a general rule that if any potential receiver of cattle has died, then his or her sons will inherit their parent's share (Evans-Pritchard 1951: 76–77).

If these receivers of bridewealth cattle are classified according to lineage affiliation, the breakdown is as follows: 27 animals go to members of the bride's F's patrilineal segment, to which must be added a further three which are given to the bride's M but presumably remain in the bride's natal household; the remaining ten animals go to the bride's M's patrilineal segment. One might be tempted to see this apparent patrilateral bias as an understandable consequence of the extreme cultural stress on patrilineality, but this is not the view of the Nuer themselves. For the purpose of reckoning bridewealth, the bride's M and uterine B are both included among the *kwi man* (maternal side) rather than the *kwi gwam* (paternal side) (ibid: 76). The paternal and maternal sides are therefore said to receive 20 animals each.

This last point illustrates the importance of classifying and understanding such prestations as the people themselves do. If you do not, then you are liable to misinterpret the situation. Note also that you will have to consider such transactions in a very much broader temporal context than that of a single wedding with which they are most directly concerned. For instance, the cattle allotted to the bride's various brothers are in fact under the control of her father, who may use them to marry off *any* of his sons, usually in order of seniority (ibid: 79). But the brother's rights by no means end there. As Nuer say, "when the bride's daughters are married more cattle will be paid to their mother's brothers" (ibid: 78). In societies which make large and elaborate marriage prestations, every transaction relates back to those of previous generations, and holds within it the seeds of transactions in generations still to come. Just how this happens depends upon other features of the social organization, and is something you will certainly need to investigate.

Lineage systems need not be segmentary in the classical sense. The south-eastern Chinese system described by Freedman (1958, 1966) is an interesting variation on the segmentary model. Traditionally, a man could establish a land-based trust for his patrilineal descendants. Alternatively, a group of relatives could establish such an estate on behalf of a mutual ancestor, who posthumously became the focus of his lineage-estate. Wealth was unevenly distributed, and wealthy individuals would try to consolidate it for use by their close agnates, in opposition to more distant ones. In setting up such estates, this meant that close focal ancestors were to be preferred over distant ones, and therefore that lineages of small span (§5.2) were economically more important than those of large span.

The point here is that cross-cutting ties, similar to those found between different kinds of groups in relation to an individual, can also be found between different levels of the same kind of group. The Chinese lineage member had to take lineage span very much into account.

7.5.3 *Locality and kinship*

David Turner (1978a; cf. 1978b, 1979) has put forward an elegant but somewhat complicated theory which attempts to reconcile the "atom of kinship" (Lévi-Strauss 1968 [1945]: 48) with the "unity of the sibling group" (Radcliffe-Brown 1950: 23), and, indeed, tries to inter-relate kinship, locality, ideology and production generally. We shall not discuss the theory as a whole, but only his distinction between the "locality-incorporative" and "kinship-confederational" principles.

Societies which are essentially locality-incorporative recognize ties of locality (often acquired through in-marriage) over ties of descent. Turner's Cree ethnography is the paradigm case. Cree hunters share rights to land within their defined range territory. Conflict and competition are reduced within one's own range, and at the same time heightened between individuals of different ranges, even if they are consanguineal kin (1978a: 227). A similar situation may have existed in the ancient Scottish clan system, though the evidence is inconclusive. In the case of clan-exogamous marriages (Scottish clans were agamous and cognatic), the foreign spouse would be incorporated into the clan in whose territory the couple resided, thus preventing the alienation of clan property (Hubert 1934: 204).

In contrast, societies which emphasize the kinship-confederational principle recognize ties of descent over ties of locality. The paradigm case here is Turner's Australian Aborigine ethnography. Conflict is reduced between the patrilineally related owners of different territories, but increased between co-producers who live together, including husband and wife (1978a: 227–228). The *modern* Scottish notion of "clanship" seems to be based on this principle too, though perhaps without the conflicting loyalties which might have stemmed from rights in clan territories if these had still existed. Recently it was stated in the press that one Scots chief was the head of a "clan" numbering some five million people, most of them scattered throughout North America and the Southern Hemisphere. Such a claim would be incomprehensible in a society where the kinship ideology is based upon the locality-incorporative principle.

The temptation must be very strong, for any ethnographer who has worked in such very different and widely separated parts of the world, to see the two societies concerned as polar opposites. But the accuracy of Turner's characterizations of the Cree and the Aborigines is not the relevant issue here. His two principles are structurally, not ethnographically opposed. Furthermore, as we saw in §5.5, an *ideology* of descent may mask the empirical fact that groups are constituted primarily on some other basis, such as co-residence. In such a case, it is the ideology which is important. That is, Turner's distinctions are best understood emically, not etically.

The chances are that both principles will operate among the people you are studying. It is worthwhile ascertaining which principle is dominant, and what conflicting ties result from the application of one principle or the other. If your people are in close contact with other ethnic groups, either related or unrelated, find out what they know about them, and how they describe these other systems. This could be especially revealing where peoples with different locality/kinship ideologies intermarry, trade, or exploit the same territory. In such cases, you may discover that there is an emphasis on one principle within the group you are studying, but that the other is applied in relation to outsiders, perhaps as a mechanism for maintaining ethnic identity (cf. Barth 1969: 15–16).

For example, Barnard (1980b: 141–143) found that Bushman groups, who traditionally think in terms of a locality-incorporative ideology, apply the kinship-confederational principle when forced to share rights to land resources with non-Bushman ranchers. That is, the non-Bushmen with whom they share their land are not treated as members of the community, whereas Bushmen temporarily resident elsewhere while employed by ranchers retain their natal group identity. Sometimes the kinship-confederational principle operates *within* Bushman society too, particularly when members of different language groups are present together in large numbers upon land which is traditionally exploited by only one group (ibid: 143–145). On some white-owned Kalahari ranches, Nharo, G/wi and G//ana are present, each group living in separate bands and maintaining its own identity despite the cultural similarities between the groups, and the mutual intelligibility of their dialects.

7.5.4 *Ramages and conical clans*

Hierarchical groups may be organized on the basis of descent. Some lines will then be regarded as superior to, or of higher social status than, others. Where descent is unilineal this should cause no complications, but where it is ambilineal (§5.2), as in much of Polynesia, the possibility of a choice in political allegiance may arise. But before looking at the implications of this, let us get some definitions straight.

One type of hierarchical descent group is that found in Polynesia, and known to anthropologists as the *ramage* or *conical descent group*. This need not in fact necessarily be ambilineal, as is shown in the different emphases of the definitions of "ramage" by Firth and Sahlins. Firth emphasizes the element of choice in group membership, whereas Sahlins stresses the hierarchical nature of the descent groups found in this area. Their essential disagreement is not over the data – both hierarchy and ambilineality are characteristic of Polynesian descent groups – but about their desire to use conceptual terms in different ways. Firth defines the relevant terms as follows:

> *Ambilateral* for the mode of attachment in which both parents are feasible as links in group membership.
>
> *Ambilineal* for the maintenance of group continuity through the generations by using male or female links without set order.
>
> *Ramage* for the kind of group constituted by using both/either parents as links in group membership. (1957: 6)

This usage of *ramage* in fact differs from Firth's earlier use of the term to describe the Tikopia patrilineal descent group (1963 [1936]: 328).

Sahlins, echoing that earlier usage, defines the "ramage system" as being "based upon internally ranked, segmentary unilineal kin groups acting also as political units" (1958: xi–xii). He opposes it to the "descent-line system", which is "characterized by discrete, localized common descent groups organized into territorial political entities" (ibid: xii), and argues throughout his book that each is associated with particular ecological conditions.

The relevant point here is that although there may be a unilineal ideology or a normative preference for one line over the other, in many Polynesian societies a person can choose to affiliate with *either* his father's "unilineal" group *or* his mother's. The choice will depend on the political gains to be made.

For the purposes of formal definition, we prefer Firth's (1957) explicit recognition of ambilineality. Sahlins' "ramage" is perhaps better described as a "conical clan", as distinct from an "equalitarian clan" (see Sahlins 1958: 139–140). Research in such hierarchical communities as those of Polynesia offers interesting possibilities for the examination of both internal and external descent-group politics. D. H. Turner's model (1978a; §7.5.3) may be applicable, as indeed may models placing more emphasis upon individual choice.

7.5.5 *Age structure and kinship*

Age, as a factor in social organization, takes many forms. The most rigid involve age sets and age grades, which frequently, where they are found, provide social links which cross-cut both descent groups and social classes. The classic examples of age sets and grades are found in Africa. Typically, those boys initiated at the same ceremony will form an age set, with a common name and identity, and often a camaraderie which binds members and sets them apart from members of other age sets. There may also be rules which impinge clearly on the kinship domain, as among the Nuer, where a man is forbidden to marry the daughter of an age-mate (Evans-Pritchard 1951: 33). Among the Nuer, age sets cross-cut the lineage organization. In some stratified African societies, such as the Swazi (H. Kuper 1947: 122) or Zulu (Gluckman 1940: 32), age sets also provide links across the social classes, since royals, aristocrats and commoners all belong to the same age set.

Age grades, the levels through which an individual passes as he grows older – initiate, warrior, adult, elder, for example – may serve a similar function, and kinship rules may be affected by a person's age-grade position relative to another. Not all societies which possess age sets also possess age grades, or vice versa; and even those societies which possess neither will frequently utilize an age principle in the jural domain of their kinship structure.

The influence of age in a very different sense and context forms the subject of Needham's famous discussion (1966) of the distinction between relative age and genealogical level. Different relationship terminologies place different degrees of emphasis upon these two criteria of classification (§3.3.3). The point is that demographic factors frequently create a situation in which ego is about the same age as or even older than alter in chronological terms, though alter's junior in terms of genealogical level. Needham's conclusion, very briefly, is that societies whose kinship systems are organized on the basis of unilineal groups would seem to favour genealogical level in their classification and behaviour, while those without the unilineal principle would seem to favour relative age. Thus the Penan, a cognatically organized people of north-central Borneo, permit marriages between genealogical levels, a practice which results in their offspring being of ambiguous genealogical status, since the status traced through one parent will be different from the status traced through the other.

7.6 Fictive and ritual kinship

In this section we consider several types of "pseudo-kinship" which you may encounter. There are two distinct possibilities here, which Pitt-Rivers (1973: 95) has called *figurative* or ritual kinship, and *fictive* or adoptive kinship, respectively. In the first case, kinship provides the idiom for relationships of other kinds, which are complementary to kinship rather than an essential part of it. In the second, the functions normally fulfilled by certain relatives are wholly or partly taken over by others. Figurative kinship is not in itself jurally recognized, although the relationship concerned may be jurally regulated from other points of view. For instance, the priest/parishioner relationship is subject to civil and ecclesiastical law, but neither treats it as if it really did involve a "father" and "son". Fictive kinship, on the other hand, *is* jurally recognized as such, in certain legal contexts. Western adoption (§7.6.3) is a case in point, where the adoptive parents take on the full legal responsibilities of the parental role.

7.6.1 *Parents and pro-parents*

Esther Goody has distinguished five aspects of the normal parental role in most societies (1971: 332). These are:

(i) biological parenthood, or the fact of being a child's genitor/genetrix (as emically defined (§8.7));

(ii) sociological parenthood, or the conferring of legitimacy and social status upon a child, by being its acknowledged pater or mater;

(iii) the provision of nurture and nursing;

(iv) the provision of moral and technical education;

(v) sponsorship, that is, helping the child acquire the position and resources associated with full adult status.

Because of its strength and importance, the parent–child relationship provides an obvious idiom in which to express relationships of other kinds, even such important ones as those linking Christians to their God. Clearly, you will have to explore such imagery whenever you come across it, although as we saw in §3.2 the "real" and the "figurative" cannot always be so readily distinguished. Moreover, the parent–child bond can easily survive the hiving-off of one or more of its aspects to fictive *pro-parents* of one kind or another (ibid: 334). Situations of both these kinds are examined below.

7.6.2 *Fosterage*

Foster parents take over, wholly or in part, elements (iii) and (iv) of the parental role-set. This may be done voluntarily or involuntarily, as the result of illness, death, divorce, etc. As Goody defines it, fosterage is merely the taking over of the *process* of rearing, without the jural status of the child being affected (ibid: 336). She cites the case of the Gonja of northern Ghana, where about half the children are brought up, from the age of 5–6 until they get married, by their grandparents or parents' siblings. This is thought beneficial to the child's moral education, and also helps children develop wide social contacts among both patrilateral and matrilateral kin (ibid: 337; 1982).

7.6.3 *Adoption*

Adoptions have three possible, overlapping functions. They may serve: (a) to provide homes and families for orphans or other deprived children; (b) to provide offspring for childless couples or individuals; (c) to provide such couples or individuals with heirs to their property (J. Goody 1976: 68). The first of these functions is the prime concern in modern, Western adoptions, which are therefore regulated by the state with the welfare of the child most in mind. This is not universally so, however. In many societies the main motive for adoption is the third, the provision of heirs to the property or offices of a family in danger of dying out. Under such circumstances, the adopted person may equally well be an adult, as in the ancient Roman practice of *adrogatio* (ibid: 70).

Clearly, these kinds of fictive parenthood serve to endow the adopted person with a new status, replacing that acquired at birth. E. Goody uses the term *adrogation* for cases like the Roman one, in which aspects (ii) and (v) of the parental role-set are wholly or partially hived off by the pro-parents, and reserves the name *adoption* for cases in which the pro-parents assume the parental role in its entirety, as in the modern West (1971: 342). These two possibilities clearly have to be distinguished, especially when both are found in the same society. However, our usual preference for polythetic definitions over monothetic ones, leads us to the view that it does not really matter whether or not you call a given institution "adoption", so long as you specify clearly what that institution entails, in both theory and practice. In other words, you should use whatever terminology is best suited to your data. You will also have to consider adoption in all three of its aspects, to assess its role in the nurture and training of children, the maintenance of continuity in lineages or other kinship groupings, the inheritance of property, and the regulation of succession to office.

7.6.4 *Sponsorship*

It is normally a parental responsibility to provide a child with the where-withal for achieving full adult status, ritually, socially, politically and economically. The most important requirement here is often the acquisition of a spouse, which in turn entails the provision of bridewealth, dowry, or other material resources. These are furnished by a sponsor, who receives the respect and long-term support of the protégé in return (ibid: 333). Although such sponsorship is usually the parents' responsibility, they may be assisted by other relatives, as in the case of Nuer bridewealth (§7.5.2). Sometimes this role may be wholly taken over by others. In Dahomey, for instance, a man's best friend may provide him with bridewealth, a debt which is finally repaid when the groom gives a daughter in marriage to his friend (L. Bohannan 1949).

Sponsorship does not only arise in connection with marriage. For instance, a Trobriand man needs a sponsor in order to enter the *kula*, the pre-eminent institution of adult life. His MB, even more than his F, is responsible for providing a youth with *kula* objects and partners, and in return receives *pokala* gifts from his protégé as a token of respect (Malinowski 1922: 279–280). But rather than provide an inevitably incomplete catalogue of such culturally specific institutions, we shall concentrate instead upon one widespread and important phenomenon, god-parenthood.

The rite of baptism is an important one in most forms of Christianity, for it gives the child a name, and a place in the Christian scheme of things, and also removes the taint of original sin. The ritual involves three sets of relationships; that between the child and its parents; that between the child and its god-parents or ritual sponsors; and that between the child's parents and god-parents (Mintz and Wolf 1950: 341). The second of these is the important one in the baptism itself, because it provides the child with a number of moral preceptors and guides, who partially take over aspect (iv) of the parental role-set. But in addition to its ritual and symbolic dimensions, god-parenthood has significant kinship functions, both in providing surrogate parents for the child, and in extending incest and exogamy restrictions. For instance, it may be forbidden to marry one's god-child, or one's god-parents' children (cf. Stirrat 1975: 595). Partly for these reasons, the relationship between god-parent and god-child has been likened to one of "complementary filiation" (Pitt-Rivers 1958; Gudeman 1971: 46).

In many Roman Catholic societies, especially those of Latin America, the institution of god-parenthood (*compadrazgo* in Spanish) is an important element in the political and economic, as well as the kinship and religious systems. In this context, it is the third set of relationships, between the child's parents and god-parents, which is crucial (Mintz and Wolf 1950: 355). These *compadres* are under mutual obligations of generalized reciprocity. They lend each other money, and give manual or moral support at festival times, or when misfortune strikes.

In non-stratified, homogeneous societies, *compadres* are usually chosen horizontally, that is, from among one's own relatives, class, or community. But where there *is* social stratification of any kind, then *compadrazgo* links tend to operate vertically, with the god-parents being of higher status than the parents (ibid: 364). This helps explain why reverse choice, in which individuals are god-parents to each others' children, may sometimes be permitted, and is even occasionally prescribed, but is far more commonly prohibited (Gudeman 1975: 233). In individual cases, god-parents may be chosen for a wide variety of reasons. Sometimes this is a device to forestall economic competition, physical aggression, or the infringing of sexual rights. Sometimes there is a more positive motive, such as the desire to cement an economic partnership. But as a general rule, *compadrazgo* "is a mechanism that can be used to strengthen existing patterns, but not to change them" (ibid: 355). Unlike adoption, it is rarely used as a means of securing heirs to property, or successors to high office.

Clearly, then, god-parenthood may have all kinds of ramifications. Stirrat shows that in Sri Lanka at any rate, where god-parenthood has no economic or political implications (1975: 596) but does affect one's marriageability, the sociological roles people play at baptism can be understood fully only when marriage, too, is taken into account. Both baptism and marriage, he argues, serve ritually to deny the "naturalness" or "animality" of man (ibid: 604).

Godparenthood is restricted to Christian countries, of course. But it is only one example of a much wider phenomenon, ritual parenthood, which is in turn only one possible type of ritual kinship. You should be on the look out for such institutions as blood-brotherhood (Evans-Pritchard 1962 [1933]), "artificial kinship" (Bloch 1973: 78), and any other form of "fictive" or "figurative" pseudo-kinship. The distinction between "true" and "pseudo-" kin is not, of course, one that can be drawn by you yourself, the fieldworker, because *all* kinship is socially rather than biologically based (§8.7), and hence ultimately a matter of cultural convention. Only your informants can determine who are their "real" relatives, and who are not.

7.7 Kinship and cosmology

There are often links between social organization on the one hand, and religion – particularly cosmology – on the other. So in societies where social structure is primarily a matter of *kinship* structure, you should be on the look out for possible parallels between kinship and cosmology. Where present, these will make an essential contribution to your understanding of the local kinship system, and its overall importance to society. The significance of such data depends upon whether these parallels are recognized locally, or purely a product of your own observation. In either case, another whole book could easily be written on the topic. Here we can touch upon it in only the briefest way, but it must be stressed that this cursory treatment in no way reflects the importance of the subject matter.

The existence of links of this kind was recognized long ago. The Victorian interest in such topics as totemism was later given sociologically respectable form in the classics of the *Année sociologique* school, such as Durkheim and

Mauss's *Primitive Classification* (1970 [1903]), Hertz's "The pre-eminence of the right hand: a study in religious polarity" (1973 [1909]), and Durkheim's *The Elementary Forms of the Religious Life* (1915 [1912]). The Durkheimian view that religious cosmology is *modelled upon* social organization (ibid: 419) is no longer thought tenable, but the congruences between the two remain clear.

Parallels between cosmological and kinship structures are especially likely in societies with "elementary" kinship structures, systematic alliance relationships, and/or universal relationship terminologies. As we saw in §6.3.2, prescription entails an extensive, clearly structured relationship terminology, distinguishing marriageable persons from non-marriageable ones. Not surprisingly, the structural principles underlying this terminology tend to appear in systems of classification used for other purposes, too. For example (§7.4.3), the Purum have a system of asymmetric alliance. Every Purum male therefore recognizes three types of social grouping: his own, and those of his wife-givers and wife-takers. But when viewed as a whole, Purum society is seen to be founded upon a more basic dyad: after all, every group is a wife-taker to its own wife-givers, and a wife-giver to its own wife-takers. In fact, such conceptual dualism is fundamental in almost every sphere of Purum life. It provides

> a mode of classification by which things, individuals, groups, qualities, values, spatial notions, and other ideas of the most disparate kind are identically ordered within one system of relations. (Needham 1962: 95)

Such findings are particularly likely in isolated, pre-literate and small-scale societies. There is, for instance, the celebrated case of "dual" or moiety organization, where the dyadic principle is much more directly evident in social structure than in the Purum case (Lévi-Strauss 1968 [1952], 1968 [1956]). But there need not be this extreme degree of consistency and uniformity in the application of structural principles. Such a state of affairs would be most unlikely in large-scale, complex societies, but even they may display some limited correspondences between cosmic structure and either the structure of the relationship terminology or, less abstractly, the empirical disposition of residential or descent groupings. The forms these correspondences will take is impossible to know in advance. We can only urge you always to be aware of such possibilities.

Kinship and cosmology may be linked rather differently in societies containing sharply defined and structurally important kin groupings, such as unilineal clans or lineages. As in the classic Tallensi case (Fortes 1953; §5.2), many such societies have important cults of ancestor worship. Here the distinction between human ancestors and divine gods inevitably gets blurred, and may even disappear altogether. Lovedu cosmology reveals a Durkheimian "coherence of the social and ancestral worlds" (Krige and Krige 1943: 239). Moreover, these ancestors are the only deities of any practical significance, so that every family has its own, separate and distinctive set of gods (ibid: 231). Not all lineage-based societies lack transcendent deities, of course. The Nuer Sky God (Kwoth) is omnipresent, all-powerful, and the creator and sustainer of both the natural and social orders. But *kwoth* also comprises a multiplicity of "social refractions of God" (Evans-Pritchard 1956: 113), structured in the same pattern as the lineages whose members worship them. Nuer use a genealogical metaphor to express the relationship between Spirit and these other, encompassed spirits. Lesser spirits are said to be agnatic relatives of Kwoth – his sons or even his grandsons – while the lowest spirits of all are related to him only cognatically, as his daughters' or even his grand-daughters' children (ibid: 119–120). So the Nuer "spirit genealogy" is immanent in, and congruent with, the empirical disposition of Nuer social groupings. This is not the only possible way of linking genealogy and cosmology, though. As we mentioned earlier (§2.4), genealogies often connect real persons or groups to mythical, divine or semi-divine ancestors. The Lugbara of Uganda, for instance, link up the genealogies of their legendary "hero-ancestors" directly with those of actual, existing lineages and human ancestors (Middleton 1954, 1960: 235–236).

One of the most widespread motifs in mythology and folklore is the portrayal of creation as an act of cosmogonic incest (Thompson 1961). This seems particularly common in unilineal societies. Usually, brother–sister incest is involved, and this of course represents a violation of exogamic rules as well as of incest prohibitions. The same is true of cosmogonic parent–child incest, though it is much less common. It seems to involve F–D incest in patrilineal societies, and M–S incest in matrilineal ones (Moore 1964). Some-times, royal or aristocratic members of such societies commit incest them-selves, symbolically or in fact, thereby re-enacting the creation of their people in accordance with the myth. Once again, the Lovedu exemplify this (Krige and Krige 1943: 5ff.). There is clearly a connection between this mythic motif and the contemporary social reality, in which the cattle-linked sister is just as responsible for the birth and legitimacy of her brother's children as is their mother.

Myths and folk-tales of all types are, of course, fruitful sources of information about many aspects of kinship. In particular, they often express the overt ideology of kinship, and dramatize the expectations and attitudes which different types of relative may legitimately hold towards one another. While this type of material takes on especial cultural importance in pre-literate societies, it is by no means restricted to them. For instance, Tamil temple myths belong to one of the oldest literary traditions in the world. None the less, Shulman's (1980) brilliant analyses of them are full of insights for the anthropologist. Just as different South Indian groupings control the sexuality of their members in ritual ways congruent with other aspects of their social structure, so do the temple myths offer differing solutions to the central problem with which all of them deal: the marriage of god and goddess, and the subsequent, though concealed, sacrifice of the former by his bride.

Human beings everywhere tend to orient their dwellings, or even entire settlements, in accordance with their cosmological notions. It is, of course, equally likely that their habitations should be structured according to kinship criteria. Durkheim and Mauss (1970 [1903]) drew attention to this possibility, citing Cushing's controversial work on the Zuñi Indians (1896). Lévi-Strauss (1968 [1952], 1968 [1956]) later examined similar evidence from North and South America, Melanesia (cf. Malinowski 1932: Fig. 1), and Indonesia. You should study village layouts and residential patterns, particularly in remote or small-scale communities, with cosmic as well as kinship questions in mind.

The design of the individual dwelling-houses themselves may also express and embody both cosmological and kinship notions. In Sierra Leone, the houses of the Temne are oriented with respect to cosmological space, and serve to protect their legitimate occupants (the family members) from harmful spiritual forces emanating from outside. They can even cure illness among their occupants: for instance, a sore throat caused by a sister-in-law's grudge can be cured if she pours water down over the eaves for the victim to drink (Littlejohn 1960: 77).

The cosmological and sociological significance of household design have now been documented many times over, for peoples as far afield as the Berber of North Africa (Bourdieu 1971), and the Atoni of Indonesian Timor (Cunningham 1973). One of the finest such studies is Tambiah's demonstration that rules pertaining to sex and marriage, the classification and edibility of animal species, and the classification of space in general, are all related to the spatial ordering of the domestic dwelling-house, in the villages of northeast Thailand (1969). The study of household design may not always yield such rich rewards, but is bound to tell you something of interest. Pay particular attention to any restrictions, injunctions, or prohibitions regarding access to or use of the various parts of the house by specific groups or categories of people.

7.8 Band societies: minimal kinship or maximal kinship?

Finally in this chapter, it is worth raising again the issue of what in fact constitutes "kinship". To illustrate our view that kinship is, or may be, so completely bound up with other social institutions that it is impossible to isolate it, we shall look briefly at one extreme case which is currently under debate, namely "kinship" in hunter-gatherer societies.

Contemporary foraging societies are typically small-scale and egalitarian, with flexible band composition and a heavy dependence on seasonal resources. Contrary to Steward (1955: 127–134) and Service (1962: 61–63), "patrilineal" or "patrilocal" bands are virtually unknown except in Aboriginal Australia. Instead, one finds residential patterns created by residence rules (§5.5), but in which a choice of residence exists. People move in and out of bands for reasons of availability of resources, and also for social reasons connected with disputes, alliances, gift relationships, marriages, and so on. Such changes should be observed carefully, and you should find out why any given individual does change his place of residence, associate with whom he does, or enter into particular alliances.

Some hunter-gatherers, such as the Mbuti Pygmies, appear to have *minimal kinship* in every sense. They possess neither lineages nor corporate, extended family groups. Kinship obligations do not extend beyond the nuclear family. Even relationship terms are used virtually only within this range, and have little sociological significance (Turnbull 1966: 110, 268–272). Meillassoux (1981: 26–30) has contrasted this situation with that in small-scale cultivating societies, which typically have lineages, clans and complementary filiation, and argues that the different attitudes to kinship are due to differing attitudes towards land and labour. These in turn stem from differences in the relations of production.

Similarly, Woodburn (1980: 98–99, 1982: 432–433) distinguishes "immediate-return" societies, in which food is procured with minimal investment of labour time and distributed immediately, from "delayed-return" societies, in which time must be spent making fishing-nets, keeping livestock, planting, and so on. In the latter case, a surplus must be generated to feed those engaged in these delayed subsistence activities. Immediate-return societies, which comprise only hunter-gatherers (and not even all of them), are characterized by considerable flexibility and a lack of kin group organization.

Yet not all immediate-return societies seem as lacking in "kinship" as the Mbuti. The Hadza, and various Bushman peoples, have similar economic relations and flexible residential arrangements, and yet apply relationship terms universally. It could be argued that this, paradoxically, does after all resemble the Mbuti case, since where *everyone* is classed as "kin", there is again no "kinship" as we usually think of it. Instead, other institutions, such as formalized gift-giving relationships among Nharo and !Kung Bushmen, cross-cut close kinship ties and the universally applied relationship categories. These kinship-like networks are based on both friendship and economic interests, and pay no necessary regard to age, sex, genealogical link or relationship category (Marshall 1976: 303–311; Barnard 1978b: 625–626).

If you encounter such systems of gift-giving (which are not, of course, restricted to immediate-return hunter gatherers), pay close attention to the relationships, of "kinship" and of other kinds, between gift-giving partners, and find out the full social implications of such transactions. This may not be as easy as it sounds. At least ten ethnographers worked with the !Kung before one (Wiessner 1977) discovered that non-subsistence gift exchange overlies a system of rights of access to water and other subsistence resources. In Sahlins' (1974 [1965]) terms, !Kung gift exchange is a form of (delayed) balanced reciprocity, and the rights to resources are a form of generalized reciprocity. The "para-kin" relationships (Barnard, *loc. cit.*) thus take over functions usually reserved for "kinship".

8 *The culture of kinship*

8.1 Introduction

It is clearly insufficient, when dealing with *action* – that is, behaviour which has meaning for the actor (Weber 1964: 88) – to be content with describing the externally observable aspects of that action, or with a statistical account of "typical action". The notions, theories, opinions and motivations of the actors themselves come into play here. In this final chapter, we concentrate upon the notions and theories concerning kinship, held by members of particular societies. As we shall see (§8.2), they raise special problems which call into question many of the premises of traditional ethnography. In particular, the relationship between such notions and actual, observed kinship practice needs to be considered (§8.3).

Cultural *rules* have been dealt with extensively above, but our present interests extend beyond purely jural factors. The emphasis here will be upon local explanations of these rules, and the indigenous biological and socio-logical theories underlying them. In particular, we shall discuss views about the mechanisms of procreation, birth, and genetic inheritance (§8.4); notions of consanguinity (§8.5); and the reasons for, as opposed to the formal logic of, the terminological distinctions drawn between different types of relative, and between relatives and non-relatives (§8.5.2). We examine various theoretical approaches to such data (§8.6), which lead us finally to reconsider the relationship between kinship and biology (§8.7), and hence the meaning of the term "kinship" itself, for both informants and anthropologists (§8.8). Much of this chapter is provisional or inconclusive. That seems inevitable, not only because the kinds of study dealt with here are in their infancy, but also because of the complex character of the material itself.

8.2 The collection of cultural data

8.2.1 *The sociology of knowledge*

Phrases of the form "The Bongo-Bongo believe that . . .", once abounded in ethnographic writing, but can no longer be considered acceptable, on two counts. First, as a fieldworker you are concerned primarily with the theories and systems of classification – in short, the collective representations – of society, not with the emotional attitudes of its individual members towards these theories and systems. It is not a matter of their "belief in" a particular set of ideas, but of their "knowledge about" them (cf. Ryle 1963: 129). This is true even when the information in question comes to you under the explicit guise of "a belief" – the Christian creed, for instance. We have no means of knowing the inner feelings of even a professed Christian reciting that creed (Leach 1968: 655). The very idea of "believing" is itself peculiar to English speaking peoples. It designates one segment within the range of emotional conditions which they habitually recognize and distinguish (Needham 1972: 50). In short, "belief" is a polythetic and culturally specific notion, which even Britons and Americans apply in subtly different ways (ibid: 40). "Knowledge", by contrast, is an externally verifiable though – as we shall see – not unproblematic condition.

Secondly, in other societies as in our own, people's knowledge is likely to differ in range and extent, and their opinions about it may be internally or externally contradictory. For instance, Geertz and Geertz (1975: 1) report that

> intelligent Balinese from the same village may give completely variant accounts of matters that the ethnologist believes are crucial to his formulation.

At the very least, every topic has its self-styled or generally acknowledged experts, as well as its laymen. There may well be disagreements both within and between these groups.

Conversely, people may have no explicit theories whatever on particular matters of interest to anthropologists. Leach (1966: 47) gives the example of the British wedding ceremony. Its overall structural logic is clear enough, but is none the less known to only a tiny fraction of bridal couples. This in no way prevents the "ignorant" majority from celebrating their weddings in legally, aesthetically and symbolically satisfactory ways, a fact which raises the whole thorny question of the relationship between knowledge and behaviour (cf. Holy and Stuchlik 1981: 26–28).

As our later discussions (especially §8.3, §8.6.4) will show, the inability of informants to provide a theoretical account of, or ideological justification for, their behaviour, is less of a drawback for the fieldworker than might at first appear, because of the problematic nature of such data. None the less, it is obviously essential that you determine and report systematically the sociology of all cultural knowledge. The basic questions are, briefly (i) *who* appeals to (ii) *what* terms of notions, and (iii) *when*? Let us consider these in order.

(i) Knowledge may be unevenly distributed among the various groupings or categories of persons of which the society is composed. For instance, it may be necessary to contrast men and women, young and old, rich and poor, high class or caste and low, and so on.

(ii) The knowledge itself is rarely a coherent, or even consistent set of terms or principles. Inconsistencies or possible alternative views should be noted. Beware of apparent lacunae in people's thinking, which are in fact merely the consequence of variations in context.

(iii) It is a commonplace in anthropology that logic is situational. So when alternative modes of explanation are available, try to clarify the circumstances under which each is used. By so doing, you will also make clear genuine cases of disagreement.

Stated generally in this way, these points seem trite and self-evident, but putting them into practice will be tedious, time consuming, and extremely demanding upon your skill as a fieldworker. The resulting detail may be equally demanding upon your future readers too (cf. Barth 1975). Yet no analysis claiming to deal with indigenous culture is of any value unless the "who?" and "when?" questions are answered, in addition to the "what?".

8.2.2 *Methods of investigation*

This brings us to the next issue, that of how to obtain the necessary data. There are established techniques for collecting genealogies (§2.5), relationship terms (§3.3), and so on, but "cultural" information cannot usually be obtained by standard procedures worked out in advance and transferable from one field situation to another. Tyler (1969) reprints several attempts to do this, but even Conklin's so-called "ethnogenealogical method" is in fact overwhelmingly concerned with the analysis of such data rather than their acquisition. On the latter he says merely that:

Depending largely on recorded conversations in local settings and on un-
intentional as well as intentional 'mistakes', I tallied and checked the use of kin
terms, personal names, nicknames, etc., with known genealogical positions.
(1969 [1964]: 102)

We have already discussed this type of activity in §3.3, and it does not seem
possible to achieve greater methodological precision without a corresponding loss of generality. For that reason, this chapter is not concerned with
explicit methods, but with discussing and illustrating the kinds of difficulty
which may arise.

You cannot even frame questions so as to elicit local theories and opinions
unless you know the correct wording to use. This may sound paradoxical,
because we are in effect saying that you cannot investigate the local culture
unless you already know what it is. Paradox or not, that is more or less the
case in practice. It may even be dangerously misleading to blunder in with a
series of direct questions, however "correct" these might appear according to
your grammars and dictionaries.

Imagine a foreign anthropologist who is investigating ideas about conception and genetics in a supposedly scientifically-minded Western society. He
waylays his informants at their homes or in the street and asks, out of the
blue: "Good morning. What is your indigenous theory of conception?"
Clearly, he will be very lucky indeed if he receives meaningful answers,
though his experiences may well shed unexpected light on many other
interesting facets of local life! For instance, even though his question is
grammatically correct and admirably precise, some people will not understand it, either because it is too abstract or because it is out of context. Others
may give him incorrect, vague, or poorly understood accounts of modern
medical thinking on the subject. It is even possible that he might record
occasional, mysterious references to storks and gooseberry bushes.

Problems are particularly likely to arise with questions requiring "yes" or
"no" answers. Such questions may not mean what you thought they meant,
in which case you will not fully comprehend the replies either. Again, they
may suggest "alternatives" which are not perceived as such by your
informants, at least in that context. Here, any answer can at best be *ad hoc*, at
worst meaningless. Remember that people may feel constrained to answer
even such meaningless questions – out of politeness, for instance. They may
also, of course, give wrong answers – whatever that means – by mistake or by
deliberately telling you a lie: you will, however, usually discover this
eventually if you question enough people. About the only general pieces of
advice we can give are: first, ask as few direct questions as possible in the early

stages of investigation; secondly, ask them in the form "What does X mean
...?" (X being some word or notion which you have come across).

Not only the form of the question is important, but also its timing. You are
likely to gain much more satisfactory results by investigating matters already
uppermost in people's minds. If you want to explore ideas concerning
marriage or procreation, ask first among families currently planning or
experiencing such events. Better still, before asking any questions at all, listen
to their discussions on these matters, trying to pick out the key words and
phrases in terms of which these discussions are conducted. Enquire into the
meanings of these terms and only then use them to phrase questions of your
own. There is, finally, the matter of "test by praxis" (Holy and Stuchlik 1981:
24). In the field of kinship, you are unlikely to be able to "duplicate actors'
performances" (ibid) in matters such as the choosing of a spouse, the con-
ducting of a wedding, or even in the organization of your domestic household. You can, however, try to infer in advance, from your knowledge of local
rules and other notions, just what is likely to happen in a given situation. To
the extent that you are successful in this, you are as close to grasping the rules
and notions current in that society as its actual members. They themselves,
remember, may disagree quite fundamentally over the models which they
employ: our search for *the* "correct" folk model is usually misconceived
(ibid: 25).

8.3 Rules and practices

As we said, traditional ethnography has been concerned largely with jural
information, a fact reflected in this book by our repeated references to rules:
rules of succession, inheritance and descent, positive and negative marriage
rules, rules governing incest and adultery, and so on. The classic general
works of kinship, such as Radcliffe-Brown's introduction to *African Systems
of Kinship and Marriage* (1950), Fortes' "The structure of unilineal descent
groups" (1970 [1953]), and even Lévi-Strauss's *Elementary Structures*
(1969), are primarily concerned with just such normative information.
Actual practices are used, if at all, to illustrate adherence to these norms, or
demonstrate the consequences of their breach.

It is hard to imagine an ethnography written without reference to jural and
normative considerations, and we certainly do not advocate such a course.
None the less, an over-emphasis on such matters raises problems on two
counts. There is first of all the matter of the precise ontological status of such
data. They are not, as we have seen, necessarily "believed in", but merely

obeyed or disobeyed. In view of this, what exactly is their explanatory status for the analyst? We shall have more to say on this in §8.3.2. Secondly, there is the relationship between them and the social practices they allegedly regulate. The tendency has been to treat behaviour which conforms to stated rules as unproblematic, and to seek further explanations (usually external to kinship itself) only when rules are "broken". Such breaches may for instance be attributed to some pre-emptive individual interest, perhaps economic or political in nature. Yet given that jural rules (as opposed to prescriptions (§6.3.2)) are *by definition* breakable, it is just as necessary to explain cases in which they are "obeyed". In any situation, an individual has two choices: either adhere to the relevant jural norms of his society, or violate them. Why, in practice, is one course chosen rather than the other?

8.3.1 *Parallel cousin marriage*

This question has recently been examined for the revealing case of parallel cousin marriage (see also §7.4.2), a phenomenon particularly common in the Islamic countries of the Middle East and North Africa. The practice presents several puzzles for conventional anthropological wisdom. For "descent theory" the difficulty is that such marriages occur *within* the patrilineage, thereby clouding the distinctions between "descent" and "filiation", and "descent" and "kinship" (§5.3). For "alliance theory" the situation is even worse, because such marriages seem to violate the fundamental notions of exogamy, alliance and exchange. It seems, then, that the existence of parallel cousin marriage shows both approaches to be geographically and conceptually localized. Neither can claim to be universal.

Perhaps because of this difficulty in reconciling it with the accepted theoretical approaches, analysts of parallel cousin marriage have tended to explain it in terms of factors from outside kinship proper. Unfortunately, the conclusions reached by different writers are in some respects contradictory. Barth (1954) sees this form of marriage as reinforcing the unity of the lineage, thereby *limiting* its tendency to undergo fission à la Fortes. For Murphy and Kasdan (1959: 24) by contrast, it *contributes* directly to the extreme fission of agnatic lines, "encysting" the resulting primary segments and encouraging a set of wider unities, which extend in the limiting case to recognition of the common origins of all Arabs. Bourdieu (1977: 32) points out that although their conclusions differ, both approaches "explain" the practice in terms of its function, not for the individuals most directly concerned but for society as a whole. This is fair enough so long as one does not claim *causal* status for such social functions, but these particular functional accounts are criticized by Bourdieu on more fundamental grounds too (see below).

Cuisenier (1962) does deal with the functional consequences of marriage choice for individuals. Using data from North Africa, he incorporates both adherence to and deviation from the patrilateral preference, into a statistical model. Thus, ideally, one brother in a family marries in, to maintain group cohesion, while another marries out, to increase the group's range of alliances. By attaching different statistical weights to these two practices, Cuisenier produces a formula which expresses the observed rate of adherence to the *bent' amm* (FBD) preference.

But this is a *post facto* formalization of the observed statistical pattern, and says nothing about the reasons for individual choices in particular cases. Moreover, Bourdieu (1977: 33) regards all these approaches as perverse, since they express themselves in terms of exogamy and endogamy, the very anthropological categories which this practice, he feels, calls most into question. His view is that lineage models and other genealogically-based constructs encountered by anthropologists in other societies, are not objective, factual statements about perceived biological and affinal connections, but depictions of "the universe of theoretical relationships within which individuals or groups define the real space of . . . *practical* relationships" (ibid: 18; orig. emphasis). In other words, the genealogical evidence adduced by a given individual in a particular social situation, depends upon both the nature of that situation and the aspirations and interests of the individual *at that particular time*. Jural analyses, being so frequently atemporal, omit a crucial element in the strategic use of rules (ibid: 5–6; cf. also Holy and Stuchlik 1981: 26–27).

This is easiest to understand with reference to an actual example, namely Peters' study of the Bedouin, which Bourdieu also cites. Bedouin describe their own society as composed of lineages in the classic Fortesian pattern (Peters 1967: 274). Parallel cousin marriage, they say, is practised wherever possible. Feuding may occur between secondary lineage segments, *unless* these contain affines or maternal relatives (ibid: 275). Deviations from these last two precepts are acknowledged to occur, but are ascribed to contingent circumstances. What Bedouin fail to recognize, Peters argues, is that "these 'contingencies' are ecologically, economically, demographically, and politically essential" (ibid). In this case, the lineage model is not sociologically valid, but merely "a frame of reference used by a particular people to give them a common-sense kind of understanding of their social relationships" (ibid: 261). It is only one of "a field of components arranged in a specific fashion to meet the interests of men at a particular time" (ibid: 281). So for Peters,

Bedouin genealogies are ideological representations of current relationships. Bourdieu agrees, and adds:

> Once family property is divided and there is nothing to recall and maintain the genealogical relationship, the father's brother's daugher may be considered no closer . . . than any other patrilateral (or even matrilateral) cousin. On the other hand, a genealogically more distant cousin may be the practical equivalent of the *bent'amm* when the two cousins are part of a strong-united 'house' living under one elder and owning all its property in common. (1977: 33)

We have encountered similar situations before, in our discussion of lineages and descent (§5.4), but Bourdieu develops the argument further. Genealogical uses of kinship, he argues, function to order and legitimize the social world. Abstract theoretical units such as unilineal descent groups constitute "the group's self-representation" (ibid: 35), and exist only in official contexts. These must be distinguished from practical kinship units, which "exist only through and for the particular functions [for] which they have been *effectively mobilised*" (ibid; orig. emphasis). For instance, it is "practical kin who make marriages; it is official kin who celebrate them" (ibid: 34).

Kinship, he argues, should be seen not as a set of normative ideals, but "in the form of the practices which produce, reproduce and use them" (ibid: 35). Those aspects of kinship practice which serve to *reproduce* the prevailing social conditions, are of course pre-eminently marriage, procreation and inheritance (§7.3.2). But that is to view things at the level of the group. For individuals, these activities are "the product of strategies . . . oriented towards the satisfaction of material and symbolic interests". These strategies occur in the context of the "determinate set of economic and social conditions" which they help reproduce (ibid). In short, social conditions and social practices exist in a dialectical relationship: the former partly determine the latter but are simultaneously shaped by them (ibid: 3).

Now the determining social conditions in Arab countries contain a basic contradiction. The relationship between brothers is the cornerstone of the family structure, and yet its weakest point. Every set of brothers is a potential point of lineage segmentation, especially since they are likely to have divergent property interests. Parallel cousin marriage unites the offspring of these brothers, and thus constitutes "the ideological resolution, sometimes realised in practice, of this contradiction" (ibid: 64). One marries according to the possibilities of the social situation one finds oneself in at the time, and the options available in the form of marriageable women. But if one can simultaneously present this mixture of self-interest and expediency in the guise of "obedience to a rule", so much the better. One will then be better respected as well as better-off. It is because it serves both strategic and ethical interests that parallel cousin marriage is "a favoured object of manipulation" (ibid: 43).

One very general and straightforward point of method emerges from this. It is not sufficient for you to record the "marriage rules" of the studied society. It is also necessary to show why, in particular cases, these rules were either obeyed or disobeyed. But there is another less obvious conclusion. The rules are not simply incomplete accounts of what actually goes on in a society, but are also, by their very nature, misleading in a way which fieldworking anthropologists, of all people, will find difficult to detect.

8.3.2 *Official and practical kinship*

Bourdieu shows wittily and convincingly just why the fieldworker is particularly attracted by the siren-song of the jural rule. When questioned by anthropologists, well-informed persons produce replies which are inadequate in several ways. First, such people are by definition extremely familiar with the matters under discussion, and so "leave unsaid all that goes without saying" (1977: 18). That is, their accounts take for granted a whole corpus of more basic knowledge, as well as an awareness of the past and of how things turn out in practice, which you as an outsider simply do not share. This is compounded by the fact that, being oriented towards an outsider, the exposition tends *deliberately* to avoid direct references to actual cases (ibid). Secondly, formal questioning inevitably produces answers which are formalized rationalizations, and "of a *semi-theoretical* disposition" (ibid; orig. emphasis). Such answers allude freely to rules and morality, but conceal the fact that social *practice* obeys quite different principles. Practice operates on the basis of "*learned ignorance* . . . a mode of practical knowledge not comprising knowledge of its own principles" (ibid; orig. emphasis). This gives the false impression that action – social practice – is the "mere execution of the model" (ibid: 29).

Indigenous "explanations" in terms of laws, rules, morals, and norms, far from being the philosopher's stone which some anthropologists have claimed (§8.6), are in fact doubly dangerous for fieldworkers. First, they provide a misleading picture of social practice, which is after all the main concern of *social* anthropology. Secondly, and more insidiously, they reinforce the intellectualist, objectivist tendencies so characteristic of modern Western thought. For instance, the fact that anthropologists themselves made so much use of genealogies (as we have done in Chapters 2 and 3), long prevented them from realizing that their informants were often using genealogical discourse in quite different ways. The anthropologist seeks "scientific objectivity", and so strives to discover the "true" genealogical relationships in a community, but actual members of that community may use their genealogies like Lévi-Strauss's celebrated *bricoleur*, taking fragments from here and there to shore up the immediate and practical concerns of their lives.

Rules, then, are not such important determinants of social action as has commonly, and largely implicitly, been assumed. Another major principle governing practice is "habitus" or practical knowledge, which your informants cannot enunciate because they are not aware of its principles. What they provide you with is a *manifestation* of habitus rather than an explanation of it. Whether you agree with Bourdieu in every particular or not, there is plenty of food for thought here. You cannot fail to recognize during your fieldwork that in some respects indigenous "explanations" create more problems than they solve. They are not privileged insights, nor the key with which to unlock your analytical understanding, but merely a category of *data* (Holy and Stuchlik 1981: 9–10) which, like any other, needs to be incorporated into your analysis. And as data, they have proved curiously intransigent.

8.4 Theories of procreation

8.4.1 *"Virgin birth"*

In the last section we saw that cultural data are both hard to collect and complicated to interpret. We can learn something about the problems of interpretation from the celebrated "virgin birth" debate. This title is something of a misnomer, since the arguments – at least in so far as we consider them here – concern parthenogenesis (Spiro 1968a: 249). Are there entire peoples in the world who are ignorant of the facts of physiological paternity?

This issue has been debated since the nineteenth century, and particularly with reference to the reports of Roth (1903) from Queensland, and Malinowski from the Trobriands (for a bibliography of earlier discussions, see Leach 1966: 46). Malinowski's interpretation of the Trobriand evidence seemed to change over time. Here we consider briefly his main ethnographic statement, in Chapter 7 of *The Sexual Life of Savages* (1932: 140–178).

When a person dies, their spirit (*baloma*) moves to the Island of the Dead for a time, but eventually returns to earth. It enters a woman's body through her head or, according to a less authoritative view, her vagina. In her womb it is nourished by blood – hence the cessation of menstruation during pregnancy. As virgins cannot conceive, sexual intercourse is clearly a necessary preliminary to conception, but its sole function is "mechanical dilation" (ibid: 155). It opens the woman's vagina and provides space for the child to grow. Male semen has no role in this process. One man is quoted as follows:

> Blood on the head makes child. The seminal fluid does not make the child. Spirits bring at night time the infant, put on women's heads – it makes blood. Then, after two or three months, when the blood does not come out, they know: 'Oh, I am pregnant!' (ibid: 160)

A second man states: "Copulation alone cannot produce a child. Night after night, for years, girls copulate. No child comes." He adds that the missionaries "talk that seminal fluid makes child. Lie! The spirits indeed bring [children] at night time" (ibid: 161; orig. gloss).

Leach has argued that this evidence does *not* demonstrate ignorance of physiological paternity among the Trobrianders of that period. After all, the persons just quoted were clearly aware of physiological theories. Instead, their explicit denial of paternity expressed a metaphysical rather than a literal truth (1966: 45). It is an article of Trobriand dogma that "the mother's husband is an affine and not a pater or a genitor in the sense that these terms are commonly used" (1968: 656). This view provoked an argument which rumbled on in the pages of *Man* during 1968–1969, raising *ad hominem* and theological issues of no concern to us here. More relevantly, Spiro disagreed that Trobrianders and Australians "really" knew all about paternity. He argued that the views elicited by Malinowski were the "true" beliefs of the Trobrianders, literal statements of the situation as they perceived it. When a man makes a statement of that kind, says Spiro, "unlike some anthropologists, I believe him" (1966: 112). Spiro and Leach use the same ethnographic evidence, but present it very differently. Both are content that you should judge for yourself which reading is the more accurate (Leach 1968: 656; Spiro 1968b: 656), and here we discuss only the interpretations they offer to account for that evidence.

Spiro suggests two alternative "functional explanations". The first, a variant of one offered by Malinowski himself, is that since Trobrianders and Australians genuinely do not know about physiological paternity, their non-procreative theories of conception satisfy their intellectual curiosity concerning this crucial and otherwise inexplicable part of their lives (1968a: 255). The purely sociological basis which they assign to paternity, is therefore "the unintended . . . function of the natives' ignorance of physiological paternity" (ibid: 256). Note that this is explicitly a matter of cause and effect.

Spiro's second suggestion is that Trobrianders may, after all, know about physiological fatherhood, but repress this knowledge to resolve their Oedipal conflicts. In this way, a man "denies the painful fact that his conception was caused by the sexual intercourse of his parents" (ibid: 251). Here Spiro seems to be saying, admittedly in a very different idiom, more-or-less what he takes such exception to in Leach's argument, namely that the Trobrianders have both a public, parthenogenetic dogma, and a private ("repressed") knowledge of physiological fatherhood. There are some difficulties with his particular formulation, though. First, it does not in itself explain why Trobriand or Australian *women* should hold similar views, if and when they do. Secondly, are you satisfied that Trobriand men – or men anywhere, for that matter – really do have Oedipus complexes? It is almost certainly beyond our power to convince you one way or the other. Thirdly, Spiro repeatedly invests society itself with a psyche. For instance, he contrasts the "personal beliefs" of individuals with the "cultural beliefs" of society as a whole. In this case, he argues, the former are repressed in favour of the latter. Again, he sees these theories of procreation as "the attempts of social *groups* to *cope* with tensions" (1968a: 258; emphases added). We agree most emphatically with Leach that, on the contrary, "social groups are no more capable of 'coping' or experiencing . . . 'tension' . . . than . . . of suffering from . . . stomach ache" (1968: 656). Beware of such psychologistic forms of expression in your own writing.

For his part, Leach connects the Trobriand "dogma" to their matrilineality, and to their myths concerning the land of Kaytalugi (Malinowski 1932: 156), which is peopled with voracious nymphomaniacs. Both the theory and the mythology belong "to a society with virilocal matriliny, likewise class stratified, in which women are given as tribute to political leaders" (Leach 1966: 44). However, Leach (1966: 39, 1968: 655) explicitly refutes the idea that there are simple, causal connections among these phenomena.

8.4.2 *Knowledge and ignorance in the case of paternity*

Leach raised another issue which others have taken up. What precisely does it *mean* to say that certain persons know or do not know that sexual intercourse "causes" pregnancy? The British cultural view is that intercourse is a necessary preliminary to pregnancy, but that conception does not automatically follow. Biologists, from whom the more precise statements of these views derive, can give no advance assurance that conception will occur in any particular case. They are merely able to specify, with increasing precision, the necessary preconditions for conception (see also Schneider 1968a: 128). Like Trobriand and Australian women, they are reduced to recognizing actual pregnancy "by certain physiological signs after the event" (Leach 1966: 47). In short, intercourse is not seen by them as *sufficient* in itself to cause pregnancy, whose actual incidence is "as mysterious to [them] as it is to any Australian" (Leach 1968: 655).

Schwimmer suggests therefore that the only difference between ourselves and the Trobrianders is that we are able to show that their theory, as reported by Malinowski, is wrong (1969: 133). However, since "our" theory has nothing to say about the ultimate cause of pregnancy, it in no way contradicts the reported Trobriand view on *that* matter. Moreover, Schwimmer places perhaps too great a faith in the ability of science to provide proof. Proof for whom? It is easy to "disprove" arguments based upon premises very different from one's own, but would such "proofs" convince the Trobrianders themselves?

Clearly, knowledge and ignorance are not the distinct and mutually exclusive opposites that they at first appear to be. In this connection, Powell's contribution to the debate is particularly interesting. He encountered among Trobrianders, not only that theory reported by Malinowski, but also a second, that "semen acts as a coagulant of menstrual blood, producing a clot which a spirit child (*baloma*) enters . . . and which [then] proceeds to grow" (1956: 277; quoted by Leach 1966: 48). This second version is entirely consistent with recognition of physiological paternity, and even with modern medical theories of conception. Powell tried to argue that the two theories were contradictory, but Trobrianders denied this. *Both* were true, but whereas Malinowski's version was valid for "formal situations, e.g., matters of land ownership", the owner was "what fathers or their sisters told children as they became old enough" (ibid). Most Trobrianders use either set of ideas as the occasion demands, thereby displaying "pragmatic, rather than academic logic" (Powell 1968: 652).

This anticipates uncannily Bourdieu's distinction between formal and practical kinship (§8.3.2). Indeed, Leach, Powell and Bourdieu seem to be saying the same thing. People's statements about kinship in general, and procreation in particular, cannot be judged by criteria of truth or falsity, knowledge or ignorance, in any absolute sense. Their formal doctrines need express neither their personal state of knowledge nor their actual kinship practices. Moreover, *pace* Spiro, these doctrines have no necessary connections with individually-held "beliefs".

Finally, notice that the most general difference between Leach and Spiro is one of philosophical approach. Spiro seeks "final cause" theories or ultimate explanations. Thus, if – as he believes – some Australians, unlike most other peoples, "have not discovered the causal link between sexual intercourse and conception" (1968a: 256), then this is a problem requiring explanation. For Leach, ethnographic details simply exist: given their existence, they require not explanation but correlation. "I just want to put the pieces of the jig-saw together. When the pieces fit, I am interested" (1966: 44). The general point at stake is thus similar to that dividing Homans and Schneider (1955) from Needham (1962), in their respective readings of Lévi-Strauss. Homans and Schneider were of course wrong to assume that "elementary structures" were explicable purely in terms of emotional alignments among first cross-cousins, but this does not affect either way the validity of their premise that one should seek "final-cause" theories to account for fieldwork findings. That is something you must judge for yourself.

8.5 Consanguinity

In most societies, relatives of certain types are regarded as having purely social relationships with ego. Trobriand fathers may come into this category (depending upon your interpretation of the evidence in §8.4) and our "in-laws" certainly do. By contrast, certain other relationships are seen as having a biological as well as a social basis. This is often expressed in terms of a sharing of common "blood", or similar physiological attribute.

Recently anthropologists have begun to pay particular attention to statements of this kind. It is clear that members of different societies define "consanguinity" in different ways, correlating to some extent (though rarely, if ever, completely) with the structural characteristics of their relationship terminology, and their kinship system in general. But the problem is, how seriously should you take such views, if expressed by your informants, and to what extent should you allow them to tailor your own analysis?

8.5.1 *American kinship*

Cultural studies have always been more central to anthropology in North America than elsewhere. It is therefore doubly appropriate that a book by and about Americans, David Schneider's *American Kinship: A Cultural Account* (1968b), should have set the trend (and provided much of the basic vocabulary) for this recent upsurge in cultural kinship studies. Schneider treats kinship not as primarily a matter of corporate groups, individual or collective behaviour, nor yet of formal structures. Instead, his book is about kinship as "a system of symbols" (ibid: 18): the approach resembles that of Geertz (1966) to religion.

Americans, he argues, take it for granted that kinship belongs to the spheres of both nature and culture. Relatives are defined by their biological inter-relationships, generally through the medium of common "blood", and by the fact that they behave in ways appropriate to relatives. As Schneider puts it, in an idiom which has become standard among his fellow Chicagoans, kinship is a matter of both *natural substance* and *code for conduct* (1968b: 29).

This is not merely a restatement of the truism that kinship has both biological and social aspects. From the cultural viewpoint, it is not the supposedly objective facts of biology which concern us, but the local recensions of these facts. American (and British) cultural ideas about "blood relationships" are symbolic, not biological statements (ibid: 116). This point marks a perhaps surprising consensus between Schneider and Leach (§8.4.1), and is crucial to the understanding of our own thinking about kinship, both as members of our native societies and as anthropologists. Since their own "emic" view of kinship is based upon a "biological" model, Western anthropologists have often found it hard to free themselves from its conceptual straightjacket. Yet that is precisely what fieldworkers are required to do. We return to the distinction between kinship and biology below (§8.7); for the moment, we wish only to re-emphasize how important – and how difficult – it is to avoid unwitting ethnocentrism in this matter.

8.5.2 *Bengali kinship*

Of those analyses following and developing Schneider's approach, many have dealt with South Asia. Presumably this reflects the rich cultural material afforded by societies with such long literary, as well as verbal traditions. In their study of Bengali kinship, for example, Inden and Nicholas (1977) use information of both types.

First they ask whether Bengalis recognize a semantic domain equivalent to our "kinship". It seems that they do, although it is differently bounded from our own. Relatives in general are termed *ātmīya-svajana* ("one's own people"). Within this loosely defined category come the more precisely specified *jñāti-kuṭumba*. The "*jñāti* class is defined by a shared body, and the *kuṭumba* class by a body given or accepted in marriage" (ibid: 86). This sounds at first like merely another way of distinguishing consanguines and affines, but Inden and Nicholas deny this for two reasons. First, the two Bengali classes are not coterminous with the two anthropological ones. For instance, a man's *jñāti* include his W and the wives of all his male *jñāti*; a married woman's *jñāti* include her H and all his *jñāti* (ibid: 12). Such people are all "affines" in anthropological parlance. Secondly, whereas American culture distinguishes "nature" from "morality", Bengali culture "postulates a single, non-dualistically conceived order of substances, each of which possesses its own inherent code for conduct" (ibid: 86). The *jñāti* are those who *share* both bodily and non-bodily substances (food, land, etc.), while *kutumba* are those who *exchange* them (ibid: 88).

Each of these terms has both a general and a restricted sense. The restricted or "par excellence" *jñāti* resemble the "agnates" of anthropological analysis: for a man, they comprise the men, unmarried daughters, and wives of his own clan (*nijer kula*), that is, his F's clan (*pitṛ-kula*). For a married woman, her par excellence *jñāti* are the members of her H's clan (*pati-kula*) (ibid: 8). The "residual" *jñāti* class is similar to the anthropological class of "cognates". For instance, it includes the parents and brothers of ego's mother (ibid: 16). In neither case, though, are the Bengali categories *exactly* co-terminous with the anthropological ones. A man's par excellence *kutumba* comprise members of his W's natal clan, as well as his ZH, DH, FZH, and other men who have married women from his own *jñāti*. His residual *kutumba* include the same persons as his residual *jñāti*, viz., the members of his M's natal clan.

Inden and Nicholas proceed from these higher-order categories to the individual relationship terms applied by Bengalis to particular sub-sets of *jñāti* and/or *kutumba*. These terms

> convey meanings relevant to several different contexts and systems of classifica-
> tion, such as sex, age, and generation, at the same time that they speak of birth
> and shared or exchanged body relationships. (ibid: 90)

They argue that this approach succeeds in giving a coherent account of the North Indian relationship terminology, which has long resisted formal anthropological analyses of more traditional kinds (ibid: 89). Its principles are to be found at the level of cultural semantics, they claim, rather than in the regularities of genealogical specification and reciprocity.

It is clear even from this very brief summary that the deliberate focus upon local culture leads to a proliferation of vernacular words and phrases in the resulting analysis. This makes great demands upon general readers with no knowledge of Bengali or Sanskrit, but if it leads them to a new, deeper understanding of kinship, then the extra effort will have been worthwhile. So we need to ask, what are the strengths and weaknesses of granting priority to "cultural" data of both jural and categorical types? It is clearly wrong to assume that you can speak meaningfully about, say, consanguineal relatives as a generic category, ignoring the fact that this class is composed differently for Americans and Bengalis. But does this mean that *all* externally-derived analytical notions and procedures are invalid? If so, then comparative anthropology is impossible. But if not, where exactly should we draw the line?

8.6. Cognitive anthropology

8.6.1 *The study of meaning*

To help answer these questions, we shall consider some of the claims made by proponents of such methods. "Ethnosociology", the label attached to their own work by authors such as Inden, is a development of "cognitive anthropology" (cf. Tyler 1969), which has a similar focus but takes a less exalted view of itself.

Cognitive anthropologists recognize that systems of classification vary from one society to another, and so set out to collect and analyse these "folk models", which are often presented by them in taxonomic form. Relationship terminologies are, of course, particularly important types of classification in many societies. When we examine how cognitive anthropologists tackle the study of such terminologies, and compare their procedures with the more formal types of analysis dealt with earlier, especially in §3.6, there turns out to be a surprisingly close connection between the two, at least in the early work of writers like Goodenough (1956) and Lounsbury (1956). The similarities lie in the methods employed, rather than in the statuses of the models obtained.

In a purely formal sense, the "best" componential model of the relationship terminology is that which accounts for all and only the observed terminological categories, using the fewest possible componential dimensions. But for a cognitive anthropologist like Goodenough, such formal criteria are subordinated to the prime requirement of revealing what these relationship terms *mean* to their native users. "To describe a community's culture," he states, "one must learn what people in the community have had to learn" (1967: 1203).

The notion of "meaning" is a complex one (§3.6.2). Relationship terms have *extensional* meanings: for instance, lists of all the individual persons to whom they may correctly be applied by ego. They also have *connotational* meanings, namely the images which they call to mind for native users. But componential analysis as practised by Goodenough deals only with "meaning" in the sense of *signification* (ibid: 1204). The signification of a term is the minimum amount of information one needs to know about a person, in order to justify applying the term to that person. In short, it is the *definition* of the term.

Even when the kind of meaning sought is restricted in this way, there may still be more than one way of defining the terms in a given terminology. In that case, we should choose the definition most likely to seem intuitively reasonable to a member of the culture. For instance, Goodenough (1969 [1965]: 257) acknowledges the *formal* validity of Wallace and Atkins' analysis of terms for consanguines in American English (1969 [1960]: 349; our Fig. 3.3). But as a potential informant, his own subjective feeling is that *brother* and *sister* somehow belong in the same set as *father, mother, son* and *daughter*, rather than with *uncle, aunt, nephew* and *niece*. There is structural support for this view, he argues, if one considers affines too, because all and only the six terms *father, mother, brother, sister, son* and *daughter* take the affixes *step-, -in-law* and *foster* (1969 [1965]: 267). This illustrates perfectly the purpose of componential analysis as Goodenough sees it, which is to provide a precise and rigorous means of portraying objectively "relationships for which otherwise we have only a subjective feel" (ibid: 285).

This amalgam of intuition and rigorous lexical analysis aims to be a "systematic, reliable technique" for making "statements about concepts in the native's 'cognitive world' " (Wallace 1969 [1965]: 397). But it does *not* purport to arrive at these statements by the same mental processes as are used by the natives themselves, nor does it seek to express them in the native format (cf. Goodenough 1967: 1207–1208). For instance, few speakers of American English will find immediately intelligible Goodenough's Rule 7, which states:

> Affinal kin types that are more than one degree of collateral distance from ego are not denoted by kinship lexemes but by two or more lexemes in descriptive constructions. (1969 [1965]: 276)

8.6.2 *Ethnosociology*

Ethnosociology goes much further than this. For example, Marriott and Inden (1977: 229) claim that India is characterized by monistic thinking of the kind reported by Inden and Nicholas (§8.5.2), and so cannot be accurately portrayed in terms of conventional, dualistic Western sociology. In particular, they summarize Indian thinking in the realm of kinship as follows. Every kinship group or category in Indian society, from entire castes to individual families, is believed to have its own peculiar defining qualities, which make up its corporate "code for conduct" (*dharma*) (Marriott and Inden 1977: 231). This code is present in the form of a particular corporeal property such as "blood" or "shared bodily substance", common to the entire group. This corporeal property is inborn just as physical characteristics are. It is transmitted from one generation to the next by a combination of physical and moral acts, such as sexual intercourse and marriage, respectively. Both types of act must be performed in accordance with certain rules, which ensure that the correct, different but complementary bodily substances are mixed and passed on to the offspring (ibid). The distinctive, monistic premise applies not only to kinship, but to all other aspects of social life. In this respect, Indian thought can be seen to be as coherent and systematic as the sociologies of Weber or Parsons, and it demands to be taken seriously on its own terms (ibid: 229). This requires anthropologists not merely to try to understand Indian thought, but to "make themselves . . . somewhat like [Indians]" (Marriott 1976: 195).

Clearly these writers are justified in insisting that you should take seriously both the systems of classification of the people whom you study, and the principles which *they* see as underlying and structuring them. As in the case of consanguinity, imposition of your own classificatory principles from the very start can only cause you to misrepresent the situation. For instance, you will certainly fail to understand indigenous ideas fully if you ignore a whole sub-set of contexts to which they are applicable, merely because these do not form part of "kinship" according to *your* criteria. But is it possible to go too far the other way?

8.6.3 *Criticisms*

The cognitive and ethnosociological approaches have been criticized on several counts. First, it has been pointed out that ethnography is rarely as clear-cut and consistent as writers such as Marriott, Inden and Nicholas imply. For instance, it is commonly held in South India that a child's body derives from the father's semen, and its "spirit" from the mother's menstrual blood (Barnett 1976: 146). An alternative theory is that blood comes from both parents while "spirit" derives from an all-pervading "life-wind" having no connection with either parent (McGilvray 1982a: 53). In both cases, the mere fact that body and "spirit" are distinguished is clear evidence of dualistic thinking in India. This kind of objection could be overcome, in part at least, if fieldworkers who emphasized "cultural" data paid comparable attention to the sociology of cultural knowledge (§8.2.1). This tends to be true of the cognitive anthropologists, but much less so of the ethnosociologists. Blanket characterizations of American or Bengali "thought" involve so much selectivity between one person's views and another's, so much systematization by the analyst, that they can no longer reflect indigenous thinking to the extent that is claimed. The same might be said of many so-called "folk" taxonomies.

Secondly, claims that cultural data give unique insights into other societies (cf. Marriott and Inden 1977), are particularly vulnerable to the kinds of criticism advanced by Bourdieu (§8.3.2). What is important for *social* anthropology is not an abstraction like "Bengali thought", but the dialectical relationship between the ideas held by individual Bengalis, and their behaviour in particular kinds of social context.

Thirdly, these types of analysis tend towards solipsism (McGilvray 1982b). It is laudable, and indeed essential, to draw attention to the unique cultural features of particular human societies, but if one emphasizes these differences too much, one can easily end up by denying (as Marriott 1976 comes close to doing) that there is any common ground at all.

8.6.4 *Culture and comparison*

Yet the very basis of social anthropology is comparison. Usually you are an outsider to the society being studied, but even if you are not, it is the outsider's viewpoint that you will eventually be required to take. Consequently, the explanations offered by members of that society cannot simply be accepted by you at face value. From your viewpoint they are not explanations, but yet more facts which *need explaining*.

Consider the kinship systems of South India and Sri Lanka. Even leaving aside such exotics as the traditional Nayar and Nambudiri Brahmans (§6.4), we are confronted with a whole range of views concerning shared "blood" and "natural substance". By some, blood is seen as an inherited characteristic of the family or sub-caste, though it is not acquired purely patrilineally as in Bengal (cf. Barnett 1976: 147). But for others it is an attribute of the entire caste (David 1973: 525), or even of the whole of humanity (McGilvray 1982a: 29). On the other hand, some do not mention blood at all, or at least not unless the matter is raised by their anthropologist (Good 1980: 47).

Consequently, some say that a woman's blood or bodily substance changes when she marries, to become like her husband's (David 1973: 530), while others say that this happens only partially (Barnett 1976: 147): both views fit in with Marriott and Inden's claim that, in India, moral actions can transmute physical substances. But others in South Asia deny this, or have no opinion either way.

In spite of this cultural variety, the groups concerned have a great many socio-structural features in common. All classify their relatives into "cross" and "parallel" sets, and most prescribe marriage with certain categories of cross relative, with particular preferences for the MBDy, FZDy, and – in most cases – eZDy. Their wedding ceremonies display remarkable similarities in form and content, whose minor variations correlate with other widespread structural features, such as the modes of descent, post-marital residence, inheritance, and so forth (Good 1982b). In short, as anthropologists we know something that our informants themselves may not be aware of, namely that similar practices are widespread but are "explained" differently by other practitioners.

Given Bourdieu's position with regard to indigenous explanations, all this seems hardly surprising. In the circumstances though, comparisons among the various peoples of the region are best conducted at the level of social structure, as abstracted from their collective behaviour.

Let us try to draw together the threads of this complex discussion. It is wrong to approach another culture with a preconceived set of pigeonholes – "consanguines", "agnates", etc. – into which the ethnographic data are immediately fitted. You have to begin by taking account of local ideas and classificatory schemes, fitting the data into *these* pigenholes rather than your own. For the reasons given by Bourdieu, the implicit categories and classifications are of more use here than the explicit rules and ideologies. Those terms or distinctions which everybody uses but no-one bothers, needs (or is able?) to spell out, provide the framework into which your data should be set. We saw in §6.3.2 that prescriptions and preferences were "facts" of quite different order: the latter may by their very nature be disregarded in particular cases, but the former apply whatever happens. Likewise, in general, this implicit or tacit knowledge, this "practical knowledge not comprising knowledge of its own principles" (Bourdieu 1977: 18), is neither true nor false, neither obeyed nor disobeyed, but provides the vocabulary in terms of which the rules are expressed.

You should begin, then, with the indigenous vocabulary, allowing it to determine the range of your analytical interests with respect to both norms and behaviour. Try as far as possible not to present this vocabulary as more systematic and internally consistent than is actually the case. At the same time, note scrupulously any variations in that vocabulary between different persons, groups or social contexts.

Ultimately you will have to analyse all these types of data in terms of external, anthropological concepts, but as we argue below (§8.8), these should be defined *formally* and analytically rather than substantively. Comparison, too, should be based upon these formal concepts rather than the substantive ones of particular cultures. For instance, anthropologists draw a logical, formal distinction between "cross" and "parallel" relatives, as we have seen. One can compare relationship terminologies on the basis of the presence or absence of this feature, irrespective of whether the societies concerned recognize such a distinction themselves. Comparison should moreover be at a high level, involving whole systems rather than their elements. In a word, one can only compare *structures* – of words, ideas, or practices – not the individual components of those structures.

We do not pretend to have disposed adequately of all the issues raised here. For example, it could be argued that the "structures" just referred to are likely to be as monolithic, idealized, and insensitive to variations as the "cultural norms" we have been criticizing. Moreover, every "structure" is of course merely an element in a structure of higher order. None the less, several positive points have emerged: (i) cultural theories are to be treated as data, not as having explanatory value for outsiders; (ii) they must none the less be taken seriously, because your investigations should cover *entire*, emically-defined semantic domains; (iii) you do not impose your own substantive definitions of what is or is not "kinship"; instead, (iv) you conduct your analyses and comparisons in terms of formally-defined anthropological concepts.

8.7 Kinship and biology

We have already mentioned the importance of distinguishing "kinship" from "biology", and the difficulty with which European and American field-workers emancipate themselves from their own cultural views (§8.5.1). As this point is so crucial it is worth exploring further.

The debate we shall consider began in rather unlikely fashion, with Gellner (1957) considering the philosophical problem of the "ideal" (completely unambiguous) language. He suggested that the study of kinship terminology might provide a suitable avenue for investigation. As it happens, he went on to confuse relationship terminologies with systems of personal naming, but we need not pursue that particular issue here. Subsequent discussion centred around his contention, almost incidental to the main argument, that the term "kinship structure" has both a biological and a sociological sense, which are logically distinct but none·less inextricably linked in practice (1957: 235–236).

In reply, Needham argued that this was erroneous: "Biology is one matter and descent is quite another, of a different order" (1960: 97). Although the two are usually congruent to some extent, institutions such as "ghost" or leviratic marriage show that they need not be. Nor is descent, as Gellner assumed, a matter of biology. A descent system is an ordered set of categories governing relations which are not necessarily biologically grounded. Recall, yet again, the Nuer case, in which a descent idiom is used with reference to what are, in effect, *co-residential* units (Evans-Pritchard 1951: 28; §5.4).

Gellner responded by grouping these arguments together as "Needham's first error". Leviratic marriage did not, he agreed, involve a biological link between the "husband" and "wife" involved. But why then call it "leviratic *marriage*" in the first place? This is done because it is distinct from plain "marriage" by virtue of its fictional character. It is precisely because there is here "a *systematic*, regulated disparity between physical and social kinship" (1960: 188; orig. emphasis), that we regard the levirate as a distinct phenomenon. In short, Gellner argues, social kinship is always a function of biological kinship, but identity is not the only possible type of functional relationship (ibid).

While there is clearly some force to this argument, most anthropologists would nevertheless agree with Needham. J. A. Barnes (1961) explains why this should be so, by clarifying just what status the biological facts of procreation have for the anthropological study of kinship. It is of course commonplace to distinguish the *pater* or social father from the *genitor* or physiological father. But whereas much effort has been devoted to demonstrating, in cases like the levirate, "ghost" marriage, and "woman–woman" marriage, that the pater's identity may indeed be systematically distinct from that of the genitor, less attention has been paid to the identity of the latter. As J. A. Barnes points out, it is necessary to distinguish the *genitor*, that person "believed by his fellows to be the physical father of the child", from the *genetic father*, "who supplies the spermatozoon that impregnates the ovum" (1961: 297).

At first sight these seem to correspond, respectively, to the biological father as emically and etically defined, but things are not quite that simple. Copulation is rarely observed, and natural impregnation cannot be. Moreover, all the resources of modern medicine cannot provide more than circumstantial evidence with regard to genetic fatherhood. The laws of genetics are general formulations, often framed in terms of statistical probabilities. Thus, although it is well established that brown eyes are genetically dominant and blue eyes recessive, this does not enable one to determine *which* brown-eyed man was the genetic father of a given brown-eyed child. One cannot even rule out the possibility that the child's father had blue eyes.

The relationship between genitor and genetic father is thus unknown – and, indeed, unknowable. There is *no* regular functional link between the two. More to the point, this relationship is irrelevant. Our concern as anthropologists is not the relationship between the social and the biological, but that between social behaviour and culturally-derived ideas about that behaviour. Kinship clearly has links with biology – and for that matter, at still greater remove, with nuclear physics – but anthropologists can afford to take these other levels for granted (cf. Beattie 1964: 102).

The distinction between pater and genitor is not, therefore, one between social and genetic kinship, but between social kinship and physical kinship *as culturally defined* by the society in question (Barnes 1961: 298). Both pater and genitor are socially-ascribed roles, and the latter is assigned not only according to indigenous theories of procreation, but also on the basis of people's knowledge of the opinions about the sexual activities of the putative parents.

To sum up, there are three levels to be considered, not the two enumerated by Gellner. These are: (i) social kinship; (ii) emically defined physical kinship; (iii) genetic relationship. Of these, the first two – and the connections between them – are the significant ones as far as social anthropology is concerned.

To return briefly to the "official" Trobriand doctrine of non-physiological paternity (§8.4), we can now describe the situation as follows. There must clearly be a genetic father, unless you are willing to adopt the extreme relativist position that Western genetics is itself just one emic model among many. There is however no genitor according to local dogma, unless one counts the *baloma* spirit. On the other hand, the pater is extremely important, so much so that to bear a child who has no social father is considered dishonourable (Malinowski 1932: 165).

8.8 What is kinship?

8.8.1 *Substantive definitions*

So kinship is not mere biology. Quite the contrary, it is a phenomenon of an entirely different order. How then are we to define and recognize it? In some ways this question should of course have begun the book rather than ended it, but our discussion will refer to all kinds of issues that have only become clear as we have gone along.

Geertz and Geertz (1975: 154) point out that there is little consensus on this matter nowadays, and much less confidence than before that "kinship" really does constitute a definite, isolable object of study. Broadly, they argue, three types of approach can be distinguished.

The *affective view*, which they trace back to Malinowski, takes as its paradigm case the set of emotional relationships within the immediate family. Other kinship usages are seen as metaphorical extensions of these. For instance, Fig. 4.4. shows that the Trobriand relationship term *ina* (possessive form, *inagu*) is used both for M and MZ. But the meaning in the second case, says Malinowski, is

> entirely different . . . something like 'subsidiary mother' . . . . In its second sense *inagu* is used with a different feeling-tone. (1932: 442–443)

He goes on to show that the MZ may act as a stand-in for the M under certain circumstances. Other, more distant uses of *inagu* involve a progressive diminution of the intimacy of the bond (ibid: 444).

This approach on its own holds few attractions, in our view. At one level it is a truism, while at another it is demonstrably false. Thus, it is indeed likely that "close" relationships will be invested with greater emotional intensity than "distant" ones. However, in general we cannot *explain* the observed structure of the relationship terminology, the forms taken by the regulatory rules, nor the practical disposition of social groupings, on this basis. As Beattie puts it, it is a matter of relevance (1964: 102). Like biology, human emotions themselves are not the concern of social anthropology, though people's ideas about them of course are.

The *normative view* is exemplified by Radcliffe-Brown and his associates. According to it, kinship is a mechanism for maintaining social order. It serves to define many of the rights and duties of social actors (Geertz and Geertz 1975: 154), and provides both the means and the justification for enforcing these rights and duties. As Radcliffe-Brown himself puts it:

> A system of kinship and marriage [is] an arrangement which enables persons to live together . . . in an orderly social life. (1950: 3)

Lévi-Strauss provides a more grandiloquent version of this approach, emphasizing the role of kinship in forming and maintaining social solidarity on a broad scale. For him:

> the rules of kinship and marriage are not made necessary by the social state. They *are* the social state. (1969: 490; our emphasis)

The limitations of such views have been dealt with at length in §8.3. Despite the ambiguity in the notion of "rules" – and in Lévi-Strauss's case, the doubt over whether he is in fact talking about rules at all (§6.3.2) – they clearly represent a valid, if partial and one-dimensional approach to the study of kinship.

Finally, the *cognitive view*, the most recent of the three and our main concern in this chapter, sees kinship as a culturally-specific intellectual scheme, whereby ego perceives other persons as standing in particular kinds of relationship to himself. Kinship is thus the cognitive map which ego uses to locate, in "the universe of logically-possible relationships [those] locally recognised to have social importance" (Geertz and Geertz 1975: 155). This approach to kinship is concerned with examining such "maps" to discover their underlying principles: Schneider's study of American kinship is a prime example (§8.5.1). Again, we have examined this approach at length, trying to assess its strengths and weaknesses (especially §8.6.4).

8.8.2 *Formal definitions*

In some ways this three-fold distinction between the affective, normative and cognitive approaches, corresponds to that between behaviour, rules and categories, respectively. But however *descriptively* accurate the Geertzs' three-fold typology may be, it is by nature *post facto* and substantive. Their typology is at the mercy of history, because the future appearance of some new analytical school would lead to the addition to their list of a fourth approach, of a kind unpredictable in advance and having no systematic connection with the first three. By contrast, and whatever its deficiencies, the second set of distinctions is at least a *formal* and logical attempt to cover the entire field, prior to any given ethnographic information or theoretical analysis. It is not dependent upon future analytical and ethnographic developments in the same way, and is subject only to modifications in the three-level model itself. Any fourth level which might be added to the model would have to have clear, formal links with the existing three, whose own inter-relationships would inevitably be modified as a result. One might say that whereas the three approaches distinguished by the Geertzs are syntagmatically linked, the three levels are linked paradigmatically.

Formally then, our provisional answer to the question "What is kinship?", is simply that it is a systematic body of categories, of rules expressed in terms of these categories, and of behaviour described in terms of the categories and assessed with reference to the rules. But the same might be said of any other aspect of social life, so "kinship" is not distinguishable with regard to its form. Is it however possible, given this formal model, to distinguish "kinship" by the characteristic *content* of its categories, rules and behaviour?

Beattie's (1964) arguments are again relevant here. After emphasizing that kinship is not, so far as anthropologists are concerned, a matter of biology, he comments that "kinship" differs from, say, "economics" and "politics" in one crucial regard. The latter two are substantively concerned with, respectively, "the production and distribution of resources", and "maintenance of territorial order" (ibid: 102). By contrast, "kinship" has no distinctive content. It is merely

> the idiom in which certain kinds of political, jural, economic, etc., relations are talked and thought about . . . . It is not a *further* category of social relationships. (ibid)

Schneider (1964), on the other hand, feels that kinship is no different from these other types of social relationship. *All* these social domains have distinctive semantic content, and can simultaneously be used as "idioms" for expressing any of the others. Bridewealth, for instance, is a kinship relation expressed in an economic idiom (ibid: 181). However, Schneider goes on to characterize the semantic content of "kinship" as being "built on consanguineal and affinal elements" (ibid). Although he recognizes that anthropology is concerned with socially, rather than biologically defined consanguinity (§8.5.1), it remains true that "kinship" cannot be substantively defined in terms of consanguinity unless one is prepared to argue that some societies – those without notions of "blood relationships" – lack "kinship" altogether.

It *is* possible to define "kinship" substantively, but only for one society at a time. Its only universal aspects are the etic biological ones which are, as Beattie says, irrelevant. We would however disagree with Beattie over whether it is possible to define "economics" and "politics" substantively either.

8.8.3 *A polythetic definition*

It is beginning to seem that at the sociological level, there is indeed "no such thing as kinship" (Needham 1971b: 5). But this is only because we have posed the problem incorrectly. Substantive definitions tend to be monothetic: that is, they set up some ultimate defining feature(s) as the *sine qua non* of the phenomenon in question. This inevitably leads, as in the case of "marriage", to fruitless debate over whether the phenomenon is, or is not, present in certain borderline societies. But in ordinary, everyday speech it is possible to use words like "kinship", "relative", "family", "marriage", and so on, without defining them precisely, and yet make statements which are perfectly intelligible *in context*. Indeed, following Bourdieu, we can say that these notions are useful in practical situations precisely because they are not rigidly defined. In anthropology too, Needham (1971b, 1975) in the case of "kinship", like Southwold (1978) and Smith (1978) for "religion", has argued that our search for monothetically defined, substantive labels to attach to social phenomena, is as philosophically misconceived as it is doomed in practice. Paradoxically, it is only by refusing to define "kinship" in any hard and fast way that we make it possible to go on using the term in comparative anthropology.

In conclusion, we would say that a relationship pertains to "kinship" if it displays some of the following characteristics. It need by no means have all of them: indeed, some are mutually exclusive. Moreover, the list is not exhaustive: we stopped quite arbitrarily after listing 12 features simply because this seemed an appropriately "round" number. Finally, some of these attributes might easily form aspects of polythetic definitions of "economics", "politics", etc., too. We tend, then, to describe in terms of "kinship" any relationship which:

(i)   is ascribed by birth and persists throughout life;
(ii)   is initiated by "marriage" (which itself needs to be polythetically defined, as in §6.1);
(iii)   is explained or justified in terms of a biological idiom;
(iv)   is invested, by its mere existence, with certain expectations regarding the conduct of both parties;
(v)   assigns the parties to an "in" group or category, in opposition to persons not so assigned;
(vi)   involves the use of relationship terms in a reciprocal, systematic way ("relationship term", too, requires polythetic definition: see §3.2);
(vii)   involves members of a single domestic unit or household;
(viii) involves systematic, enduring relationships between members of different domestic units or households;
(ix)   entails the joint ownership or use, and/or the serial inheritance, of property and resources;
(x)   serves as a medium for assigning hereditary social positions or offices;
(xi)   involves the nurture and upbringing of small children;

(xii) involves the making of prestations without expectation of im-
       mediate or direct return.

Clearly much of this is vague and imprecise. But as we have just argued,
greater precision would be a hindrance rather than a help. We hope to have
demonstrated throughout this book that it is possible to make intelligible
analytical statements about ethnographic issues of great complexity, without
it being necessary to define the precise, substantive essences of the phenomena
under investigation.

Bibliography

Ackerman, C. (1976). Omaha and 'Omaha'. *Am. Ethnol.* **3**, 555–572.

Adam, L. (1948). 'Virilocal' and 'uxorilocal'. *Man* **48**, 12.

Aiyappan, A. (1934). Cross-cousin and uncle-niece marriage in South India. In *Int. congr. anthrop. ethnol. sci.*, vol. I, pp. 281–282.

Alexandre, P. (1967). *Langues et langage en Afrique noire.* Paris: Payot.

Allen, N. J. (1976). Sherpa kinship terminology in diachronic perspective. *Man* (NS) **11**, 569–587.

Anderson, M. (ed.) (1971). Introduction. In *Sociology of the Family*, pp. 7–14. Middlesex: Penguin Books.

Anderson, T. R. and Zelditch, M. (1975). *A Basic Course in Statistics with Sociological Applications* (3rd edn). New York: Holt, Rinehart and Winston.

Bailey, F. G. (1957). *Caste and the Economic Frontier.* Manchester: Manchester University Press.

Banton, M. (ed.) (1966). *Anthropological Approaches to the Study of Religion* (ASA Monographs 3). London: Tavistock.

Barnard, A. J. (1975). Australian models in the South West African highlands. *Afr. Stud.* **34**, 9–18.

Barnard, A. J. (1978a). Universal systems of kin categorization. *Afr. Stud.* **37**, 69–81.

Barnard, A. J. (1978b). The kin terminology system of the Nharo Bushmen. *Cah. Etud. afr.* **18**, 607–629.

Barnard, A. J. (1980a). Convergent structures in Nama and Dutch-Afrikaans kinship terminologies. *V.O.C.* **1**, 25–34.

Barnard, A. J. (1980b). Basarwa settlement patterns in the Ghanzi ranching area. *Botswana Notes and Records* **12**, 137–148.

Barnard, A. J. (1980c). Sex roles among the Nharo Bushmen of Botswana. *Africa* **50**, 115–124.

Barnes, J. A. (1961). Physical and social kinship. *Philosophy of Sciences* **28**, 296–299.

Barnes, J. A. (1962). African models in the New Guinea highlands. *Man* **62**, 5–9.

Barnes, J. A. (1967a). Genealogies. In *The Craft of Social Anthropology* (ed. A. L. Epstein), pp. 101–127. London: Tavistock.

Barnes, J. A. (1967b). The frequency of divorce. In *The Craft of Social Anthropology* (ed. A. L. Epstein), pp. 47–99. London: Tavistock.

Barnes, J. A. (1969). Networks and political process. *Social Networks in Urban Situations* (ed. J. C. Mitchell), pp. 51–76. Manchester: Manchester University Press.

Barnes, R. H. (1974). *Kédang: A Study of the Collective Thought of an Eastern Indonesian People.* Oxford: Clarendon.

Barnes, R. H. (1976). Dispersed alliance and the prohibition of marriage: a reconsideration of McKinley's explanation of Crow–Omaha terminologies. *Man* (NS) **11**, 384–399.

Barnes, R. H. (1977). Kédang: kintypes and categories. *Man* (NS) **12**, 172–174.

Barnes, R. H. (1978). The principle of reciprocal sets. *Man* (NS) **13**, 475–476.

Barnett, S. (1976). Coconuts and gold: relational identity in a South Indian caste. *Contrib. Ind. sociol.* (NS) **10**, 133–156.

Barth, F. (1954). Father's brother's daughter marriage in Kurdistan. *SWest. J. Anthrop.* **10**, 164–171.

Barth, F. (1967). Economic spheres in Darfur. In *Themes in Economic Anthropology* (ed. Raymond Firth), pp. 149–174 (ASA Monographs 6). London: Tavistock.

Barth, F. (ed.) (1969). Introduction. In *Ethnic Groups and Boundaries*, pp. 9–38. London: George Allen and Unwin.

Barth, F. (1975). *Ritual and Knowledge among the Baktaman of New Guinea.* New Haven, Conn.: Yale University Press.

Beattie, J. H. M. (1957). Nyoro kinship. *Africa* **27**, 317–340.

Beattie, J. H. M. (1960). *Bunyoro: An African Kingdom.* New York: Holt, Rinehart and Winston.

Beattie, J. H. M. (1964). Kinship and social anthropology. *Man* **64**, 101–103.

Benson, S. W. (1960). *The Foundations of Chemical Kinetics.* New York: McGraw-Hill.

Berreman, G. D. (1972). *Hindus of the Himalayas: Ethnography and Change* (2nd edn). Berkeley: University of California Press.

Bleek, D. F. (n.d.) I !Kuṅ + Naron 1–53 (unpublished field notes, 1920–1921).

Bloch, M. (1973). The long term and the short term: the economic and political significance of the morality of kinship. In *The Character of Kinship* (ed. J. Goody), pp. 75–87. Cambridge: Cambridge University Press.

Bohannan, L. (1949). Dahomean marriage: a revaluation. *Africa* **29**, 273–287.

Bohannan, P. and Bohannan, L. (1968). *Tiv Economy.* Evanston, Ill.: Northwestern University Press.

Boissevain, J. (1968). The place of non-groups in the social sciences. *Man* (NS) **3**, 542–556.

Boremanse, D. (1981). A comparative study of two Maya kinship systems. *Sociologus* **31**, 1–37.

Borland, C. H. (1979). Kinship term grammar: a review. *Anthropos* **74**, 326–352.

Boswell, D. M. (1969). Personal crises and the mobilization of the social network. In *Social Networks in Urban Situations* (ed. J. C. Mitchell), pp. 245–296. Manchester: Manchester University Press.

Bott, E. (1971). *Family and Social Network* (2nd edn). London: Tavistock.

Bourdieu, P. (1973). The Berber house. In *Rules and Meanings* (ed. M. Douglas), pp. 98–110. Middlesex: Penguin Books.

Bourdieu, P. (1977). *Outline of a Theory of Practice*. Cambridge: Cambridge University Press.

Carter, A. T. (1974). A comparative analysis of systems of kinship and marriage in South Asia. *Proc. R. anthrop. Inst.* 1973, 29–54.

Chagnon, N. (1974). *Studying the Yąnomamö*. New York: Holt, Rinehart and Winston.

Chayanov, A. V. (1966 [1925]). *The Theory of Peasant Economy*. Homewood, Ill.: Richard D. Irwin.

Cline, W. (1936). *Notes on the People of Siwah and el-Garah in the Libyan Desert*. Menasha: George Banta Publ. Co.

Colson, E. (1967). The intensive study of small sample communities. In *The Craft of Social Anthropology* (ed. A. L. Epstein), pp. 3–15, London: Tavistock.

Conklin, H. C. (1969 [1964]). Ethnogenealogical method. In *Cognitive Anthropology* (ed. S. A. Tyler), pp. 93–122. New York: Holt, Rinehart and Winston.

Conté, E. (1979). Politics and marriage in South Kanem (Chad): a statistical presentation of endogamy from 1895 to 1975. *Cahiers de L'ORSTOM, série sciences humaines* 16, 275–297.

Cuisenier, J. (1962). Endogamie et exogamie dans le mariage Arabe. *L'Homme* 2, 80–105.

Cunningham, C. E. (1973). Order in the Atoni house. In *Right and Left* (ed. R. Needham), pp. 204–238. Chicago: University of Chicago Press.

Cushing, F. H. (1896). Outlines of Zuñi creation myths. *Ann. Rept. Bureau of Ethnology* 13, 321–447.

Damas, D. (1963). *Igluligmiut Kinship and Local Groupings: A Structural Approach*. Nat. Mus. of Canada, Bulletin No. 196: Ottawa.

Das, T. C. (1945). *The Purums: An Old Kuki Tribe of Manipur*. Calcutta: Calcutta University Press.

David, K. (1973). Until marriage do us part: a cultural account of Jaffna Tamil categories for kinsmen. *Man* (NS) 8, 521–535.

du Boulay, J. and Williams, R. (1984). Collecting life-histories. In *Ethnographic Research: A Guide to General Conduct* (ed. R. F. Ellen) London and New York: Academic Press.

Dumont, L. (1953). The Dravidian kinship terminology as an expression of marriage. *Man* 53, 34–39.

Dumont, L. (1957). *Hierarchy and Marriage Alliance in South Indian Kinship* (R.A.I. occ. Paper no. 12). London: Royal Anthropological Institute.

Dumont, L. (1964). Marriage in India, the present state of the question: postscript to part I. Part II: marriage and status; Nayar and Newar. *Contrib. Ind. sociol.* 7, 77–98.

Dumont, L. (1966). Descent or intermarriage? A relational view of Australian section systems. *SWest. J. Anthrop.* 22, 231–250.

Dumont, L. (1971). *Introduction à deux théories d'anthropologie sociale*. Paris/The Hague: Mouton

Dumont, L. (1980). *Homo hierarchicus* (revised ed.). Chicago: University of Chicago Press.

Durkheim, E. (1915 [1912]). *The Elementary Forms of the Religious Life*. London: George Allen and Unwin.

Durkheim, E. and Mauss, M. (1970 [1903]). *Primitive Classification*. London: Routledge and Kegan Paul.

Eggan, F. (1950). *Social Organization of the Western Pueblos*. Chicago: University of Chicago Press.

Ellen, R. F. (ed.) (1984). *Ethnographic Research: A Guide to General Conduct* (ASA Res. Meth. Ser. 1). London and New York: Academic Press.

Epstein, A. L. (ed.) (1967). *The Craft of Social Anthropology*. London: Tavistock.

Epstein, A. L. (1969). The network and urban social organization. In *Social Networks in Urban Situations* (ed. J. C. Mitchell), pp. 77–116. Manchester: Manchester University Press.

Epstein, A. L. (1981). *Urbanization and Kinship: The Domestic Domain on the Copperbelt of Zambia, 1950–1956*. London and New York: Academic Press.

Epstein, T. S. (1967). The data of economics in anthropological analysis. In *The Craft of Social Anthropology* (ed. A. L. Epstein), pp. 153–180. London: Tavistock.

Evans-Pritchard, E. E. (1933). Zande blood-brotherhood. *Africa* 6 (also in Evans-Pritchard (1962), pp. 131–161).

Evans-Pritchard, E. E. (1940). *The Nuer*. Oxford: Clarendon.

Evans-Pritchard, E. E. (1951). *Kinship and Marriage Among the Nuer*. Oxford: Clarendon.

Evans-Pritchard, E. E. (1956). *Nuer Religion*. Oxford: Clarendon.

Evans-Pritchard, E. E. (1962). *Essays in Social Anthropology*. London: Faber and Faber.

Firth, Raymond (1936). *We, the Tikopia*. London: George Allen and Unwin.

Firth, Raymond (1956). *Two Studies of Kinship in London* (LSE Monographs 15). London: Athlone Press.

Firth, Raymond (1957). A note on descent groups in Polynesia. *Man* 57, 4–8.

Firth, Raymond (1963). Bilateral descent groups: an operational viewpoint. In *Studies in Kinship and Marriage* (ed. I. Schapera), pp. 22–37. London: Royal Anthropological Institute.

Firth, Raymond (1965). *Primitive Polynesian Economy* (2nd edn). London: Routledge and Kegan Paul.

Firth, Raymond, Hubert, J. and Forge, A. (1969). *Families and Their Relatives. Kinship in a Middle Class Sector of London*. London: Routledge and Kegan Paul.

Firth, Rosemary (1943). *Housekeeping Among Malay Peasants* (LSE Monographs 7). London: Percy Lund, Humphries and Co.

Fischer, H. T. (1952). Polyandry. *Int. Arch. Ethnog.* **46**, no. 1.

Forde, D. (1950). Double descent among the Yakö. In *African Systems of Kinship and Marriage* (eds A. R. Radcliffe-Brown and D. Forde), pp. 285–332. Oxford: Oxford University Press.

Forde, D. and Douglas, M. (1971). Primitive economics. In *Man, Culture and Society* (ed. H. L. Shapiro), pp. 402–416. Oxford: Oxford University Press.

Fortes, M. (1945). *The Dynamics of Clanship Among the Tallensi.* Oxford: Oxford University Press.

Fortes, M. (1949a). *The Web of Kinship Among the Tallensi.* Oxford: Oxford University Press.

Fortes, M. (ed.) (1949b). Time and structure: an Ashanti case study. In *Social Structure: Studies Presented to A. R. Radcliffe-Brown.* Clarendon (also in Fortes (1970), pp. 1–32).

Fortes, M. (1953). The structure of unilineal descent groups. *Am. Anthrop.* 55 (also in Fortes (1970), pp. 67–95).

Fortes, M. (1955). Radcliffe-Brown's contributions to the study of social organization. *Brit. J. Sociol.* 6 (also in Fortes (1970), pp. 260–278).

Fortes, M. (1958). Introduction. In *The Development Cycle in Domestic Groups* (ed. J. Goody), pp. 1–14. Cambridge: Cambridge University Press.

Fortes, M. (1959). Descent, filiation and affinity. *Man* 59 (also in Fortes (1970), pp. 96–126).

Fortes, M. (1970). *Time and Social Structure, and Other Essays.* London: Athlone Press.

Fortes, M. and Evans-Pritchard, E. E. (1940). *African Political Systems.* Oxford: Oxford University Press.

Fourie, L. (1928). The Bushmen of South West Africa. In *The Native Tribes of South West Africa*, pp. 79–105. Cape Town: Cape Times.

Fox, R. (1967). *Kinship and Marriage.* Middlesex: Penguin Books.

Freedman, M. (1958). *Lineage Organization in Southeastern China.* London: Athlone Press.

Freedman, M. (1966). *Chinese Lineage and Society: Fukien and Kwangtung.* New York: Humanities Press.

Freeman, J. D. (1961). On the concept of the kindred. *J. R. anthrop. Inst.* 91, 192–220.

Friedman, J. (1974). Marxism, structuralism and vulgar materalism. *Man* (NS) 9, 444–469.

Friedman, J. (1975). Tribes, states, and transformations. In *Marxist Analyses and Social Anthropology* (ed. M. Bloch), pp. 161–202 (ASA Studies 2). London: Malaby Press.

Fuller, C. J. (1976). *The Nayars Today.* Cambridge: Cambridge University Press.

Fuller, C. J. (1979). Gods, priests and purity: on the relation between Hinduism and the caste system. *Man* (NS) 14, 459–476.

Geertz, C. (1966). Religion as a cultural system. In *Anthropological Approaches to the Study of Religion* (ed. M. Banton), pp. 1–46. London: Tavistock.

Geertz, H. and Geertz, C. (1975). *Kinship in Bali.* Chicago: University of Chicago Press.

Gellner, E. (1957). Ideal language and kinship structure. *Philosophy of Science* 24, 235–242.

Gellner, E. (1960). The concept of kinship. *Philosophy of Science* 27, 187–204.

Gibson, G. (1956). Double descent and its correlates among the Herero of Ngamiland. *Am. Anthrop.* **58**, 109–139.

Gluckman, M. (1940). The kingdom of the Zulu of South Africa. In *African Political Systems* (eds M. Fortes and E. E. Evans-Pritchard), pp. 25–55. Oxford: Oxford University Press.

Gluckman, M. (1950). Kinship and marriage among the Lozi of Northern Rhodesia and the Zulu of Natal. In *African Systems of Kinship and Marriage* (eds A. R. Radcliffe-Brown and D. Forde), pp. 166–206. Oxford: Oxford University Press.

Gluckman, M. (1955). *Custom and Conflict in Africa.* Oxford: Blackwell.

Godelier, M. (1973). Modes de production; rapports de parenté et structures démographiques. *La Pensée* **172**, 7–31.

Good, A. (1978). The principle of reciprocal sets. *Man* (NS) **13**, 128–130.

Good, A. (1980). Elder sister's daughter marriage in South Asia. *J. Anthrop. Res.* **36**, 474–500.

Good, A. (1981). Prescription, preference and practice: marriage patterns among the Kondaiyankottai Maravar of South India. *Man* (NS) **16**, 108–129.

Good, A. (1982). The female bridegroom: rituals of puberty and marriage in South India and Sri Lanka. *Social Analysis* **11**, 35–55.

Goodenough, W. H. (1956). Componential analysis and the study of meaning. *Language* **32**, 195–216.

Goodenough, W. H. (1967). Componential analysis. *Science* **156**, 1203–1209.

Goodenough, W. H. (1969 [1965]). Yankee kinship terminology: a problem in componential analysis. *Am. Anthrop.* **67** (also in *Cognitive Anthropology* (ed. S. A. Tyler), pp. 255–288. New York: Holt, Rinehart and Winston).

Goody, E. N. (1971). Forms of pro-parenthood: the sharing and substitution of parental roles. In *Kinship* (ed. J. Goody), pp. 331–345. Middlesex: Penguin Books.

Goody, E. N. (1982). *Parenthood and Social Reproduction: Fostering and Occupational Roles in West Africa.* Cambridge: Cambridge University Press.

Goody, J. R. (1956). A comparative approach to incest and adultery. *Brit. J. Sociol.* **7**, 286–305 (also in J. Goody (1969) and J. Goody (ed.) (1971)).

Goody, J. R. (ed.) (1958). *The Developmental Cycle in Domestic Groups.* Cambridge: Cambridge University Press.

Goody, J. R. (1969). *Comparative Studies in Kinship.* London: Routledge and Kegan Paul.

Goody, J. R. (ed.) (1971). *Kinship.* Middlesex: Penguin Books.

Goody, J. R. (ed.) (1973a). *The Character of Kinship.* Cambridge: Cambridge University Press.

Goody, J. R. (1973b). Bridewealth and dowry in Africa and Eurasia. In *Bridewealth and Dowry* (eds J. Goody and S. J. Tambiah), pp. 1–58. Cambridge: Cambridge University Press.

Goody, J. R. (1976). *Production and Reproduction: A Comparative Study of the Domestic Domain.* Cambridge: Cambridge University Press.

Goody, J. R. and Tambiah, S. J. (1973). *Bridewealth and Dowry.* Cambridge: Cambridge University Press.

Gough, E. K. (1952). Changing kinship usages in the setting of political and economic change among the Nayars of Malabar. *J. R. anthrop. Inst.* **82**, 71–87.

Gough, E. K. (1955). Female initiation rites on the Malabar coast. *J.R. anthrop. Inst.* **85**, 45–80.

Gough, E. K. (1959). The Nayars and the definition of marriage. *J. R. anthrop. Inst.* **89**, 23–34.

Gray, A. (1979). The working class family as an economic unit. In *The Sociology of the Family: New Directions for Britain* (ed. C. C. Harris), pp. 186–213 (Sociol. Rev. Monograph 28). Keele: Sociol. Review.

Gudeman, S. (1971). The *compadrazgo* as a reflection of the natural and spiritual person. *Proc. R. anthrop. Inst.* 1971, 45–71.

Gudeman, S. (1975). Spiritual relationships and selecting a godparent. *Man* (NS) **10**, 221–237.

Hackenberg, R. A. (1967). The parameters of an ethnic group: a method for studying the total tribe. *Am. Anthrop.* **69**, 478–492.

Hajnal, J. (1963). Concepts of random mating and the frequency of consanguineous marriage. *Proc. Roy. Soc.* **B159**, 125–177.

Hart, C. W. M. and Pilling, A. R. (1960). *The Tiwi of North Australia*. New York: Holt, Rinehart and Winston.

Heinz, H. J. (1966). The Social Organization of the !kō Bushmen. Unpublished M. A. thesis, University of South Africa, Pretoria.

Héritier, F. (1979). Symbolique de L'inceste et de sa prohibition. In *La fonction symbolique: essais d'anthropologie* (eds M. Izard and P. Smith), pp. 209–243. Paris: Gallimard.

Héritier, F. (1981). *L'exercise de la parenté*. Paris: Gallimard.

Hertz, R. (1909). La préeminence de la maine droite: étude sur la polarité religieuse. *Rev. philosophique* **68**, 553–580 (trans. in Needham (ed. 1973b), pp. 3–31).

Hobart, M. (1978). The path of the soul: the legitimacy of nature of Balinese conceptions of space. In *Natural Symbols in South East Asia* (ed. G. Milner), pp. 5–28. London: S.O.A.S.

Hocart, A. M. (1933). *The Progress of Man*. London: Methuen and Co.

Hocart, A. M. (1937). Kinship systems. *Anthropos* **32**, 545–551.

Hoernlé, A. W. (1925). The social organization of the Nama Hottentots of Southwest Africa. *Am. Anthrop.* **27**, 1–24.

Holston, J. (1977). Kédang: kintypes and categories. *Man* (NS) **12**, 170–172.

Holy, L. (1979). The segmentary lineage and its existential status. In *Segmentary Lineage Systems Reconsidered* (ed. L. Holy), pp. 1–23. Belfast: Queen's University. Papers in Soc. Anthrop. 4.

Holy, L. and Stuchlik, M. (1981). The structure of folk models. In *The Structure of Folk Models* (eds L. Holy and M. Stuchlik), pp. 1–34 (ASA Monographs 20). London and New York: Academic Press.

Homans, G. C. and Schneider, D. M. (1955). *Marriage, Authority and Final Causes: A Study of Unilateral Cross-Cousin Marriage*. Glencoe: Free Press.

Hopkins, K. (1980). Brother–sister marriage in Roman Egypt. *Comp. Stud. in Society and History* **22**, 303–354.

Hubert, H. (1934). *The Greatness and Decline of the Celts.* London: Kegan, Paul, Trench and Trubner.

Inden, R. B. and Nicholas, R. W. (1977). *Kinship in Bengali Culture.* Chicago: University of Chicago Press.

Kaplan, J. O. (1975). *The Piaroa: A People of the Orinoco Basin.* Oxford: Clarendon.

Kirchhoff, P. (1931). Die Verwandtschaffsorganisation der Urwaldstämme Südamerikas. *Z. für Ethnol.* **63**, 85–193.

Knight, C. D. (1978). The origins of woman: a Marxist-structuralist view of the genesis of culture. *Critique of Anthropology* **3**, 58–87.

Kolenda, P. M. (1968). Region, caste and family structure: a comparative study of the Indian "joint" family. In *Structure and Change in Indian Society* (eds M. Singer and B. S. Cohn), pp. 339–396. Chicago: Aldine.

Kolenda, P. M. (1970). Family structure in village Lonikand, India: 1819, 1958 and 1967. *Contrib. Ind. Sociol.* (NS) **4**, 50–72.

Kopytoff, I. (1977). Matrilineality, residence, and residential zones. *Am. Ethnol.* **4**, 539–558.

Korn, F. (1973). *Elementary Structures Reconsidered: Lévi-Strauss on Kinship.* London: Tavistock.

Krige, E. J. (1939). The significance of cattle exchanges in Lovedu social structure. *Africa* **12**, 393–424.

Krige, E. J. (1975). Asymmetric matrilateral cross-cousin marriage: the Lovedu case. *Afr. Stud.* **34**, 231–257.

Krige, E. J. and Krige J. D. (1943). *The Realm of a Rain Queen.* Oxford: Oxford University Press.

Kroeber, A. L. (1909). Classificatory systems of relationship. *J. R. anthrop. Inst.* **39**, 77–84.

Kuhn, T. S. (1970). *The Structure of Scientific Revolutions* (2nd edn). Chicago: University of Chicago Press.

Kuper, A. (1975a). The social structure of the Sotho-speaking peoples of southern Africa. *Africa* **54**, 67–81, 139–149.

Kuper, A. (1975b). Preferential marriage and polygyny among the Tswana. In *Studies in African Social Anthropology* (eds. M. Fortes and S. Patterson), pp. 121–134. London and New York: Academic Press.

Kuper, A. (1982a). Lineage theory: a critical retrospect. *Ann. Rev. of Anthropology* **11**, 71–95.

Kuper, A. (1982b). *Wives for Cattle: Bridewealth and Marriage in Southern Africa.* London: Routledge and Kegan Paul.

Kuper, H. (1947). *An African Aristocracy.* Oxford: Oxford University Press.

Kuper, H. (1963). *The Swazi: A South African Kingdom.* New York: Holt, Rinehart and Winston.

La Fontaine, J. (1973). Descent in New Guinea: an Africanist view. In *The Character of Kinship* (ed. J. Goody), pp. 35–51. Cambridge: Cambridge University Press.

Lakatos, I. (1976). *Proofs and Refutations: The Logic of Mathematical Discovery.* Cambridge: Cambridge University Press.

Leach, E. R. (1951). The structural implications of matrilateral cross-cousin marriage. *J.R. anthrop. Inst.* **81** (also in Leach (1961a), pp. 54–104).

Leach, E. R. (1954). *Political Systems of Highland Burma*. London: Athlone Press.

Leach, E. R. (1955). Polyandry, inheritance and the definition of marriage. *Man* **55** (also in Leach (1961a), pp. 105–113).

Leach, E. R. (1957). Aspects of bridewealth and marriage stability among the Kachin and Lakher. *Man* **57** (also in Leach (1961a), pp. 114–123).

Leach, E. R. (1958). Concerning Trobriand clans and the kinship category 'tabu'. In *The Developmental Cycle in Domestic Groups* (ed. J. Goody), pp. 120–145. Cambridge: Cambridge University Press.

Leach, E. R. (1960). Descent, filiation and affinity. *Man* **60**, 9–10.

Leach, E. R. (1961a). *Rethinking Anthropology*. London: Athlone Press.

Leach, E. R. (1961b). *Pul Eliya: A Village in Ceylon*. Cambridge: Cambridge University Press.

Leach, E. R. (1962). On certain unconsidered aspects of double descent systems. *Man* **62**, 130–134.

Leach, E. R. (1966). Virgin birth. *Proc. R. anthrop. Inst.* 1966, 39–49.

Leach, E. R. (1968). Virgin birth (letter). *Man* (NS) **3**, 655–656.

Leach, E. R. (1969). 'Kachin' and 'Haka Chin': a rejoinder to Lévi-Strauss. *Man* (NS) **4**, 277–285.

Leach, E. R. (1970). *Lévi-Strauss*. London: Fontana.

Leach, E. R. (1976). *Culture and Communication*. Cambridge: Cambridge University Press.

Leach, E. R. (1982). *Social Anthropology*. Glasgow: Fontana.

LeClair, E. E. (1968 [1962]). Economic theory and economic anthropology. In *Economic Anthropology* (eds E. E. LeClair and H. K. Schneider), pp. 187–207. New York: Holt, Rinehart and Winston.

Lee, R. B. (1979). *The !Kung San: Men, Women and Work in a Foraging Society*. Cambridge: Cambridge University Press.

Lévi-Strauss, C. (1945). L'analyse structurale en linguistique et en anthropologie. *Word* **1** (trans. in Lévi-Strauss (1968), pp. 31–54).

Lévi-Strauss, C. (1949). *Les structures élémentaires de la parenté*. Paris: Presses Universitaires de France.

Lévi-Strauss, C. (1952). Les structures sociales dans le Brésil central et oriental. In *Indian Tribes of Aboriginal America* (ed. Sol Tax), pp. 302–310. Chicago: University of Chicago Press.

Lévi-Strauss, C. (1956). Les organisations dualistes existent-elles? *Bijdr. tot de Taal-, Land-, en Volkenkunde* **112** (trans. in Lévi-Strauss (1968), pp. 132–163).

Lévi-Strauss, C. (1968). *Structural Anthropology*. Middlesex: Penguin Books.

Lévi-Strauss, C. (1969). *The Elementary Structures of Kinship* (2nd edn). London: Eyre and Spottiswoode.

Little, K. (1966). The strange case of romantic love. *The Listener,* 7 April 1966.

Littlejohn, J. (1960). The Temne house. *Sierra Leone Studies* 63–79.

Lounsbury, F. G. (1956). A semantic analysis of the Pawnee kinship usage. *Language* **32**, 158–194.

Lowie, R. H. (1920). *Primitive Society*. New York: Horace Liveright.

Lowie, R. H. (1928). A note on relationship terminologies. *Am. Anthrop.* 30, 263–268.

Lowie, R. H. (1929). Relationship terms. *Encycl. Brit.* (14th edn) **19**, 84–86.

Lyons, J. (1977). *Semantics*, Vol. 1. Cambridge: Cambridge University Press.

Madan, T. N. (1965). *Family and Kinship: A Study of the Pandits of Rural Kashmir.* Bombay: Asia Publ. House.

Maddock, K. (1972). *The Australian Aborigines: A Portrait of Their Society.* London: Allen Lane.

Maine, H. S. (1861). *Ancient Law*. London: John Murray.

Mair, L. (1971). *Marriage*. Middlesex: Penguin Books.

Malinowski, B. (1922). *Argonauts of the Western Pacific*. New York: Dutton.

Malinowski, B. (1932). *The Sexual Life of Savages in North-western Melanesia* (3rd edn). London: Routledge and Sons.

Marriott, McK. (1976). Interpreting Indian society: a monistic alternative to Dumont's dualism. *J. Asian stud.* **36**, 189–195.

Marriott, McK. and Inden, R. B. (1977). Towards an ethnosociology of South Asian caste systems. In *The New Wind: Changing Identities in South Asia* (ed. K. David), pp. 226–238. Paris/The Hague: Mouton.

Marshall, L. (1976). *The !Kung of Nyae Nyae*. Cambridge, Mass.: Harvard University Press.

Martin, J. F. (1981). Genealogical structures and consanguineous marriage. *Curr. Anthrop.* **22**, 401–412.

Maybury-Lewis, D. H. P. (1960). Parallel descent and the Apinayé anomaly. *SWest. J. Anthrop.* **16**, 191–216.

Maybury-Lewis, D. H. P. (1965). Prescriptive marriage systems. *SWest J. Anthrop.* **21**, 207–230 (also in J. Goody (ed.) (1971)).

Mayer, A. C. (1960). *Caste and Kinship in Central India.* London: Routledge and Kegan Paul.

Mayer, A. C. (1966). The significance of quasi-groups in the study of complex societies. In *The Social Anthropology of Complex Societies* (ed. M. Banton), pp. 97–122 (ASA Monographs 4). London: Tavistock.

McGilvray, D. B. (1980). The matrilocal household system of eastern Sri Lanka. Paper read at 79th Annual Meeting of Amer. Anthrop. Assoc., Washington.

McGilvray, D. B. (1982a). Sexual power and fertility in Sri Lanka: Batticaloa Tamils and Moors. In *Ethnography of Fertility and Birth* (ed. C. P. MacCormack), pp. 25–73. London and New York: Academic Press.

McGilvray, D. B. (ed.) (1982b). Mukkuvar vannimai: Tamil caste and matriclan ideology in Batticaloa, Sri Lanka. In *Caste Ideology and Interaction*, pp. 34–97. Cambridge: Cambridge University Press.

Mead, M. (1939). Sex and temperament in three primitive societies. In *From the South Seas: Studies of Adolescence and Sex in Primitive Societies*. New York: William Morrow.

Meggitt, M. J. (1965). *The Lineage System of the Mae Enga of New Guinea.* Edinburgh: Oliver and Boyd.

Meillassoux, C. (1981). *Maidens, Meal and Money: Capitalism and the Domestic Economy.* Cambridge: Cambridge University Press.

Middleton, J. (1954). Some social aspects of Lugbara myth. *Africa* **24**, 189–199.

Middleton, J. (1960). *Lugbara Religion.* Oxford: Oxford University Press.

Mintz, S. W. and Wolf, E. R. (1950). An analysis of ritual co-parenthood (compadrazgo). *SWest. J. Anthrop.* **6**, 341–365.

Mitchell, J. C. (1961). Social change and the stability of African marriage in Northern Rhodesia. In *Social Change in Modern Africa* (ed. A. Southall), pp. 316–329. Oxford: Oxford University Press.

Mitchell, J. C. (1967). On qualification in social anthropology. In *The Craft of Social Anthropology* (ed. A. L. Epstein), pp. 17–45. London: Tavistock.

Mitchell, J. C. (ed.) (1969). The concept and use of social networks. In *Social Networks in Urban Situations: Analyses of Personal Relationships in Central African Towns*, pp. 1–50. Manchester: Manchester University Press.

Mitchell, J. C. (1984). Case studies. In *Ethnographic Research: A Guide to General Conduct* (ed. R. F. Ellen). London and New York: Academic Press.

Mitchell, W. E. (1963). Theoretical problems in the concept of kindred. *Am. Anthrop.* **65**, 343–354.

Monkhouse, F. J. and Wilkinson, H. R. (1963). *Maps and Diagrams.* London: Methuen.

Moore, S. F. (1964). Descent and symbolic filiation. *Am. Anthrop.* **66**, 1308–1320.

Morgan, L. H. (1871). *Systems of Consanguinity and Affinity of The Human Family.* Washington: Smithsonian Institution.

Morgan, L. H. (1877). *Ancient Society.* New York: Henry Holt.

Murdock, G. P. (1949). *Social Structure.* New York: Macmillan.

Murdock, G. P. (1967). *Ethnographic Atlas.* Pittsburgh: Pittsburgh University Press.

Murphy, R. F. and Kasdan, L. (1959). The structure of parallel cousin marriage. *Am. Anthrop.* **61**, 17–29.

Needham, R. (1958). The formal analysis of prescriptive patrilateral cross-cousin marriage. *SWest. J. Anthrop.* **14**, 199–219.

Needham, R. (1960). Descent systems and ideal language. *Philosophy of Science* **27**, 96–101.

Needham, R. (1962). *Structure and Sentiment.* Chicago: University of Chicago Press.

Needham, R. (1966). Age, category and descent. *Bijdr. tot de Taal-, Land- en Volkenkunde* **122**, 1–33.

Needham, R. (1967). Terminology and alliance, II: Mapuche, conclusions. *Sociologus* **18**, 39–53.

Needham, R. (ed.) (1971a). Introduction. In *Rethinking Kinship and Marriage* pp. xiii–cxvii, (ASA Monographs 11). London: Tavistock.

Needham, R. (ed.) (1971b). Remarks on the analysis of kinship and marriage. In *Rethinking Kinship and Marriage*, pp. 1–34 (ASA Monographs 11). London: Tavistock.

Needham, R. (1972). *Belief, Language and Experience.* Oxford: Blackwell.

Needham, R. (1973a). Prescription. *Oceania* **42**, 166–181.

Needham, R. (ed.) (1973b). *Right and Left*. Chicago: University of Chicago Press.

Needham, R. (1975). Polythetic classification: convergence and consequences. *Man* (NS) **10**, 349–369.

Notes and Queries on Anthropology (4th edn, 1912). London.

Notes and Queries on Anthropology (6th edn, 1951). London: Routledge and Kegan Paul.

Parry, J. P. (1979). *Caste and Kinship in Kangra*. London: Routledge and Kegan Paul.

Pelto, P. J. and Pelto, G. H. (1978). *Anthropological Research: The Structure of Enquiry* (2nd edn). Cambridge: Cambridge University Press.

Peters, E. L. (1960). The proliferation of segments in the lineages of the Bedouin of Cyrenaica. *J.R. anthrop. Inst.* **90**, 29–53.

Peters, E. L. (1967). Some structural aspects of the feud among the camel-herding Bedouin of Cyrenaica. *Africa* **37**, 261–282.

Pitt-Rivers, J. (1958). Ritual kinship in Spain. *Trans. N.Y. Acad. Sci.* II, **20**, 424–431.

Pitt-Rivers, J. (1973). The kith and the kin. In *The Character of Kinship* (ed. J. Goody), pp. 89–105. Cambridge: Cambridge University Press.

Pollard, A. H., Yusuf, F. and Pollard, G. N. (1981). *Demographic Techniques* (2nd edn). Oxford: Pergamon Press.

Popper, K. R. (1972). *The Logic of Scientific Discovery*. London: Hutchinson.

Powell, H. S. (1956). An analysis of present day social structure in the Trobriand Islands. Unpublished Ph.D. thesis, University of London.

Powell, H. S. (1968). Virgin birth. *Man* (NS) **3**, 651–653.

Preston-Whyte, E. (1981). Model-building in action: genealogical characters in white South Africa. In *The Structure of Folk Models* (eds L. Holy and M. Stuchlik), pp. 183–208. London and New York: Academic Press.

Radcliffe-Brown, A. R. (1924). The mother's brother in South Africa. *SAfr. J. of Sci.* **21**, (also in Radcliffe-Brown (1952), pp. 15–31).

Radcliffe-Brown, A. R. (1930). A system of notation for relationships. *Man* **30**, 121–122.

Radcliffe-Brown, A. R. (1940). On social structure. *J.R. anthrop. Inst.* **70** (also in Radcliffe-Brown (1952), pp. 188–204).

Radcliffe-Brown, A. R. (1941). The study of kinship systems. *J.R. anthrop. Inst.* **71** (also in Radcliffe-Brown (1952), pp. 49–89).

Radcliffe-Brown, A. R. (1950). Introduction. In *African Systems of Kinship and Marriage* (eds A. R. Radcliffe-Brown and D. Forde), pp. 1–85. Oxford: Oxford University Press.

Radcliffe-Brown, A. R. (1952). *Structure and Function in Primitive Society*. London: Cohen and West.

Radcliffe-Brown, A. R. and Forde, D. (1950). *African Systems of Kinship and Marriage*. Oxford: Oxford University Press.

Reid, R. M. (1974). Relative age and assymetrical [*sic*] cross-cousin marriage in a South Indian caste. In *Genealogical Mathematics* (ed. P. A. Ballonoff), pp. 257–273. Paris/The Hague: Mouton.

Richards, A. I. (1934). Mother-right in Central Africa. In *Essays Presented to C. G.*

Seligman (eds E. E. Evans-Pritchard, R. Firth, B. Malinowski and I. Schapera), pp. 267–280. London: Kegan Paul, Trench, Trubner and Co.

Richards, A. I. (1940). The political system of the Bemba tribe – North Eastern Rhodesia. In *African Political Systems* (eds M. Fortes and E. E. Evans-Pritchard), pp. 83–120. Oxford: Oxford University Press.

Richards, A. I. (1950). Some types of family structure amongst the Central Bantu. In *African Systems of Kinship and Marriage* (eds A. R. Radcliffe-Brown and D. Forde), pp. 207–251. Oxford: Oxford University Press.

Richards, A. I. (1961 [1939]). *Land, Labour and Diet in Northern Rhodesia* (new edn). Oxford: Oxford University Press.

Rivers, W. H. R. (1900). A genealogical method of collecting social and vital statistics. *J. anthrop. Inst.* **30**, 74–82.

Rivers, W. H. R. (1910). The genealogical method of anthropological inquiry. *Sociol. Rev.* **3** (also in Rivers (1968), pp. 97–109).

Rivers, W. H. R. (1968 [1914]). *Kinship and Social Organization*. London: Athlone Press.

Rivers, W. H. R. (1924). *Social Organization*. London: Kegan Paul, Trench and Trubner.

Riviere, P. G. (1966). Oblique discontinuous exchange: a new form of prescriptive alliance. *Am. Anthrop.* **68**, 738–740.

Rivière, P. G. (1969). *Marriage Among the Trio*. Oxford: Clarendon.

Romney, A. K. and D'Andrade, R. G. (1969 [1964]). Cognitive aspects of English kin terms. *Am. Anthrop.* **66** (also in *Cognitive Anthropology* (ed. S. A. Tyler), pp. 369–396. New York: Holt, Rinehart and Winston).

Rose, F. G. G. (1960). *Classification of Kin, Age, Structure and Marriage Amongst the Groote Eylandt Aborigines*. Berlin: Akademie-Verlag.

Roth, W. E. (1903). *Superstition, Magic and Medicine*. Brisbane: Vaughan.

Ryle, G. (1963). *The Concept of Mind*. Middlesex: Penguin Books.

Sahlins, M. D. (1958). *Social Stratification in Polynesia*. Seattle: University of Washington Press.

Sahlins, M. D. (1965). On the ideology and composition of descent groups. *Man* **65**, 104–107.

Sahlins, M. D. (1974). *Stone Age Economics*. London: Tavistock.

Sarma, J. (1964). The nuclearization of joint family households in West Bengal. *Man in India* **44**, 193–206.

Schapera, I. (1950). Kinship and marriage among the Tswana. In *African Systems of Kinship and Marriage* (eds A. R. Radcliffe-Brown and D. Forde), pp. 140–165. Oxford: Oxford University Press.

Scheffler, H. W. (1966). Ancestor worship in anthropology: or, observations on descent and descent groups. *Curr. Anthrop.* **7**, 541–551.

Scheffler H. W. (1977). On the 'rule of uniform reciprocals' in systems of kin classification. *Anthrop. Linguistics* **19**, 245–259.

Scheffler, H. W. (1978). *Australian Kin Classification*. Cambridge: Cambridge University Press.

Scheffler, H. W. and Lounsbury, F. G. (1971). *A Study in Kinship Semantics: The Siriono Kinship System*. Englewood Cliffs, NJ: Prentice-Hall.

Schneider, D. M. (1964). The nature of kinship. *Man* **64**, 180–181.

Schneider, D. M. (1968a). Virgin birth. *Man* (NS) **3**, 126–129.

Schneider, D. M. (1968b). *American Kinship: A Cultural Account*. Englewood Cliffs, NJ: Prentice-Hall.

Schneider, D. M. (1968c). Rivers and Kroeber in the study of kinship. In *Kinship and Social Organization* (W. H. R. Rivers), pp. 7–16. London: Athlone Press.

Schwimmer, E. G. (1969). Virgin birth. *Man* (NS) **4**, 132–133.

Service, E. R. (1962). *Primitive Social Organization*. New York: Random House.

Sharma, U. (1980). *Women, Work and Property in North-west India*. London: Tavistock.

Shulman, D. D. (1980). *Tamil Temple Myths: Sacrifice and Divine Marriage in the South Indian Saiva Tradition*. Princeton: Princeton University Press.

Smith, R. T. (1973). The matrifocal family. In *The Character of Kinship* (ed. J. Goody), pp. 121–144. Cambridge: Cambridge University Press.

Smith, W. C. (1978). *The Meaning and End of Religion*. London: S.P.C.K.

Southwold, M. (1978). Buddhism and the definition of religion. *Man* (NS) **13**, 362–379.

Spier, L. (1925). The distribution of kinship systems in North America. *Univ. of Washington Publ. in Anthrop.* **1**, 69–88.

Spier, R. F. G. (1970). *Surveying and Mapping: A Manual of Simplified Techniques*. New York: Holt, Rinehart and Winston.

Spiro, M. E. (1966). Religion: problems of definition and explanation. In *Anthropological Approaches to the Study of Relgion* (ed. M. Banton), pp. 85–126. London: Tavistock.

Spiro, M. E. (1968a). Virgin birth, parthenogenesis and physiological paternity: an essay in cultural interpretation. *Man* (NS) **3**, 242–261.

Spiro, M. E. (1968b). Virgin birth (letter). *Man* (NS) **3**, 656.

Steward, J. H. (1955). *Theory of Culture Change*. Urbana, Ill.: University of Illinois Press.

Stirrat, R. L. (1975). Compadrazgo in Catholic Sri Lanka. *Man* (NS) **10**, 589–606.

Strathern, A. J. (1972). *One Father, One Blood: Descent and Group Structure Among the Melpa People*. London: Tavistock.

Strathern, M. (1982). The place of kinship: kin, class and village status in Elmdon, Essex. In *Belonging: Identity and Social Organisation in British Rural Cultures* (ed. A. P. Cohen), pp. 72–100. Manchester: Manchester University Press.

Tambiah, S. J. (1969). Animals are good to think and good to prohibit. *Ethnology* **8**, 424–459.

Tambiah, S. J. (1973a). Dowry and bridewealth and the property rights of women in South Asia. In *Bridewealth and Dowry* (eds J. Goody and S. J. Tambiah), pp. 59–169. Cambridge: Cambridge University Press.

Tambiah, S. J. (1973b). From varna to caste through mixed unions. In *The Character of Kinship* (ed. J. Goody), pp. 191–229. Cambridge: Cambridge University Press.

Tax, S. (1955 [1937]). Some problems of social organization. In *Social Anthropology of North American Tribes* (ed. F. Eggan), pp. 3–32 (2nd edn). Chicago: Chicago University Press.

Thompson, S. (1961). *Motif-index of Folk-literature*. Bloomington, Ind.: Indiana University Press.

Trautmann, T. R. (1981). *Dravidian Kinship*. Cambridge: Cambridge University Press.

Turnbull, C. M. (1966). *Wayward Servants*. London: Eyre and Spottiswoode.

Turner, C. (1969). *Family and Kinship in Modern Britain*. London: Routledge and Kegan Paul.

Turner, D. H. (1978a). Ideology and elementary structures. *Anthropologica* **20**, 223–247.

Turner, D. H. (1978b). *Dialectics in Tradition: Myth and Social Structure in Two Hunter-gatherer Societies* (R.A.I. Occ. Paper no. 36). London: Royal Anthropological Institute.

Turner, D. H. (1979). Hunting and gathering: Cree and Australians. In *Challenging Anthropology* (eds D. H. Turner and G. A. Smith), pp. 195–213. Toronto: McGraw-Hill Ryerson.

Tyler, S. A. (ed.) (1969). *Cognitive Anthropology*. New York: Holt, Rinehart and Winston.

Verdon, M. (1982). Where have all their lineages gone? Cattle and descent among the Nuer. *Am. Anthrop.* **84**, 566–579.

Wallace, A. F. C. (1969 [1965]). The problem of the psychological validity of componential analyses. *Am. Anthrop.* **67** (also in *Cognitive Anthropology* (ed. S. A. Tyler), pp. 396–418. New York: Holt, Rinehart and Winston).

Wallace, A. F. C. and Atkins, J. (1969 [1960]). The meaning of kinship terms. *Am. Anthrop.* **62** (also in *Cognitive Anthropology* (ed. S. A. Tyler), pp. 345–369. New York: Holt. Rinehart and Winston).

Weber, M. (1964). *The Theory of Social and Economic Organization*. New York: Free Press.

Webster, D. (1977). Spreading the risk: the principle of laterality among the Chopi. *Africa* **47**, 192–207.

Wiessner, P. W. (1977). Hxaro: a regional system of reciprocity for reducing risk among the !Kung San. Unpublished Ph.D. thesis, University of Michigan, Ann Arbor; 2 vols.

Wiessner, P. W. (1982). Risk, reciprocity, and social influence in !Kung San economics. In *Politics and History in Band Societies* (eds E. Leacock and R. B. Lee), pp. 61–84. Cambridge: Cambridge University Press.

Woodburn, J. (1980). Hunters and gatherers today and reconstruction of the past. In *Soviet and Western Anthropology* (ed. E. Gellner), pp. 95–117. London: Duckworth.

Woodburn, J. (1982). Egalitarian societies. *Man* (NS) **17**, 431–451.

Wouden, F. A. E. van (1968 [1935]). *Types of Social Structure in Eastern Indonesia* (trans. R. Needham). The Hague: Martinus Nijhoff.

Yalman, N. (1962). The structure of the Sinhalese kindred: a re-examination of the Dravidian terminology. *Am. Anthrop.* **64**, 548–575.

Yalman, N. (1963). On the purity of women in the castes of Ceylon and Malabar. *J.R. anthrop. Inst.* **93**, 25–58.

Yalman, N. (1967). *Under the Bo Tree: Studies in Caste, Kinship and Marriage in the Interior of Ceylon.* Berkeley: University of California Press.

Yellen, J. E. (1977). *Archaeological Approaches to the Present: Models for Reconstructing the Past.* New York and London: Academic Press.

Young, M. and Willmott, P. (1962). *Family and Kinship in East London.* Middlesex: Penguin Books.

Author index

Subject index